61L

Made Simple ... TION

Dolores Serrat

Londres - junio 1972

In the same series

Accounting
Advanced Algebra & Calculus
Anthropology
Art Appreciation
Biology
Book-keeping
Chemistry
Commerce
Electricity
Electronic Computers
Electronics
English
French
German
Intermediate Algebra & Analytic Geometry
Italian
Latin
Law
Mathematics
New Mathematics
Organic Chemistry
Philosophy
Physics
Psychology
Russian
Spanish
Statistics
Typing

ART APPRECIATION
Made Simple

Barbara Whelpton

Made Simple Books
W. H. ALLEN London

Made and printed in Great Britain
by Richard Clay (The Chaucer Press) Ltd., Bungay, Suffolk
for the publishers W. H. Allen & Company Ltd.,
Essex Street, London W.C.2

ISBN 0 491 00015 4 Casebound
ISBN 0 491 00025 1 Paperback

Foreword

This book is designed to serve as background reading for all students of 'O' or 'A' level G.C.E. and for those members of the general public who are anxious to extend their knowledge and understanding of art. It covers a very wide field in a general way, but the suggested further reading at the end of each chapter will give any student helpful guidance towards more detailed and specialized study.

Throughout the book the reader is encouraged to look at works of art for himself and to form his own judgments. Accordingly, lists of Art Galleries and Museums in Britain, Australia, and New Zealand are given, although, for reasons of space, these have had to be confined to main ones only, but readers will easily be able to find the names of those nearest them in their own districts.

The book can be read as a continuous narrative, or may be dipped into at will. The side headings are there for easy reference; they are not intended to break up the continuity of the text.

I should like to express my sincere thanks to James Burr who, despite the fact that he may well disagree with some of my opinions, gave me generous encouragement as well as constructive criticisms and suggestions which were of invaluable help in the final stages of this book.

BARBARA WHELPTON

To Patricia Aldington in gratitude for her unfailing help in the preparation of this book

Table of Contents

	FOREWORD	v
1	HOW TO USE THIS BOOK	1
2	HOW TO LOOK AND SEE	4
	The impact of Impressionism	4
	Art is timeless	4
	'Beauty' in a work of art	5
	Art and craft	6
	Materials and technique	6
	Examples from different periods	7
	Prehistoric	8
	African	8
	Etruscan	8
	Medieval glass	9
	Steel	10
	Venetian sixteenth-century painting	10
	French Romanesque carving	11
	English Romanesque carving	11
	Medieval tapestry	12
	Chinese T'ang pottery	13
	Greek fifth-century relief	13
	Seventeenth-century Flemish painting	14
	Picasso	14
	Fourteenth-century Sienese painting	14
	Possible essays, discussion and research	16
3	DIFFERENT ASPECTS OF ART	17
	Easel painting	17
	The technique of fresco	17
	Mosaic	18
	Stained glass	19
	Carving	19
	The work of goldsmiths and silversmiths	19
	Modern media	20
	Drawings	20
	Water colours; Gouache	20
	Pastels	20
	Engravings, woodcuts, etchings, lithography	21

Tapestry 21
Sculpture 22
Major and minor arts 22
Examples of different media 23
Prehistoric Lascaux 23
The Parthenon frieze 24
The Book of Kells 25
Twelfth-century mosaic 25
Fresco 26
Woodcuts 26
Seventeenth-century Spanish painting 27
Seventeenth-century drawing 27
Nineteenth-century Pointillism 27
Twentieth-century sculpture 28
Possible esssays, discussion and research 29
Suggested further reading 29

4 THE BEGINNINGS 30
The cave paintings of Altamira 30
The art of the hunter 31
The first farmers 33
Megalithic monuments 34
Nuraghic bronzes 35
Ancient civilizations 36
The Ancient Middle East 36
Oriental art 39
Indian cave paintings 40
Chinese ceramics 42
Chinese paintings 42
Japanese colour prints 43
Possible essays, discussion and research 44
Suggested further reading 44

5 EARLY MEDITERRANEAN ART 45
Minoan and Mycenaean art 45
The orders of Greek architecture 47
Greek sculpture 49
The Etruscans 49
Roman grandeur 50
The early Christians 51
The basilica 52
Early church architecture 53
Byzantine splendour 54
Mosaics of Ravenna 54
Manuscripts 56
Early Christian chalices 57
Possible essays, discussion and research 59
Suggested further reading 59

6 THE MIDDLE AGES 60
Carolingian art 60
Romanesque sculpture and architecture 60
Vézelay 62
Processional crosses and altarpieces 64
St. Trophime 65
The pointed arch 65
Chartres cathedral 67
Stained glass in Europe 67
The Madonna and Child in the Middle Ages 68
The Sainte Chapelle 68
Portuguese architecture 68
Tapestry 69
Illuminated manuscripts 70
Possible essays, discussion and research 71
Suggested further reading 71

7 EARLY PAINTING, MOSAICS, AND SCULPTURE IN EUROPE 71
Flemish painting 71
Portuguese painting 73
Landscape as a background 73
Schools of Italian painting 74
Mosaics in Rome 74
Painting in Siena 74
Giotto's frescoes 77
Sculpture and the Pisano family 78
The Baptistery doors in Florence 79
Gothic painting 81
Possible essays, discussion and research 82
Suggested further reading 82

8 THE EARLY YEARS OF THE RENAISSANCE 83
Masaccio 83
Uccello 84
Pisanello (Verona) 85
Hubert and Jan Van Eyck 86
Nineteenth-century return to 'before Raphael' 87
Sixteenth-century French tapestry 88
Three fourteenth-century carved Madonnas 89
Possible essays, discussion and research 91
Suggested further reading 91

9 THE RENAISSANCE IN FLORENCE 92
Patrons of the arts 92
Italian Gothic architecture 92
Renaissance architecture and Brunelleschi 93

Sculpture and Donatello 93
Painting 94
Fra Angelico 94
Piero di Cosimo 95
Piero della Francesca 95
Botticelli 96
Nativity scenes compared 97
Great masters of the Renaissance 98
Leonardo da Vinci 99
Michelangelo 100
Raphael 101
Possible essays, discussion and research 103
Suggested further reading 103

10 VENETIAN PAINTING 104
Venetian love of colour 104
The Bellini family 104
Mantegna (Padua) 105
El Greco compared with the Venetians 106
Crivelli 106
Venetian pageantry and Carpaccio 107
Great Venetians 108
Giorgione 108
Titian 109
Tintoretto 110
Veronese 111
Italian art as a criterion 112
Possible essays, discussion and research 113
Suggested further reading 113

11 THE RISE OF LANDSCAPE PAINTING 114
The northern schools 114
Joachim Patenir 114
Altdorfer 114
Dürer's use of landscape 115
Brueghel 115
Flemish and Italian love of nature 116
Seventeenth-century French landscape 117
Poussin and Claude 117
Seventeenth-century painting in Holland 118
The new patrons 118
Dutch landscape 119
Pissarro compared with Hobbema 119
The eighteenth-century Italians 120
Comparison with Richard Wilson 121
Possible essays, discussion and research 123
Suggested further reading 123

12 THE SEVENTEENTH AND EIGHTEENTH CENTURIES IN EUROPE 124
Genre in Holland 124
Jan Vermeer 124
Pieter de Hooch 124
Frans Hals 125
Rembrandt 125
Rubens in Flanders 126
Velasquez in Spain 127
Versailles 127
Eighteenth-century France 128
Fragonard 128
Watteau 129
Baroque sculpture and architecture 129
Bernini in Italy 130
The palace of Caserta 130
Baroque and Rococo in Austria, Bavaria, and Spain 131
Mansart in France 132
Wren in England 132
Eighteenth-century England 133
Portraits 133
Van Dyck 133
Hogarth 134
Reynolds 134
Gainsborough 134
William Blake 134
The country scene 135
Possible essays, discussion and research 137
Suggested further reading 137

13 A PERIOD OF TRANSITION 138
El Greco 138
Goya 138
From Classicism to Romanticism 139
David and Delacroix 139
Corot 140
The great age of English landscape 140
Turner and Constable 140
The Norwich School 143
The Pre-Raphaelites 145
Treatment of landscapes at different times compared 145
Treatment of animals compared 148
Equestrian statues 148
Possible essays, discussion and research 150
Suggested further reading 150

14 IMPRESSIONISM 151
Manet and the Salon 151
Aspects of Impressionism 153
Seurat and Pointillism 153
Monet 154
Degas 155
Renoir 155
Toulouse-Lautrec 156
Sisley and Pissarro 156
Cézanne 157
Van Gogh and Gauguin 158
Rousseau 160
Achievements of the Impressionists 162
Possible essays, discussion and research 165
Suggested further reading 165

15 A BRIEF SURVEY OF ARCHITECTURAL TRENDS FROM THE EIGHTEENTH CENTURY TO THE PRESENT DAY 166
Eighteenth-century architecture in Britain 166
The Adam brothers 166
John Nash 166
Revivals: Classical and Gothic 166
Art Nouveau 167
The advent of steel 167
The Crystal Palace 167
Reinforced concrete 168
William Morris 168
Gropius and the Bauhaus 169
Le Corbusier 170
Restoration and rebuilding after the Second World War 170
Employment of progressive artists 171
Renaissance of stained glass and tapestry 171
John Ruskin 172
Contribution by engineers and designers 172
Possible essays, discussion and research 173
Suggested further reading 173

16 MODERN ART 174
The expansion of patronage 174
Great changes in the approach to art 175
Cézanne, the first modern 175
L'École de Paris 175
Utrillo 176
The Fauves 176
Matisse 177
Vlaminck 177
Rouault 178

Cubism: Picasso and Braque 178
Expressionism 179
Respect for medium 180
Abstract art: Kandinsky 181
Surrealism: Chagall 182
Action painting: Jackson Pollock 183
Kinetic art and Op art: Vasarely 183
Minimal art 184
Quality of colour in contemporary art 184
Australian painting 185
Pop art and Roy Lichtenstein 186
Four Moderns 187
Ben Nicholson 187
Albert Marquet 187
Paul Klee 187
L. S. Lowry 187
Experience and new discoveries 188
Possible essays, discussion and research 189
Suggested further reading 189

APPENDIX ONE—ART GALLERIES AND MUSEUMS IN GREAT BRITAIN 191

APPENDIX TWO—ART GALLERIES AND MUSEUMS IN AUSTRALIA AND NEW ZEALAND 195

ANSWERS 197

INDEX 201

Chapter One

HOW TO USE THIS BOOK

A great many authors have written on the appreciation of art, but most of them presuppose a good deal of knowledge not necessarily possessed by even the most intelligent reader.

This book is intended to serve as an introduction to the appreciation of art. It is not a history of art, but there is a loose chronological thread and very brief historical notes are introduced in some sections. It does not pretend to give any technical knowledge but is designed to encourage appreciation of a wide range of art as a general background for any study of the humanities. For more detailed information there is a list of suggested books at the end of each chapter. These tend to be more specialized and more advanced towards the end of the book.

It is obvious that the generalization necessary when covering a period from prehistory to the present day in a short book is dangerous and may lead to misconceptions; also, as there is no space for more than one or two examples of any individual's work, the value of his contribution to art can be wrongly assessed. For instance, Picasso's tremendous achievement cannot be judged by studying two paintings, since his forms of expression have passed through so many phases.

In each section I have put forward some ideas, some accepted facts and some of my own reactions to specific works of art. After reading each section, the beginner should have widened his experience and should have at least a glimmering of the tremendous scope of art appreciation. Each chapter is followed by some suggestions for essays, discussions, and the discovering of new things of interest. In the main, there are no correct nor incorrect answers to these, but you will find, at the end of the book, lines along which your arguments might have run, and possible avenues of research.

Half-way through the book and at the end you will find reproductions without titles, dates or any information; these are for you to study so that you can form your own opinion in the light of the experience you have gained.

As they are limited in number, each reproduction or photograph is referred to in several places and compared with others.

In describing and appreciating the works of art, I have, in the main, kept to those periods and movements previously dealt with, so that there is a gradual building-up of appreciation and a widening of the field.

When other considerations are equal, I have chosen works which are easily available to the public. Since museums in Great Britain have collections of outstanding value, many examples are taken from the London museums and from galleries all over the country. Others come from the capitals of Europe and a few from the Commonwealth. It is to be hoped that everyone using this book will find means of visiting several major collections or a number of monuments and will seek out either the originals of the works described or others of the same style and period.

Since there are no colour reproductions, it has not been found advisable to include examples of those modern paintings which depend almost entirely on colour for their effect. In order to include less familiar works, I have left out photographs of very well-known buildings such as the Eiffel Tower. In some cases I have sketched a familiar painting or piece of sculpture as a reminder, or I have made a diagram to show some point of composition, design or comparison.

Above all, it is hoped that this book will make the reader more fully and more clearly aware not only of works of art as such, but of everything around him. After all, artists are specialists at seeing: whether they be painters, poets, sculptors or architects, they see more clearly and feel more intensely about what they have seen than other people.

What I have to say has inevitably a personal bias. How much I am stimulated by a work of art is important to me. My reactions are, I hope, liable to change. The really important thing is to experience what the artist has to give and to increase *your* ability to receive or reject it, according to whether it is significant or commonplace.

As you see more to stimulate you in art, you will find more to interest you, and you should see the things around you more intensely. You will gradually develop a personal taste and discernment, the kind of discernment which, should you have half-an-hour to spend in a small provincial gallery with no major works (although most of them have some), will enable you to know how to spend your time, and the significant paintings will draw your attention. A half-hour spent like this will give intense enjoyment.

For those in large towns with easy access to collections, it is an excellent idea to make short visits, to concentrate on seeing just a few paintings or perhaps only one at a time. Even the specialist requires exceptional stamina to spend hours in a museum. I derive a great deal of personal pleasure from minor or little-known provincial museums anywhere, and taking the time to enjoy painting or sculpture as though I had all the leisure in the world. There are many lovely 'major' works of minor artists to be found and savoured, and much to be discovered even in very minor works.

During the Second World War, some of the major collections in London displayed one picked work at a time, near the main entrance, so that anyone with ten minutes to spare between raids or stress of work could get solace by becoming part of the tremendous creative power which reasserts itself and forget, for a while, the negative destructive forces of war.

Do not despise anything that is to hand, even a show by amateur painters or a private house opened for charity for one day. Go and see and test your discernment and your capacity for enjoyment.

Whenever a painter or work of art is mentioned, there will usually be a reference to where you can get further information, and the bibliography will help you to find more advanced reading. This book is really meant to stimulate *you* to seek specialist knowledge for yourself, but above all it gives a wide canvas so that you should be better able to enjoy art in all its aspects. After all, if you have only seen the paintings of, say, Michelangelo, you cannot truly assess their value unless you have also seen, say, Rembrandt's or Picasso's. If you have only travelled to Rome, you cannot say with truth that it is the best or worst city in Europe.

The human mind has an infinite capacity for rejecting what it does not want, so there is no fear of getting indigestion from taking in too much. By acquiring more experience, taste becomes more fastidious and automatically rejects what is trivial. At least we can hope that this is true since it is the best we can do.

Chapter Two

HOW TO LOOK AND SEE

In the year 300 B.C. certain philosophers and scholars came to the conclusion that civilization had reached its apogee and that man could not expect any further progress in the realms of Art, science, and philosophy. I am not quite sure how this pronouncement was made but it is certainly credible that there were men who could believe in its validity. Twenty-two centuries later, Spengler came to a similar conclusion, asserting that western civilization had reached its peak towards the end of the eighteenth century and that the decline of all human values began at that time.

THE IMPACT OF IMPRESSIONISM

Certainly in the last quarter of the nineteenth century, when the French Impressionists exhibited their light-flooded paintings to an astonished public, conventional opinion proclaimed them insane and asserted that all these artists stood for was a negation of the art of painting; doubtless the same was felt about contemporary movements in sculpture and architecture. Impressionism broke the chains which bound painters to the accepted academic style if they wanted to exhibit in the Paris *Salon* (the French equivalent of the Royal Academy exhibitions of art in London), almost the only place where they could exhibit at that time. It also opened the way for further experiments and movements such as the post-Impressionism of Cézanne. It is Cézanne who is the real creator of modern art, and he himself said: 'I am the primitive of the way I have discovered', leaving his successors to develop his ideas still further and to explore the possibilities of even newer forms of expression.

ART IS TIMELESS

There are endless examples of public outcry against revolutions in art, since most people like repetition and no effort is needed to accepted oft-repeated and familiar forms; there is no shock of impact, but neither is there any real satisfaction nor any expansion of the mind. This does not, of course, mean that only unfamiliar forms are exciting, nor that representational art is dull. Repeated use of popular means of expression, with no conviction behind it and no impelling force, *is* dull, for live art is presented in an impelling way: the only way that the artist feels able to express himself. Anything else is small-talk and trivial; there is no achievement and therefore no important communication between the beholder and the painter. All works of art, to whatever period of history they belong, express permanent values, and if they have the quality of life, they are timeless in their appeal.

It follows that it is possible for the same person to enjoy a prehistoric cave painting, the Parthenon, Michelangelo's *David*, a Flemish Nativity, Gothic carving, Impressionist paintings, and abstract paintings of the twentieth century; for each has something different to contribute to the stream of art, a flow which is ever reaching back further into the past in the light of new archaeological discoveries and into the future with the birth of new genius. It may have its periods of decline, but will nevertheless gather and renew itself as long as humanity survives.

Obviously no one would expect to get the same reaction to the Parthenon as to one of Matisse's statements in pure colour, nor from a twelfth-century processional cross and a portrait by Rembrandt, but there is no doubt that all these have the essential qualities of a great work of art, and it is just these qualities which are so difficult to define.

'BEAUTY' IN A WORK OF ART

Many people seek beauty in a work of art, and 'beautiful' is the description most often heard in a museum or gallery. This is a much misused word, usually implying that the subject depicted conforms to conventional standards of perfection or to personal preferences and has little to do with the object's quality as a work of art. Few of us can define beauty beyond the pedestrian combination of qualities delighting the eye, and still fewer use the word with discretion. A 'beautiful portrait' generally means a portrait of a beautiful woman or handsome man, and a 'beautiful landscape painting' is usually a painting, irrespective of its quality, of a stretch of beautiful countryside, and the qualifying word really states whether the 'beautiful' object has been convincingly represented in the picture.

Despite the fact that the public has been seeing experiments in art which not only dispense with the need to represent familiar forms meticulously, but also use entirely new materials, the vast majority of people are still obsessed by representational painting and sculpture, and traditional styles in building. One of the aims of this book is to get rid of prejudices (although in doing so it will probably create others) and to bring a fresh approach not only to the more 'difficult' modern works of art, but also to the appreciation and enjoyment of works of art of any period and any style. Obviously everyone has his own likes and dislikes. Nothing could be worse than negative indifference except, perhaps, 'good taste' which amounts to no taste as it allows for nothing that does not conform or harmonize, for no shocks, no brave experiments with colours and shapes, no fun, no errors nor splendid failures. It only changes with fashion and is usually dictated by 'experts'.

Nevertheless, no one but a fool would disregard tradition entirely nor ignore the accepted masterpieces of art which have become part of our heritage, and it is obvious that anyone who cannot find delight in most of the works of art which have stood the test of time is missing great experiences.

Great works of art have no fashion for the discerning. An open-minded critic can appreciate any work of quality even if it is of a period or style that is passing through a stage of unpopularity with the public or specialists; he can appreciate that a 'popular' school of painting or a 'popular' artist does not always run to form, and however trivial some of the work produced may be, it is also possible for something of outstanding merit to appear.

ART AND CRAFT

In the past the field of art was divided into sections at different levels. The term 'Fine Arts' meant paintings, architecture, and sculpture for public or private delight; the 'Minor Arts' defined the work of goldsmiths, illuminators, ivory workers; 'crafts' were produced by craftsmen or skilled workmen and included wood carving, folk art, primitive art, and ironwork. 'Commercial Art' referred to designs and decorations produced to promote commerce, and was, until recently, far down the scale of values.

MATERIALS AND TECHNIQUE

Now the attitude has changed and it is recognized that a superbly wrought chalice, an illuminated manuscript, a peasant's wood carving or a prehistoric cave painting are not necessarily lesser works of art than frescoes or portraits or religious compositions. With 'Pop Art', considered by some to be an important contribution to modern art, commercial art has been drawn into the field, for Pop artists are expressing the age we live in: an age where advertising plays such a large part. Similarly in the past, painting was carried out in oils, water-colour or tempera on a wall or flat surface, while sculpture was carved from stone or wood, or cast in bronze. Now we are used to any material, cloth, paper, metal, plastics, even selected junk, being employed for either 'painting' or sculpture.

Since these new materials and techniques have come into use, a whole new language has been born, not only of essential new terms for new things, but new or coined phrases to explain away obscurities. These, when originally employed, had some meaning; but they have now become a jargon which only adds to the confusion, and descriptions have become clichés which convey nothing.

It is possible to appreciate a work of art without any knowledge of its background, without any knowledge of its place of origin and without any practical knowledge of art, but this is a rare gift. For most people it is certainly an advantage to understand even a little about the circumstances in which a work of art was produced and something about those who produced it. Expert knowledge of any technique obviously sharpens the perceptions of the beholder, but when it comes to the instant magic of those rare expressions of genius which combine popular appeal with genius, it is readily accessible to all.

However the object of this book is to carry appreciation of art much further than this and, to help to achieve this object, there are two essentials: a growing experience and an open mind.

Experience can only come with constant effort in really looking and valuing everything around. Clearly the more different kinds of art are appreciated, the greater the enlargement of experience, though to try to take too much in at once is always dangerous. Ten minutes of enjoyment are worth two hours of study at saturation point, and concentrating on one particular school or period of architecture or painting is usually more valuable to the beginner than darting about from one type to another since different styles need a little getting used to. As comparison always plays a part in appraising anything, if only inferior works are seen there can be no judgment. So it is extremely important to look as soon as possible at some originals of high standing: works of art which, by the assessment of time, are without doubt of the highest order.

Secondly, it is essential to keep an open mind and accept what the artist has to offer, with no preconceived prejudice, for an artist works in the way he feels compelled to work, and expresses whatever he has to say in the only way he can. Although he will develop and change with experience, he cannot successfully work in any other way. Nevertheless no one can be entirely free from personal bias and would not wish to be; everyone will at times be out of sympathy with even acclaimed masterpieces.

This book will necessarily be biased and it will express some views different from those I might have expressed a few years ago or may express in the future, for, with increased experience and knowledge and new things seen, there is a constant adjustment of taste and a gradual appreciation of things which did not appeal earlier.

EXAMPLES FROM DIFFERENT PERIODS

In this chapter I have chosen examples in different fields of art from prehistoric times to the present day which are not presented chronologically nor with more than the briefest mention of their origin. Most of them are timeless, but they include some which are half in the realms of engineering or design and they are not all of the same standards of excellence. These may be referred to again from time to time in comparison with others described later and in the light of any knowledge which may have been gained.

PREHISTORIC

Bronze Cult Chariot (*about* 700 B.C.). *Joanneum, Graz, Austria* (Plate 1). Even to the least interested of laymen this bronze from Strettweg in Austria is clearly a primitive and religious work. It is equally evident that the artist or artists responsible have given an intense life to the group: a surge of vitality and enthusiasm for whatever aspect of religion is being celebrated. Each of the figures has astonishing grace stressed by the subtle movement of long athletic limbs. The figures and stags and armed horsemen press forward in emotional fervour, looking like pronged spears. The force of movement seems to turn the chariot's wheels, but the whole composition is given stability by the immensely tall, very slender, figure of a goddess or priestess who places her upraised arms beneath a great dish resting on her head. Animals' heads, possibly deer, decorate the wheel shafts.

The figures are so composed as to look impressive from any angle, and the contrast between the gently curved bodies of men and animals with the straight lines of the chariot and the sharply spiked antlers is most effective. Although it would be interesting to discover exactly what this represents, it has an immediate appeal to the least knowledgeable. It makes one long to run a hand down over these vital forms and feel the tautness of the limbs and the proud carriage of head and shoulders.

AFRICAN

Bronze Head of Queen Mother (*probably* 16*th century*). *British Museum, London* (Plate 2).This head from Benin, Nigeria, probably cast over 2,000 years later than the Strettweg chariot, has the same tremendous power but also a classical perfection and refinement. Since Europe and Africa were in contact in very early times, it is possible that the magnificent bronzes of the Benin period were influenced by classical antiquity. There is no unnecessary elaboration here, but an astonishing grasp of the essentials of form and restraint in the treatment of the decorative head-dress. Dignity and majesty are both expressed in this head so regally set on the slender encircled neck, and, as in most of these bronzes, there is a look of thoughtfulness and great intelligence in the eyes and sensitivity in the mouth and nostrils. Here again one wants to feel the subtly rendered form and pass a hand up the sweeping curve of the pointed head-dress.

ETRUSCAN

Etruscan Winged Horses (4*th to* 3*rd century* B.C.). *National Museum, Tarquinia, Italy* (Plate 3). Although this pair of horses was probably created to form part of a temple pediment, it stands in its own right as an important terracotta. Strong and pulsing with life, these superb animals are tensed to rush forward. An immense reserve of strength would seem to enable them to lift their bodies effortlessly into the sky with the help of finely tapered wings, and to speed on into the mists of the Etruscan afterlife. Their splendid heads are drawn back for an instant in arrested movement, but their pointed ears and wide-open eyes, the hooves already lifting from the ground and the continuous flow of rippling muscles show them alert and full of purpose. They are indeed horses of the gods, reined back from Olympus for a brief moment that we may wonder, and for a spell, enter into the mysterious world of Etruscan art.

MEDIEVAL GLASS

Samuel (12*th century*). *Stained glass in Canterbury Cathedral* (Fig. 1). The medieval stained-glass worker has shown full respect for his

Fig. 1

medium and has not attempted any elaborations which might have spoilt the boldness of effect. He had only a small range of colours in this case: a saffron yellow for the large area of the robe, broken by the thick dark lines of the lead used both to hold the glass together and to outline the figure and drapery; a background blue, a red and a green, and clear glass. The colours are limited in number but there are subtle irregularities and unevenness in the thickness of the glass which the craftsman exploited to the full to give richness of effect and to trap the light.

The glass worker has to play with light and colour. The 'portrait' of Samuel has to be interesting and decorative in itself and to fit in with the other panels to make a larger decoration which must in turn enhance the architecture. Above all, the artist must concern himself with light coming through the glass and being trapped by it. In this panel he has depicted a solemn, enthroned figure in green, yellow, and red against a blue background; the light coming through in varying intensity gives it a mystical, shimmering life.

STEEL

The Eiffel Tower (1889). *Paris.* This was erected for an exhibition and although primarily accepted as a feat of engineering, it is also entirely successful from the point of view of elegance and proportion as it soars effortlessly into the sky, with the grace of a Gothic cathedral. It is a miracle of lightness, yet monumental at the same time. The laciness of the lattice-work on the four immense pylons which gently taper into one and the arches on the low level counteract the austere lines of the structure and make this monument not only a landmark and symbol of Paris—so simple as to be easily remembered—but a work of genius.

VENETIAN SIXTEENTH-CENTURY PAINTING

The Madonna Enthroned. *Giorgione* (1476–1510). *Castelfranco Cathedral, Northern Italy* (Plate 4). Even a casual glance at this glowing painting proclaims the fact that the artist was primarily interested in the putting on of colour and in the possibilities of paint: an interest that was characteristic of the Venetians. He seizes every oportunity of giving us the richness of drapery, the shine of armour, the warm heavy texture of the monk's robe. The structure of the picture, though based on the often-used pyramid, is extremely subtle and full of variety, and the dramatic force of the composition is overwhelming. The perspective lines of a simple black-and-white floor lead the eye to the throne, which is little more than a series of superimposed boxes relieved by an elaborate strip of green brocade and a striped rug, where Mary is lifted majestically above the saints standing on either side. The group is set against a romantic background of castle and woods and gentle, swaying, feathery trees with far-off blue hills fading into the distance against a luminous sky.

The strong blue and deep red folds of the Virgin's dress and mantle fall softly over the throne, and the warm golden skin of the Baby contrasts with this depth of colour. The strong oblique line of the standard and the downward droop of the pennon link the saints with the rest of the picture and save the three rectangular sections at the top from monotony.

Even without taking the picture apart to see how it works, all these facts are unconsciously observed for they combine to give a monumental quality and complete unity to the theme. The solemn dignity of the figures is enhanced by the spaciousness of the setting and yet relieved by the delight that Giorgione experienced in giving us the radiance of the gentle countryside, the silver highlights on the armour and the shine of the gilding in the brocade.

FRENCH ROMANESQUE CARVING

Romanesque Capital. *Musée Municipal, Poitiers* (Fig 2). This dramatic interpretation of discord is typical of the fascinating carvings on capitals and cathedral portals of the Romanesque period. Closely knit, the composition fills a necessarily small space without being cramped. Admittedly the bodies are distorted, but this only gives more fury to the expression of the heads. A unifying flow of design runs through the conventionally treated draperies and hair, but there is just enough diversity in the pose of each figure to avoid monotony. The central figures grip each other's beards with extraordinary ferocity, in contrast to the rather gentle attempt of the smaller

Fig. 2

figures to draw them apart. Decorative architectural features and decorative foliage complete the design held together beneath the scrolled top of the capital, only broken by the heads of the quarrelling figures which are so full of life as to be rising out of the stone. This is a carving of exceptional quality which stands in its own right as a work of art, yet it was one of a series, all different, and fitting in with an architectural whole.

ENGLISH ROMANESQUE CARVING

Romanesque Capital. *Crypt of Canterbury Cathedral* (Fig. 3). This too was carved to add to the beauty of the architecture as a whole, but is quite differently treated. An entirely decorative and lively, though harmless-looking, lion is carved in relief against a flat surface; it is simply a picture of a lion and tells no story apart from some facts about the make-up of the animal. But as a carving it shows astonishing freedom and boldness, and like the capital in Poitiers, it fills the allotted space admirably, the simplicity of handling giving it a kind of majesty. Here too, details are conventional: the hair of the mane and coat are treated conventionally and the tail makes a wonderful swinging curve round the body to end in a fanciful tuft.

Fig. 3

How much more delightful is this beast of the imagination than some of the later carved lions which try to give a replica of the common view of the animal.

MEDIEVAL TAPESTRY

Tapestry: Departure for the Hunt (*early* 16*th century*). *Cluny Museum, Paris* (Fig. 4). In this delightful scene from the series *La Vie Seigneuriale* ('The Lordly Life'), the artist has produced a design entirely suitable for tapestry or embroidery and has not attempted to 'paint pictures'. His figures and animals are given prominence but are flat, decorative, and bold against a *mille fleurs* background of woodland bestrewn with flowers and plants, each

Fig. 4

one treated as an exquisite design, but also imbued with life. The falcon, with all the delicate markings of its wings, is poised ready for flight as soon as the nobleman frees it, while a greyhound sits gazing up at the halbardier who is expectantly awaiting the flight. The deep, simple colouring of blue, red, green, and dusky browns has kept astonishingly fresh and has as much appeal today as it had over 400 years ago; it could just as well decorate a modern house as a Renaissance château.

CHINESE T'ANG POTTERY

Chinese Pottery: Fighting Horse (*T'ang period*). *British Museum, London* (Fig. 5). This grave statuette was produced at some time between the seventh and tenth centuries A.D., but these objects were

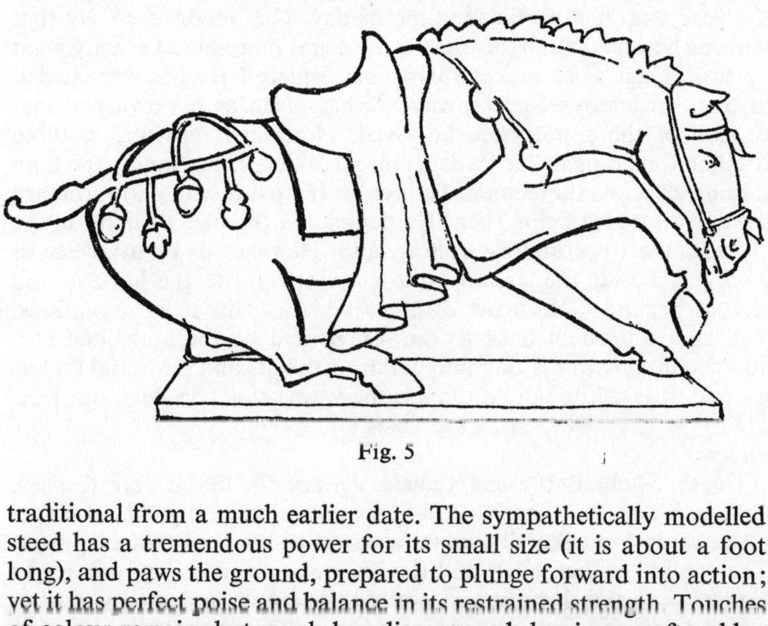

Fig. 5

traditional from a much earlier date. The sympathetically modelled steed has a tremendous power for its small size (it is about a foot long), and paws the ground, prepared to plunge forward into action; yet it has perfect poise and balance in its restrained strength. Touches of colour remain, but much has disappeared, leaving a soft golden ochre. Notice how the forward movement of the off foreleg is balanced by the firm stance of the near leg and how the backward swing of the saddle-cloth counteracts the too-positive forward thrust of the hind leg and helps to give stability to the whole. Though to some extent stylized and an oft-repeated theme, this small model has the life and quality of timelessness.

GREEK FIFTH-CENTURY RELIEF

The Birth of Aphrodite (*Greek, 5th century* B.C.) *Museo delle Terme*, Rome (Plate 5). In this relief, a sculptor with a magical sense of rhythm suggests the flow and transparency of water in the sensitive lines of the draperies of the figures who lift Aphrodite from the sea.

This is accentuated by the ripples over the goddess's shoulders and the flow of her waving hair as she turns her head to gaze at the graceful goddess on her right whose limbs are revealed by the clinging fall of the gown. Aphrodite's young, firm body is treated with the utmost simplicity and half-hidden behind the curved lines of the drapery in which she is being wrapped. The perfect balance of the flanking figures and the subtle lift of Aphrodite's shoulders as she rises, combine with the easy flow of line to express an indefinable charm in the relationship between the figures which makes this one of the masterpieces of fifth-century Greek art.

SEVENTEENTH-CENTURY FLEMISH PAINTING

Château de Steen. *Rubens* (1577–1640). *National Gallery, London* (Plate 6). A painting of a recognizable place at a definite season of the year and at a particular time of day. One might even say that Rubens had held a mirror up to nature and represented exactly what he saw. Then what makes this a masterpiece? He has recreated it in paint in his own special way; he has given us his own personal version of the countryside he loved. Nothing is obvious, nothing is taken for granted. He leads us into a wider, richer landscape than we ourselves would see, and he lays on the paint with extraordinary dexterity without being slick. He delights in the play of light on the château, the trees, and the rolling land. He takes us on a voyage of discovery beside the streams and willows, right to the horizon and almost beyond it, into the distance which seems to be boundless. Yet we are brought back to the foreground by the horse and cart and the man with his dog and details of plants and birds and undergrowth. It is as though he spreads the whole countryside at our feet.

PICASSO

Goat's Skull, Bottle and Candle. *Picasso* (*b.* 1881). *Tate Gallery, London* (Plate 7). A painting in black and white and grey and rather melancholy but, like all Picasso's work, it has tremendous power. The colour (or lack of it) and the interrelation of curves and angles express fear and disturbance, not with nervous, hesitant shapes but with a terrifying certainty and conviction. This is not for those who prefer tranquillity to violent stimulus in a picture, though no one can deny its impact, its architectural unity and inventive genius. It is a work which reveals itself more and more as one looks at it, and it is strange that it can be pictorially so entirely satisfying and emotionally so disturbing. The very definite framework of shapes gives a stained-glass effect and confines the different tones within its latticing.

FOURTEENTH-CENTURY SIENESE PAINTING

The Finding of Christ in the Temple. *Simone Martini* (*c.* 1284–1344), *Walker Art Gallery, Liverpool* (Plate 8). A conception which keeps some of the dignity and majesty of the austere and remote Byzantine style to be seen in ikons, but adds a certain tenderness and emotional concern and the involvement of the three figures with each other. There is no attempt at perspective or the third dimension. The haloes are exquisitely decorative burnished golden plates: decoration which is delicately echoed around the edges of the draperies, accentuating the turn of a wrist or framing a head and shoulders or simply stressing the rhythmic flow of the robes, leading the eye from one figure to another. The painting is finished with the jewel-like brilliance characteristic of the Sienese school, of which Simone Martini was one of the foremost members.

POSSIBLE ESSAYS, DISCUSSION AND RESEARCH

There are no correct or incorrect answers to these questions, but at the end of the book you will find suggested lines along which you might have thought before answering.

1 What common factors make works of art as far removed as the Strettweg Chariot and the Romanesque capitals both masterpieces?

2 Why is the quality of 'life' so important in painting or sculpture?

3 How far do you think it of value in learning to appreciate art to have a knowledge of the artist, his background and his period?

4 Can you make a definite distinction between the major and minor arts, or do you think that they overlap?

5 When, in your opinion, does art become 'commercial'?

6 Why is a good painting better than one of the excellent modern colour photographs?

7 What differences are there between the Etruscan Horses and the Chinese Horse?

8 Rubens' *Sunset* would be unsatisfactory if used as a design for a tapestry. Is this true?

9 Can you find stimulus in both Giorgione and Picasso?

Chapter Three

DIFFERENT ASPECTS OF ART

It is obviously impossible to cover the whole expanding field of art in a limited space, so I shall deal mainly with painting, mosaics, and sculpture; some reference will be made to architecture, but chiefly in so far as it is concerned with these arts. Tapestries, embroideries, metalwork, and stucco will also be mentioned as they form an important part of the decoration of churches, palaces, and cathedrals.

EASEL PAINTINGS

By far the largest part of this book will be devoted to easel paintings, i.e. portable pictures on wooden panels or canvas, since most people have access to originals in museums and galleries in or near their home town, even if they are not able to travel to the large cities or to the continent of Europe.

Easel painting can be carried on in a number of media, the most popular being oil painting on canvas or on prepared panels of wood. The alternative which was used extensively in the early days of European painting, especially in Italy, was to paint on wood in tempera: a powder pigment made fluid by the addition of white of egg. Both these media allow a great deal of freedom of handling and both allow of alterations, but oil paint is more easily handled than tempera and gives a richer result.

The first paintings we know anything about were carried out at some period between 5000 and 2000 B.C. These had developed from meandering designs engraved on the damp clay walls of caves, probably as early as 30,000 B.C., and are in charcoal and simple earth colours. Gradually these designs became recognizable shapes of animals outlined in black and filled in, with one colour to begin with and later with several. The bumpy surface of the rock was often exploited to give actual form to the animals. Some of these 'primitive' works are of an astonishingly high order and must have been created by men of intelligence. Nevertheless, thousands of years passed before the most important schools in European painting—the Italian—produced their early and much more complicated approach to wall paintings in the shape of the very special technique of fresco.

THE TECHNIQUE OF FRESCO

In early frescoes the painter applied pigment to a fresh layer of wet plaster which the paint penetrated and became one with. Only enough plaster could be laid for the day's work and no satisfactory nor permanent alterations could be made. Strokes on the wet plaster are immediately absorbed and, as soon as the plaster is dry, the paint will not adhere properly to the wall unless mixed with special vehicles such as glue, to make it grip. Many of the later wall paintings were not true frescoes—that is, painted *a fresco* (on wet plaster)—but the pigments were mixed with an adhesive and applied *a secco* to a dry wall. Nevertheless the term 'fresco' is loosely used for many types of wall decorations.

In true fresco the wall was first covered with a fairly thick rough layer of plaster and on this the master made a bold sketch of the composition in charcoal. This was then lightly traced in red (*sinopia* red—hence the name *sinopie* for the sketches) and the charcoal was brushed away. This left a clear outline of the intended composition which could be shown to the patron for his approval. The finished design was not a tracing nor a filling in of this, since the area for each day's work was covered with a concealing layer of wet plaster. It was of course a relatively simple matter to redraw the covered portion since it could be linked with the rest of the design which was still visible. Painting could not be continued successfully on the plaster after it had dried, so unpainted plaster was cut away and new laid the next day.

With modern methods of removing frescoes from walls, some of these *sinopie*, which have been hidden for five centuries or more, have been revealed in excellent condition and can be studied alongside the finished fresco. Many of the *sinopie* are extraordinarily fine in their boldness of conception and handling and, as sketches on paper were not made until later, are among the earliest examples of Italian drawings. The same system of *sinopie* was employed for carrying out mosaics which were so much in use by the early Christians for decoration in Byzantium, in Rome and in Venice. In Plates 9 and 10 you can compare the finished frescoes with the *sinopie*.

Oil painting was in use in Flanders even in the fourteenth century and in general use in Europe a little later, although a great deal of work was still carried out in tempera. It is a stronger, richer medium than fresco or tempera and was increasingly employed for easel painting from about the fifteenth century.

MOSAIC

Mosaic, used by the Romans for pavements and rather differently by the Byzantines for walls, requires great skill in handling. This difficult technique was used to perfection in the walls of early Christian and Byzantine churches. A mosaic is made up of *tesserae*, pieces of coloured glass and stone and gold set unevenly into plaster so that they catch the light at different angles and shimmer in the mysterious gloom of the almost windowless churches and baptisteries. Mosaics were used to represent in gleaming golden majesty God the Father or God the Pancreator, huge and remote in the dome or apse of a basilica; or smaller scenes in detail, of the life of Christ or the saints or even of the Empress Theodora, the great sixth-century patron of the arts in Ravenna.

STAINED GLASS

Since the Church was the main patron of the arts in Europe, from early Christian times until the Renaissance, the demand was for decorating the churches with illustrations of the Bible stories for those who could not read, so almost all art was of a religious nature. When expense was a consideration, vast areas of church walls were decorated with frescoes, since they were less costly than mosaics; and when the style of architecture developed from the Romanesque to the lofty Gothic, which permitted the construction of huge windows to let in the light, wall space was much smaller and the pale emptiness of the building was enlivened with the glowing stained glass that has become the glory of European cathedrals. These stained-glass windows told the Bible stories and not only provided separately designed incidents which could be read consecutively, but were continued into a whole large design knit together with lead and the decorative tracery of the framework.

CARVING

Carvings, statues, and reliefs on façades, portals, and capitals were also religious in subject, but often included fanciful creatures of the mason's imagination—as can be seen so well in the fierce animals and grotesque figures which enlivened the capitals in the churches and provided the gargoyles on the roof of Notre Dame in Paris.

THE WORK OF GOLDSMITHS AND SILVERSMITHS

Goldsmiths and silversmiths, wondrously skilled in their craft, fashioned reliquaries, caskets, and processional crosses, and set them with jewels and enamels just as rich and glowing as the magnificent crown jewels; church vestments were richly embroidered in brilliant designs, and even lenten cloths were painted on huge strips of linen in bright colours. Ivory was carved in infinite detail and delicacy, in contrast to the bolder relief of stonework, and used to depict such scenes as the Navity or Crucifixion.

Examples of all these crafts can be found even in small churches in Britain and on the Continent, and no one should go into a cathedral to look at a splendid altarpiece and ignore the other marvels of art and craftmanship around him or preserved in the treasury or sacristry.

MODERN MEDIA

During the present century there has been a great deal of experimenting with all kinds of new and mixed media: metal, paper, cloth, and wood being affixed in collage to the painting surface and new kinds of synthetic paint have been added to the range. Artists feel free to use gloss paint, distemper or dyes, even all of them in the same painting. Plastic emulsion paints are still in the experimental stage but have already shown great potentialities, for they can be mixed with water or a special medium and used thin or thick, transparent, glossy or matt; the main disadvantage, which is at times an advantage, is that they dry rather too quickly for easy handling. We cannot yet say how permanent they are.

DRAWINGS

For centuries ink, charcoal, chalk, wash, and pencil have been used for sketches and for detailed studies of anything from minute plant forms such as Dürer depicted so delicately, to large cartoons (working designs) such as Raphael painted for his tapestries and Michelangelo used for his paintings and frescoes.

WATER-COLOURS; GOUACHE

Water-colour was very popular as a medium for landscape painting with the eighteenth-century English artists, pure and transparent, or opaque when the colours are mixed with white. This opaque colour, or *gouache*, is a medium which is very much favoured today and is usually considered easier to handle than water-colour since it is possible to make alterations which cannot be done effectively in water-colour.

PASTELS

Pastels are rather transitory as a medium unless very well fixed and protected. The medium is made from coloured powder bound with gum and moulded into sticks which are very fragile to handle. The powder breaks down when applied so that areas or lines of colour adhere to the paper. Children's cheap chalks are a harder form of pastel.

In the nineteenth century, Degas produced some exquisitely delicate pastels. His ballet girls in their slightly tawdry costumes take us right on to the stage, the satin shimmering in the footlights and described by him as: 'The dancing girls have sewn my heart into a satin bag—pink satin, a little faded like their ballet shoes.' These sensitive and lovely drawings have no relation to the slick modern portraits of children and animals sketched in pastels by society portraitists.

ENGRAVINGS, WOODCUTS, ETCHINGS, LITHOGRAPHY

We are here concerned only with the artist's employment of the technique.

Engraving is a system of cutting a design into a plate of stone, metal or wood, so that numbers of prints may be taken from it. Its employment for commercial purposes is obvious when craftsmen reproduce an artist's work, but it also stands in its own right as an art when the artist himself engraves upon the plate a design he has specially prepared for the purpose. When colour is used, several blocks are needed for the different colours and each has to be registered so that they do not overlap. Overprinting of, say, yellow on blue to produce green reduces the number of plates needed.

Woodcuts (and lino-cuts and the child's potato cuts) are produced by cutting away unwanted material and leaving the areas and lines to be printed untouched. When covered with ink these areas will print, but the gouged-out areas will remain white. Similarly a white line on black can be achieved by engraving lines into the block so that a white design appears on a black or coloured ground.

In engraving on metal, the area cut away is reproduced in black and this system includes a number of different techniques. The engraved plate is covered with ink and is then wiped so that the ink clings only to the engraved lines. In etching, the metal plate is covered with resin which is scratched with a needle to expose areas to a bath of acid which eats into the engraved lines, then the resin is removed and the plate printed as with line engraving.

Woodcuts were used at the end of the fourteenth century, and Dürer produced superb woodcuts a century later, but wood engraving came into use in the eighteenth. Etching had its greatest period with Rembrandt (1606–69) although it was used a century earlier.

Mention must be made here of lithography, a process invented at the end of the eighteenth century; it is not engraving, but relies on the fact that water and grease do not mix. The design is made with a greasy chalk on a stone or metal plate; the plate is then damped, but the water flows off the grease. The plate is then covered with greasy ink which will not cling to the damp surface but only to the greasy lines. This is a very free technique and at first glance is like an original drawing. This was the forerunner of the much more sophisticated litho technique now used extensively for modern posters and book illustrations.

TAPESTRY

Tapestries often constitute part of the decoration of a church as well as serving to warm the cold stonework, and they can be major works of art. The same cannot be said of printed material, however attractive it may be, for even if printed by hand the pattern can be repeated indefinitely. Tapestry is usually the result of the co-operation of artist and craftsmen just as a pianoforte performance is the combined effort of pianist and composer. It is made by weaving coloured wools and follows a design specially prepared by an artist. Less successfully, it can also reproduce an existing painting in wool. The famous Bayeux Tapestry is erroneously termed: it is actually a strip of cloth *embroidered* with wool; it is not woven.

SCULPTURE

Sculpture is produced by two methods: (*a*) by carving in the round or in relief, (*b*) by modelling. In the first, material is chipped away to leave the desired form; in the second, shapes are built up from nothing with clay and, since clay soon crumbles when dry, a plaster cast is taken from it in which process the original clay is destroyed. Subsequently bronze casts can be made from the plaster cast.

Bronze casting has a very long history, but medieval artists used to carve in wood and cover this area with plates of metal. Modern sculptors tend to carve rather than to model, since a direct approach with respect for the limitations of the medium is preferred and the sculptor likes to be in contact with the finished work of art (Plate 13).

MAJOR AND MINOR ARTS

It is generally accepted that the major arts are painting, sculpture, and architecture, and that 'crafts' such as wrought iron, ivory carving, glass-making, and embroidery are minor arts. I have not confined this book to major arts.

I shall refer to some things which are not generally classified as works of art, if they are capable of 'lifting the spirit', such as the splendid sweeps of an arterial road which sculptures the bones of a landscape with its curves, its bridges, and its flyovers and is capable of complementing the grandeur of the landscape. So, too, can a machine stimulate the senses in its functional perfection—the lines of the Concorde, not entirely bird-like but the re-creation of a bird on a huge scale, with swiftness and grace as it pierces the clouds but seems one with the atmosphere. We shall probably become so used to its rhythmic curve that it will arouse less wonder than the stately lines of pylons which stride so majestically over the countryside.

Clearly perceptive people will look with discerning eyes at a viaduct, a motor road or a roll of printed silk. They will, however, probably find greater stimulus in the work of the painter or sculptor who uses his personal vision of the world around him and translates it on to canvas or into stone, giving it life and a degree of magic. Whether it be abstract or representational, whether it be of familiar forms or an experiment into new realms of colour, the result will enlarge the experience of the beholder.

Ceramics hover between being an art or a craft, but I am loath to dismiss the sensitively handled Chinese grave figures (Fig. 5) and animals as being incapable of arousing emotion or taking us into a world of wider horizons. The same applies to the beautiful Greek figurines made in thousands, and those from the civilizations of Crete and Mycenæ and the wondrously fashioned golden masks. Yet the necklets of golden flowers, the bracelets and clasps so beautifully conceived and skilfully wrought are the work of craftsmen and, except in very rare cases, their function is decorative rather than creative.

The craft of overlapping brilliantly coloured feathers to make head-dresses, rugs, and even shields, as practised by the pre-Columbian South Americans, is fascinating but not a major art; and although many primitive carvings and even totem poles can be inspiring, many more are, although attractive, mainly repetitive.

EXAMPLES OF DIFFERENT MEDIA

At this stage I am taking specific examples of some of these types of art, looking at them closely in order to see where their greatness (or, in some cases, their inadequacy) lies.

PREHISTORIC LASCAUX

The Leaping Wild Ox. *Lascaux*, *France* (Fig. 6). Carried out at some period between 15,000 and 10,000 B.C., this reveals an astonishing understanding of animals and a feeling for movement and

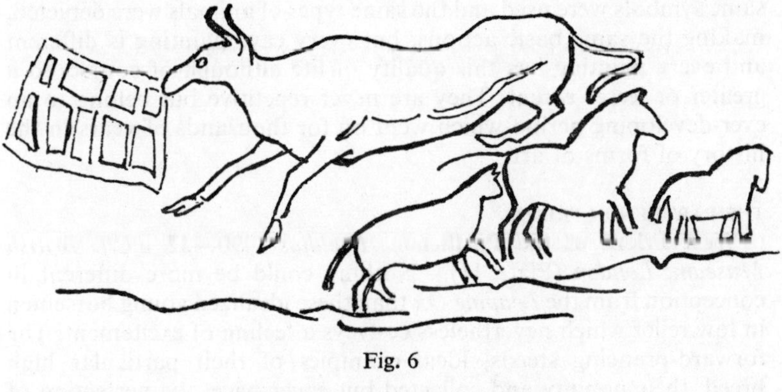

Fig. 6

dramatic force. The great leaping ox, with his decoratively drawn hooves and horns and his swishing tail, is definitely wild and also obviously much admired by the hunter who painted it. He had certainly memorized its movements, the better to re-create it on the walls of the cave: to hold it imprisoned there, perhaps even to capture its soul with the curious symbol of a trap. Though their manes are flowing, the gentle-looking ponies move quite slowly in the opposite direction, in contrast to the strong leap of the ox.

Clearly the uneven surface of the wall has been exploited to give texture, form, and an almost luminous quality to the skins of the animals. Indeed the very roughness of the stone may have dictated some of the shapes. The ox's body is painted in black over red, and his internal organs are visible; the ponies are brown with black outlines. Why should the primitive hunters have painted such animals in their dark caves where it is difficult to see them? It is probable that they were making magic and making it for a variety of reasons, but mainly, surely, to ensure a perpetual supply of animals for food and skins, and for bones for implements.

As they destroyed the animals, they wanted to re-create them, and more especially their souls, so that they could have life apart from the body. Maybe there was, too, a kind of boosting of morale for the hunter, so that with a picture of the splendid animals in his mind he would venture out to hunt confident of success: even this was a kind of magic. So these early men did what their artist successors were to do: they made magic, probably for their own satisfaction rather than for the benefit of the beholder.

Perhaps the tremendous impact of these creatures upon us is due to the fact that their creators really lived among them, and the wild life surrounding them was their whole world. For instance, it is believed that spots increased fertility, so some animals are covered in spots; antlers have been meticulously observed and the softness of hair and fur convincingly portrayed. They were certainly not 'backward' as regards artistic genius, for a painting such as this can rank with the greatest achievements of any time. It is true that the same symbols were used and the same types of animals were depicted, making the same basic actions, but every cave painting is different and every painting has this quality of life although of course, to a greater or lesser extent. They are never repetitive but belong to an ever-developing period which went on for thousands of years in the history of forms of art.

THE PARTHENON FRIEZE

West Frieze of the Parthenon. *Pheidias* (490–432 B.C.). *British Museum, London* (Plate 11). Nothing could be more different in conception from the *Leaping Ox* than these idealized young horsemen in low relief which nevertheless conveys a feeling of excitement. The forward-prancing steeds, ideal examples of their particular high breed, their nobility and collected but eager pace, the perfection of form in the riders' bodies and the well-knit, satisfying composition of each group of figures contributes towards this. The onward rush is stopped from being precipitous by the backward twist of the first rider's torso and head, and the riders are linked by the horses' movement and the flow of drapery from the foremost rider. Yet this detail of a larger scene has excitement more intensely conveyed than reality. It not only displays the ideals of a highly civilized nation at the peak of its artistic development but, as with the horses and the oxen of Lascaux, it recreates the excitement of a splendid procession and the importance of the Goddess Athene to the Athenians to a similar degree as the magic of the animals, the very lifeblood of the hunters' existence, is conveyed in the cave paintings.

THE BOOK OF KELLS

Portrait of Christ from the Book of Kells (*9th century*). *Trinity College Library, Dublin* (Plate 12). This page, from a book of the Gospels probably brought unfinished from Iona by Irish monks, combines majesty and a monumental quality of design with the most delicate and intricate imaginative detail which in itself has almost barbaric splendour. There is no waywardness in the strong, firm, dark outlines of the figure of Christ and of His features. The body is absolutely flat, the limbs being merely indicated by the fold of the drapery; the hair patterns the forehead in a strong black outline, but is also an interlacing of scrolls in keeping with the elongated beasts interlaced round the framework. Primitive-looking birds with decorative wings and feathers flank the head of Christ but do not break its isolation and remoteness. The colour has the depth and richness of fire and earth and rock: deep red and brown, dense green and deep purple, black ochre, all combining in richness almost equal to a mosaic. It is astonishing how such depth and splendour can be effected without the use of gold. Everything is stated uncompromisingly, from the most minute detail to the broadest sweep of a fold in the drapery and, although the artist or artists have obviously taken a delight in the flow of the interlacing ornamentation and the invention of strange grotesque beasts, none of the detail detracts in the slightest from the grand conception of the whole.

An illustration to a book, certainly, and descriptive enough for those who cannot read, but nevertheless an illustration raised to the heights of great art.

TWELFTH-CENTURY MOSAIC

Mosaic: Christ Pantocrator (*12th century*). *Cefalù Cathedral, Sicily* (Fig. 7). This huge mosaic in the dome of the apse has a power and majesty which could not have been so successfully expressed in any other medium. Formal and austere, the majesty of Christ is not only conveyed by mere size, but by a grand conception of every detail of the head and shoulders and drapery. Every fold of the mantle and robe is stressed by a strong rhythmic line flowing into the outline of hair and neck and even the upraised hand, even the circle of the halo continuing round the neck of the robe, just sufficiently broken to be astringent. The rectangular shape of the open book gives just the right contrast to the curved lines to be satisfying. Even in a small reproduction some of the awe-inspiring impact of this magnificent mosaic can be felt, but to stand before it in the vast and bare cathedral is to be utterly overwhelmed by its power.

Fig. 7

FRESCO

St. Ansanus. *Francesco d'Antonio di Bartolommeo* (1393–*c.* 1433). *Church of San Nicholò, Florence* (Plate 9: Fresco. Plate 9a: *sinopia*). Painted by a minor and little-known Florentine, this fresco, though attractive enough in colour and general design and decorative frame, has no great impact and lacks life; but the *sinopia*, is bold and more convincing. Note the assurance with which the saint's right leg is drawn and particularly the slim ankle and foreshortened foot. This assurance is entirely lost in the painting.

Crucifixion. *Master from Pistoia* (mid-thirteenth century). *Church of San Domenico Pistoia* (Plate 10: Fresco. Plate 10a: *sinopia*). This shows the interesting changes in the fresco made by the artist perhaps, as Prof. Umberto Baldini suggests, by the patron, for it is possible to discern on the *sinopia* faint marks of the alterations. The drawing suggests a dramatic scene with the soldier one side and St. John and the Virgin on the left. The painting is much more austere, much more conventional and far less human.

WOODCUTS

Woodcut: The Four Horsemen of the Apocalypse. *Albrecht Dürer* (1471–1528). *Albertina, Vienna* (Plate 76). The tremendous gallop of onrush, the intense vitality of every line, Dürer's own invention for conveying hair and feathers in a woodcut and his respect for the limitations of the material, make this one of the finest illustrations in existence. Look at the marvellous rendering of the hands, the overwhelming power of the horsemen, the collapse of the figures they are trampling upon, yet the staggering man in the right-hand corner serves to prevent the riders from going headlong out of the picture.

Looking at this woodcut it is obvious that Dürer was an astonishingly accomplished draughtsman.

SEVENTEENTH-CENTURY SPANISH PAINTING

Don Balthazar Carlos. *Velasquez* (1599–1660). *The Prado, Madrid* (Plate 16). A wonderful equestrian portrait without any of the pompousness and majesty usually found in portraits of kings, but regal nonetheless, as the obviously royal prince rushes across the canvas in a surge of vitality evident in the pony and in the child's erect and proud little body. The gay tilt of the ridiculous hat, the sash flowing out in company with the tough bay pony's tail, the flowing mane, the pretty trappings all set against a swinging landscape and a racing sky. This painting reveals the absolute command Velasquez had over the medium of oil, which in a lesser artist would have amounted to a fatal facility. Velasquez has such a mastery of tone, and his colour is orchestrated so superbly that despite his lack of imagination and his unemotional acceptance of things as they are, the result is of such stupendous and satisfying achievement that the painting must rank with the greatest. We can only wonder and admire this remarkable achievement, at the way in which he states the drama of the scene, and the genius with which he can express grandeur and dignity even in a child.

SEVENTEENTH-CENTURY DRAWING

Girl Sleeping. *Rembrandt* (1606–69). *British Museum, London* (Plate 17). This drawing of a woman deeply sleeping conveys complete relaxation with a few decisive yet sensitive strokes of the brush. The varying thickness of line caresses the form beneath the drapery and with the greatest economy conveys a solid body. The weight of the head on the arm is strongly expressed by the solid mass resting on the one sharp angle in the drawing, and the firmly stated end of the sleeve, from which comes the scarcely suggested forearm with a beautifully subtle droop of the wrist. Strong vertical brush strokes counteract the oblique slope of the figure, while the wash in the upper corner suggests light and accentuates the atmosphere of utter quietness.

Even in this 'lightning sketch' Rembrandt expresses that arresting radiance which comes from within his figures rather than from an independent source of light.

NINETEENTH-CENTURY POINTILLISM

The Circus. *Georges Seurat* (1859–91). *Louvre, Paris* (Plate 14). Though possessing architectural unity, this has a most exhilarating continuous movement, miraculously held within the four sides of the canvas, but confined within and by it. The girl on the white horse, the leaping acrobat, the clown in the foreground, and the suave ringmaster are all caught up in a kind of exciting spiral, completely controlled and yet suggesting absolute abandon. Even the two minute figures of the orchestra in the top right-hand corner are swaying in time as they play, but the spectators sit more or less upright and still, giving weight to the composition, though all of them have the appearance of being entranced by what is going on. This technique of Pointillism or neo-Impressionism was a system of using pure colours of the spectrum without mixing and the resultant loss of brilliance. Spots and dashes of blue close to spots and dashes of yellow were optically mixed by the spectator. In the words of his friend Signac, Seurat set out to 'assure the benefits of luminosity, colour and harmony by the optical mixture of uniquely pure pigments, all the tints of the prism and all their tones'.

How far he succeeded in brilliance of colour cannot be judged from this painting as it is unfinished, though in my view, predominance of yellow and dusky reds admirably conveys the dusty heat of the circus. It is remarkable that with Seurat's almost classical rendering of form and balance of verticals and horizontals, he should also convey not only the terrific pace of the circus but also such great vitality in the painting itself.

TWENTIETH-CENTURY SCULPTURE

Reclining Figure (1929). *Henry Moore* (*b*. 1898). *City Art Gallery, Leeds* (Plate 13). Not many people would call the subject of this sculpture beautiful, though this depends on the individual's conception of beauty; but it can still claim to be a great and beautiful work of art, for it has that vital life within itself—organic life. This does not portray the accepted feminine form nor the ideal proportions associated with it, but it expresses a power and a simplicity which is completely uncluttered with extraneous detail. It has a Romanesque directness and does not attempt the refinements nor the decorative Gothic additions to fundamentally elegant form. The limbs have a statuesque weight and show respect for the material used. Although so heavy, the figure is utterly relaxed, but the right arm has to bear the weight of the body and is uncompromisingly fitted for that purpose. There is extraordinary subtlety in the modelling of the breasts and the lift of the left arm, simplified as it is; the alert head and left arm prevent the rest of the figure from being too passive. Make the experiment of covering the arm and head and see how much energy is lost.

POSSIBLE ESSAYS, DISCUSSION AND RESEARCH

1 What are the merits of a fresco compared with an oil painting?

2 Do you think that some subjects are better conveyed by drawing than painting?

3 Which of the works of art described in this section appeals to you most?

4 Can you make any suggestions as to why the prehistoric artists were so well able to portray animals?

5 Do you agree that a sketch such as a *sinopia*, can sometimes be more satisfying than a finished painting?

6 What has Rembrandt's *Girl Sleeping* in common with Lorenzetti's sinopia of the *Angel of the Annunciation*?

7 Why is it possible to accept as works of art, two such different interpretations of human figures as the *Frieze of the Parthenon* and Henry Moor's *Reclining Figure*?

Suggested Further Reading

Arts Council of Great Britain: *Frescoes from Florence.* (Catalogue of exhibition of Florentine frescoes and *sinopie* held at the Hayward Gallery): London, 1969.

Murray, Peter and Linda: *A Dictionary of Art and Artists.* Penguin Reference Books: London, 1968.

Rice, David Talbot: *A Concise History of Painting* (prehistoric to thirteenth century). Thames & Hudson: London, 1967

Chapter Four

THE BEGINNINGS

By now even the beginner should have a more confident approach and will have begun to gain experience, to form his own opinions, and to disagree with some of the opinions and prejudices put forward in these first chapters. We have examined, more or less at random and without taking any background knowledge into account, a number of entirely different works of art. Let us therefore attempt at this stage a chronological approach to the contribution made by various civilizations to our cultural heritage.

Since very early cultures belong to the realms of archaeology and anthropology they can have only a passing reference in this book. But some cultures have created stimulating works of art of the highest excellence, so it is not out of place to discuss a few examples in some detail.

Ethnological museums dealing with primitive cultures from all over the world are to be found in most of the capitals of Europe and in some of the provinces. These collections are now beginning to attract large numbers of visitors, especially young art students who are entirely sympathetic towards these primitive people's direct and powerful approach to art. The word 'primitive' is now used so loosely that it may lead to confusion, but in this context it denotes cultures of man's prehistoric past which developed over long periods and produced great works of art; it also includes the primitive cultures existing in many parts of the world today which produce repetitive and non-creative folk art. The word 'primitive' is often applied to very early works in European schools of painting, and it is also applied loosely to naïve or childlike paintings of any period.

THE CAVE PAINTINGS OF ALTAMIRA

Almost every year new traces of artistic achievement are unearthed which prove that art was understood and practised at an even earlier date than had been believed. For our purpose we may take the earliest to be the cave paintings of Altamira, in northern Spain. These date back to a period between 30,000 and 40,000 years ago when men began to trace curves and meandering lines on the damp walls of their caves, possibly actually following their irregularities and discovering the shapes of animals in the scratches they had made with their fingers. The next step was building up in relief with clay and the production of wall engravings, incised drawings or *graffiti*. (The same kind of incised-drawing technique is used in our own era for decorating houses, in Austria for instance.)

THE ART OF THE HUNTER

Then came painting with earth colours: red and yellow and black and the white of chalk, mixed with animal fat to form a kind of oil paint, the brilliance of which has survived to this day. The really astonishing thing is that uncivilized hunter tribes, supposedly with no great mental equipment or intelligence, could have produced works of art of such extraordinary power and inspiration. They are not simply wonderful achievements for prehistoric man, but for any man of any century. How this can be so remains unsolved and adds to the mystery of what makes a work of art, but it is certain that these men had intelligence, if only of a different quality than man possesses now. It is probable that they looked on painting as magic, possibly both the ability to recreate a creature on the wall and the spell this worked to ensure plenty of food for the hunter. They did not, apparently, capture the little woolly ponies to carry them on their hunting expeditions, but to eat their flesh which was considered to be particularly tasty. Even today there are old goatherds in the remoter parts of Greece who look upon drawing or painting as magic and will prize a rough sketch of a goat, believing that if preserved, it will give the animal a longer span of life. A peasant will sometimes ask to have his portrait sketched while standing behind the artist: he believes that Hephaistos, the god of craftsmen, will provide the 'magic' or 'eyes' in the back of the head.

You have only to look at the rough sketch (Fig. 8) of the clay relief of bisons mating, in a cave on the French side of the Pyrenees, to see at once that these splendid animals are modelled so powerfully in order to create a spell that will ensure a continued supply of food. Look, too, at the engraving of mating elks in Norway, with their hearts and other organs seen through their skins. These lines of internal organs were at one time considered to be a lasso with which the animals were captured, but they undoubtedly represent the 'living' organs, thus adding to the magic of eternal life.

But what particular senses are needed for the fuller appreciation of prehistoric paintings? Since they represent more or less familiar forms, there is no question of not understanding what the pictures are about, at least in their most limited meaning, and anyone, however slight his experience, can sense their magic. In this particular case, the awe-inspiring knowledge that the cave was inhabited thousands of years ago prepares one for 'entering into' the picture and experiencing it. The really important thing is to have an open mind, not just to rid yourself of personal likes and dislikes—that would make everything dull—but to be prepared for an entirely new experience and an enlargement of the world you can enjoy.

One obvious way of appreciating a work of art is to get to know it. To do this, there is no need for any practical knowledge of the technique employed. The layman can perfectly well explore the points of a painting or building or carving, though he may not be able to

Fig. 8

express his feelings in art critics' language. For an experiment ask yourself a few questions about these cave paintings. What is the relationship between the various animals and symbols: the pictorial relationship? How far do you find the design of the painting stimulating? Is it a continuous flow or is it an excited, nervous kind of progression? Try to be carried away along the confident black outline which seems to have been done with one continuous stroke of the brush. Notice how it exploits or avoids the uneven surface. In Fig. 6, what gives such a strong feeling of atmosphere as though the creatures were galloping along through limitless space? Notice the soft technique for the mane and the contrast between this and the firm line of the body, and the very definite and accurate drawing of the hard-looking hooves.

Now you are getting right into the picture and you can explore the differing density of colour, strong and deep, light and almost transparent, all of the intensity of earth colours in a limited range but capable of producing a deeply glowing effect. This is the work of men whose life was lived in an entirely natural environment: an environment of human beings and animals, of caves and earth and sky. No buildings, no roads, no agriculture, no farms: in this environment man *really knew* about animals.

Since it is not possible for everyone to see any of these paintings in the original, the best thing is to make do with a compromise and get hold of some of the first-class colour photographs which are available. Then try to see some of the originals if you are travelling in Europe.

Hunter painting originated in the caves of France and Spain, but from about 15,000 B.C. onwards it spread to North and South Africa and eventually northwards to Scandinavia. About 2000 B.C. it probably reached Australia, where it still influences Aboriginal art. In 1000 B.C. the 'animal-style' was apparent in the use of the elephant, the bear and the white deer as motifs in Chinese art, but since the Shang Yin Emperors then in power were themselves great hunters in a less primitive sense, the use of the animal motif would seem to be quite normal.

The practice of tracing the heart and internal organs is found in early Chinese paintings, and a decorative form of it is sometimes seen in the work of the Australian aborigines of this century.

The Atlas mountains of North Africa are particularly rich in caves with rock paintings and there are a number scattered over South America.

Gradually over a period of several years the style changed and human figures (which had been a rarity) were introduced into the hunting scenes. In areas where agriculture and farming gradually spread as a way of life, symbols of the soil and of fertility appear—female fertility in which there is no sign of perfection of form such as the Greeks expressed but of the exaggerated fitness of the body to procreate, hence the enormous hips.

THE FIRST FARMERS

It was generally thought that these first farmers emerged around 2000 B.C. in Europe, but recent excavations in Yugoslavia have revealed that by 5000 B.C. hunters and fishers in the Balkans were already producing sculpture in the round (the earliest known of this type) as the farmers with their new way of life were beginning to influence them from the south. These people produced monumental sculpture from boulders, chipping laboriously away at the stone to give it the details of a head. Owing to their rough stone tools, they were obliged to keep the original form of the boulder which, presumably, they selected for its resemblance to the general shape of a head. We can see from the following sketches (Fig. 9) how impressive

Fig. 9

this carving is: how the sculptors understood the limitations of their medium and exploited it. Colin Renfrew, in his introduction to the catalogue of an exhibition of these works in London, suggests that they had a religious significance, since they were set near the hearth in the houses that were excavated. Other authorities believe their rather fish-like features may signify that they are representations of a fish god. This theory is given some credibility by the fact that the people were dependent on fish from the Danube.

Lady of Aleksandrovac (*terracotta from Vitkovo*). *Aleksandrovac Secondary School, Yugoslavia* (Fig. 10). This is more sophisticated, with a definite sense of style. Her carefully modelled cheek bones

Fig. 10

and pointed chin, her hair piled neatly on her head, and the decorations incised on her shoulders show that there was an advanced stage of culture among these artists.

MEGALITHIC MONUMENTS

The Megalithic (great stone) style is superbly exemplified in England by Stonehenge, which is either 'architecture' or a colossal form of sculpture. In Europe there are huge standing stones in Brittany, Spain, France, and Ireland.

We know little about the great structure of Stonehenge and we can only admire and wonder at this fantastic achievement of the second millennium B.C. Huge blocks of upright stone, forming walls and pillars, are often linked by great lintels (horizontal slabs) all arranged in a circle of earth. Even archaeologists are not yet certain exactly what it signifies. It is obviously a temple, but it also probably has some sort of astronomical significance, since the stones are directionally arranged. However, here we can only wonder at the astonishing magic, the aura of deep religious significance and the extraordinary barbaric scale of this monument wrapped in mystery—a mystery which adds to its great appeal.

No photograph or sketch can possibly give more than a very hazy idea of megalithic monuments, for it is size and setting and the different shapes and groupings which emerge when actually walking around and inside it and savouring it from every aspect. Since you can actually roam around and within Stonehenge, it is much easier to suggest ways and means of 'getting to know' this kind of art than of getting to know a painting which has to be 'entered' or understood through visual means.

NURAGHIC BRONZES

During the first millennium B.C. bronze human figurines and animals reached a very high standard notably in the Hallstat period in Austria (Plate 1) and the Nuraghic Bronzes in Sardinia (Figs. 11 and 12) of which many examples are to be seen in the museum of Cagliari.

Fortunately many of these fascinating works of art can be studied in the original by visiting caves and museums; modern manifestations of the same styles are still current in large areas of the world. Admittedly these latter almost always lose the force and intrinsic magic of the early work since they are repetitive. However, many of

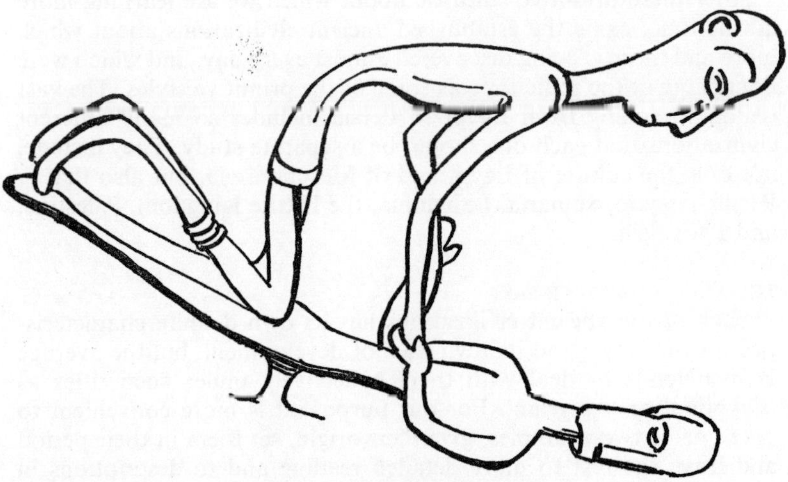

Fig. 11

Fig. 12

the masks and images are still specifically used as charms against evil and to help hunters and fishermen and to increase fertility.

ANCIENT CIVILIZATIONS

After these primitive cultures, about which we are learning more all the time, came the established ancient civilizations about which more and more is being discovered almost every day, and which were flourishing at the same time as some of the primitive styles. The vast region stretching from Egypt to Persia includes so many different civilizations that each one should be a separate study. They include, not only the culture of Egypt and of Mesopotamia, but also that of Persia, Assyria, Sumaria, Babylonia, the Hittite Kingdom, Palestine, and Phoenicia.

THE ANCIENT MIDDLE EAST

Each of the ancient civilizations has its own definite characteristics, its own style and its own pace of development, but the average laymen tends to deal with them collectively under such titles as 'Egyptian' or 'Assyrian'. For our purpose it is more convenient to take one or two examples, give their origin, set them in their period and leave the rest to more detailed reading and to descriptions in later chapters.

The Pyramids of Giza (2600–2480 B.C.). *Egyptian.* The silhouette of these monuments in their uncompromising strength and simplicity must be familiar all over the world. Even so, they are not devoid of subtlety, and the uneven stone of which they are built shows a constant tremble of light even in the shadows; their disposition and differing heights, partly due to being built on different levels, gives a varying skyline. It took over two million limestone blocks to build the largest of the three, the Great Pyramid of Cheops. The Pyramid of the Pharaoh Chephren is on higher ground but not so immense; the smallest one, the Pyramid of Mycerinus, has minor pyramids built for three of the pharaoh's queens.

The huge Sphinx of Cephren stands, more than ten times the height of a man, in the varied stone of golden-cream and olive. To me it is impressive rather than stimulating.

Relief: Imugud from Ubaid (2600–2400 B.C.). *Sumerian. British Museum, London* (Plate 18). This relief seems partly mysteriously mythical and partly medieval in spirit, having something in common with the cathedral tympanums. Admittedly the theme is entirely different, but the component parts fit superbly into the given space, yet 'grow' out of the background. The mythological lion-headed Sumerian eagle rears its kindly head from the framework and spreads its great protective wings over the two stages. Notice how the rather formless elongated body of each stag helps to focus attention on the proudly held heads and antlers. Constructed of copper over a wooden base, this relief was probably set above the entrance to a temple. The rather lovable, but slightly grotesque, creatures would not look out of place among the carvings of a Romanesque church.

Lion Hunt of King Assurnasirpal (883–859 B.C.). *Assyrian. British Museum, London* (Plate 19). In this relief from a palace at Nimrod, the king is aiming to shoot at a lion. Unlike most Assyrian reliefs, the figure of the king is full of vitality and the muscles are tensed for action, but true to form, the soldiers and the charioteer are stiff and lifeless. In contrast to the lifelike lions, oddly enough, the horses are stiff and stylized. It is the king himself in this instance who is full of life he turns to attack the splendid lion and the lion crouches beneath the horses. It is almost as though two artists had worked on this relief: one with a great knowledge of wild animals and a command of portraying rhythmic movement was responsible for the lion and the king; while the other, capable of producing a pleasing design but unable to infuse any kind of life into his work, carved the three stylized horses and the stiff soldiers.

The Seated Scribe (*c.* 2470 B.C.). *Egyptian. Louvre, Paris* (Fig. 13). Carved in limestone by a sculptor with complete assurance, this compact figure sits cross-legged. The solid, firmly rounded limbs are perfectly disposed; the body is erect and distinguished, and the head is set magnificently on shoulders which, though squared, seem relaxed. Every part of the body is perfectly, almost geometrically, balanced, and the remarkably alive head has a steadfast, deeply thoughtful gaze, stressed by inset coloured stones. Even a sketch of this impelling statuette has great impact, but the original in its

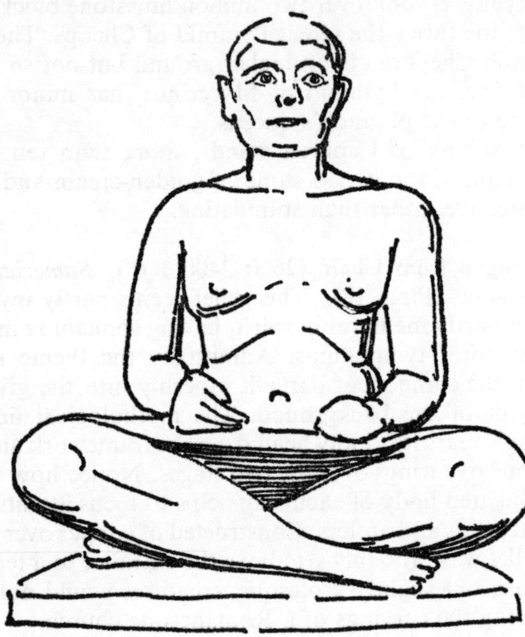

Fig. 13

superb setting in the Louvre draws the spectator right into the presence of this nobleman depicted as a scribe. Although simple and almost modern in style, it has the aura of antiquity—of the living past which it still seems to breathe.

Queen Nefertiti (fourteenth century B.C.). *Egyptian. Staatliche Museum, Berlin* (Plate 20). This painted limestone and plaster head was produced during the Armana period when portraits as such first appeared. It is one of the most truly beautiful portrait busts in existence: beautiful in subject and perfect in the subtlety and delicacy of its execution. Surely no head was ever more regally poised on gently sloping shoulders and no neck more delicately curved. The necklet gently outlines the form of the neck as it meets the shoulders and then stresses this with more decorative curves. The head-dress is superbly set and not too heavy, with simple decoration breaking up the mass; the lovely line of the profile is entirely serene and the full, red-painted lips have just the trace of a smile about to break.

Two of the Daughters of Akhenaton (1370–1358 B.C.). *Egyptian. Ashmolean Museum, Oxford* (Plate 21). This charming painting on plaster is part of a larger group but does in itself produce a complete composition. The outlines of the two girls' bodies flow rhythmically and easily to convey family affection and to produce a design which is entirely satisfying. How wonderfully the slender arms are interlaced and the suppleness of the limbs is conveyed! The strange, doe-like eyes are depicted frontally in the formal profile view, and ear-rings and necklets emphasize the subtle form of neck and shoulders. Even the bright toenails and fingernails play their part in drawing attention to the delicately drawn hands and feet.

Works of art from the ancient Middle East tend to be repetitive and remote, but Egyptian art was for a while under Akhenaton infused with a certain tenderness as can be seen in *Queen Nefertiti* and in *Two of the Daughters of Akhenaton.* Even those impersonal and formal sculptures and paintings which adhere strictly to conventional rules are arresting and have the quality of timelessness.

ORIENTAL ART

In the Far East, India, China, Korea, and Japan there is a very long history of achievement in art. A study of any one country's civilization would take a lifetime, but, as a very broad generalization, they do have some definite ideals in common and they do all differ fundamentally from the West in their approach to nature and in their manner of representing the world around them.

The history of Eastern art follows an entirely different course from Western art since oriental artists were never interested in some of the problems of representation which the Europeans were struggling to resolve. For instance, the oriental artist does not bother himself with presenting perspective *visually*; he does not necessarily make people and objects in the distance smaller than those in the foreground, though he may do so for decorative purposes. He assumes that the spectator 'reads' the painting from the bottom (the foreground) to the top (the background), so he places distant things at the top. He may or may not attempt to show us sky, but he does not attempt to show us horizontal and vertical planes. He does not make the land a horizontal plane; the whole effect is almost of a flat drop curtain.

Nor is the oriental artist interested in representing solid form; he uses a caressing, sensitive line in figures and animals, and his instinctive feeling for the use of a freely flowing design enables him to suggest movement: the deer leap, the horses canter, the elephants lumber along, even water flows, and in some miraculous way mists gather and disperse.

Whereas, until the twentieth century, painters have confined their compositions within a panel or a frame, the oriental often paints continuously in a scroll to be unrolled and enjoyed gradually. It is a decoration, but one in which nature has been faithfully observed and contemplated. The artist thinks out the painting in his mind. He tells us a great deal of what he knows of nature but he does not record a particular place at a particular time.

Obviously these broad generalizations do not apply in the same degree to the art of all the oriental countries, but they do show that the Eastern approach to painting is fundamentally different from the art of the Old Masters, though a little nearer to modern art.

Chinese painters have extraordinary skill in handling ink and can produce a painting of, say, bamboos in such variety of greys and blacks as to convey subtle colour. But they can also exploit the most delicate and pure colours unbroken by the use of shadows, since theirs is a shadowless, two-dimensional world.

The Persians designed enchanting miniatures in jewel colours, again unhampered by any need to use modelling of forms.

In India, the Moguls draw with an exquisitely sensitive line or they can paint in water-colour or gouache, decorative illustrations of lives of their gods and heroes in the most sophisticated range of pure colour.

The Japanese became familiar to the West through the flood of more-or-less commercial, coloured woodcuts that came into Europe in the eighteenth and nineteenth centuries; but beautiful as many of these are, they represent only a small part of Japanese achievement in art.

Oriental art is, then, decorative and two-dimensional; it uses natural forms but does not represent them visually. In Moslem countries the stress is entirely decorative since, by the laws of their religion, they cannot represent the human form.

Oriental art did not 'progress' in a continuous stream towards more complete visual and three-dimensional representation of nature like the European schools, but followed traditional rules; hence it is much more difficult to assign an oriental work of art to its right century. There is also the difficulty of adjusting values: not, of course, in what constitutes a great work of art, but in assessing style and technique. We may, for instance, say truthfully that the landscape background to an early Italian Madonna and Child is 'flat' and like a drop curtain, but it is not flat if we compare it with a Persian miniature.

One might imagine that the oriental sculptor would confine himself to bas reliefs and stone engravings, but he did in fact produce sculpture in the round and we have already seen an example of superb clay modelling in the Chinese war horse (Fig. 5).

INDIAN CAVE PAINTINGS

The famous paintings in the caves of Ajanta in central India, executed between the fifth and sixth centuries A.D., show the sympathetic Indian drawing of animals (Fig. 14). They constitute an amazing record of the life of the time, with groups of people and episodes subtly linked together to form a kind of continuous strip which is

Fig. 14

not divided into separate shapes on panels. These paintings were produced during the Gupta dynasty (320–600 A.D.). At the end of the sixteenth and during the seventeenth and eighteenth centuries under the Moguls, superb miniatures abounded with animals and birds and detailed drawings of flowers, trees, and foliage all decoratively treated to fill a given shape.

Radha and Krishna (*late eighteenth century*). *Victoria and Albert Museum, London* (Plate 22). This decorative illustration from northern India depicts an incident in the life of Krishna, a deified hero of Hindu mythology associated with Radha. The two figures are flat; form is only hinted at by the expressive lines, and movement by glowing arabesques. The couple are swaying in their embrace, and this swaying line is repeated in the hillock, the plants, the birds, and some of the trees, while other vertical trunks give it stability. Flowing waters surround the island. Notice how the water flows along and out of the picture, but the eye is caught by the detail of flowers curving round in the left-hand corner and carried, through other flowers and a twisting creeper, to the figures. See too the pull to the right of the marvellously placed oval leaves and flowers, creating the same effect on the right. The exquisite detail of the blossom and the placing of the birds spread a kind of enchantment over this 'lotus land' and give infinite pleasure to the eye, but always bringing it to rest on the central theme.

CHINESE CERAMICS

In China during the T'ang dynasty, figurines were modelled which bear witness to the elegance and luxury of the time, and we have already seen an example of a war horse (Fig. 5). Artists of this period and of later dynasties, notably the Sung (tenth–thirteenth century), also had a great feeling for animals and birds and flowers and indeed for nature as a whole. Mere man was only an infinitesimal but integral part of the whole, completely at the mercy of the mountains, the mists, and the waters.

CHINESE PAINTINGS

What might to a Western mind seem almost trivial as a subject for a painting—such as a soft black cat with gleaming eyes watching a flower grow, or a dragonfly just about to alight on a water lily—were drawn and painted as things of great importance centuries before Western painters employed them as more than incidental details in compositions. Ducks swim around in a pool beneath opening lotus flowers, puppies frolic on the ground: the Chinese could even paint such subjects as the wind or the mist. Three swimming fish make a satisfying composition, and the miraculous 'Hundred Geese' are painted in ink on a long, horizontal scroll in a continuous graceful sweep as they flutter above the tops of lightly sketched trees and grasses. Chinese art is a contemplative art. The artist contemplates the geese and the growth of a flower. He gazes on the mountains and the waters, and they are infinite. A horizon would curb the boundless distance: so range after range of mountains tower above each other, lost in cloud. Feathery trees sweep down to a stream, and a tiny horseman may cross a bridge over a torrent. The title may be 'fishing', but the fisherman is lost in the world of nature. These characteristics did not change radically for centuries, although there are differences of style and quality. Infinite landscapes of great beauty were being painted on scrolls as late as the seventeenth and eighteenth centuries.

Space and atmosphere play an important part in Chinese painting. The silence of a space enhances the precise details of the composition; what is left unsaid, and the empty spaces, play their part. The Chinese can leave much to the imagination of the beholder, perhaps best summed up in Laurence Binyon's statement in 'The Flight of the Dragon' where he tells us that one of the subjects for a competition was 'The hoof of his steed comes charged with the scent of flowers'. The winning painting was of a rider, with a cluster of butterflies following at the horse's heels!

Landscape painting on silk (1636–37). *Gulbenkian Collection, Durham* (Plate 23). In this hanging scroll of the Ch'ing dynasty, decorative trees with delicate branches and foliage twist their roots into the rocks above a torrent crossed by a minute bridge. Beyond, the seams of a towering mountain let the silver threads of a waterfall drop delicately into the valley, while in the far distance mountain ranges dissolve into the sky. This is a painting which seems to lead the eye upwards from the stones and rocks of the foreground to infinity.

JAPANESE COLOUR PRINTS

Japanese colour prints, which became much sought after in Europe during the nineteenth century, also give a feeling of infinity and space, a sense of the importance of the wind or the rain and the waves. But though they can be decorative, the very nature of the medium of colour printing gives much more definite forms and outlines, and less of the misty infinity expressed by the best Chinese artists.

POSSIBLE ESSAYS, DISCUSSION AND RESEARCH

1 Do you think it possible that prehistoric cave paintings could have originated from a kind of doodling?

2 Find a good coloured photograph of animal paintings in a cave and describe it.

3 Do megalithic stones impress you as temple architecture or monumental sculpture?

4 Can you describe some examples of standing stones in Brittany or Ireland?

5 Are you more impressed by standing stones or the Pyramids?

6 How do Assyrian reliefs of animals compare with cave paintings?

7 Compare the Chinese landscape (Plate 23) with Rubens' *Château de Steen* (Plate 6).

Suggested Further Reading

Auboyer, J., and Goepper, R.: *The Oriental World.* Paul Hamlyn: London, 1967.

Brodrick, Alan Houghton: *An Outline of Chinese Painting*. Avalon Press: London, 1949.

Garbini, Giovanni: *The Ancient World.* Paul Hamlyn: London, 1966.

Lissner, Ivan: *The Living Past.* Penguin: London, 1957.

Lommel, Andreas: *Prehistoric and Primitive Man.* Paul Hamlyn: London, 1966.

Silcock, Arnold: *Introduction to Chinese Art and History.* Faber & Faber: London, 1936.

Chapter Five

EARLY MEDITERRANEAN ART

Until comparatively recently, Greek art was considered to be of no great interest before the seventh century B.C., and only of really high importance in the fifth century B.C. with the building of the Parthenon in Athens and the temple of Zeus at Olympia. The momentous finds of Heinrich Schliemann and Arthur Evans in the prehistoric Minoan and Mycenaean civilizations within the last hundred years have completely changed this attitude.

MINOAN AND MYCENAEAN ART

Schliemann's discovery in 1876 of the shaft graves at Mycenae, and Arthur Evans' later discovery of the palace of Knossos (or Cnossus) in Crete, opened up a new world of art and brought to light golden ornaments and masks, bronzes and clay figurines, pottery and wall paintings of astonishing power and perfection of handling. After the fall of these civilizations there was a period of non-creativeness (as far as we know) from the twelfth to the seventh centuries B.C., but even this period is beginning to link up with Mycenaean art and that of the Greek city states of the eighth century B.C.

The remains of the palace at Knossos, and the colourful reconstruction of other parts where the original wooden columns have been copied in concrete, are very much in keeping with the graceful and naturalistic female figures of goddesses and the obvious delight in dancing and colour shown in the wall paintings (*c.* 1500 B.C.).

Wall Painting: The Toreadors. *Palace of Knossos, Crete* (Fig. 15). This celebrated composition shows the characteristics of Minoan art admirably. The astonishing grace and strength of the bull, the

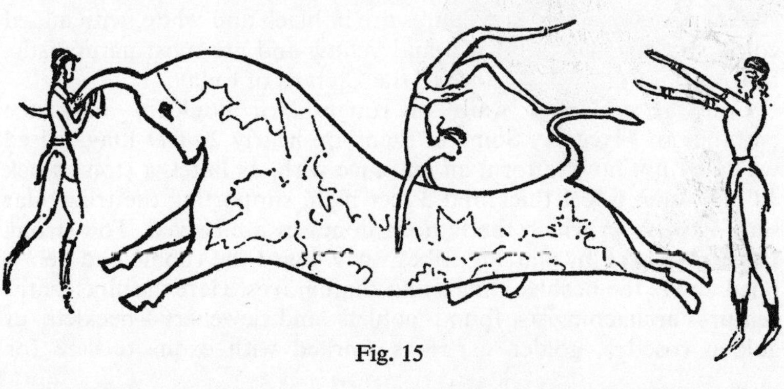

Fig. 15

magnificent swerve of the line from the horns to the swirling tail, the stretch of the body and spread of its legs, and the confident ease of the acrobat about to be caught by the slender dancer are a miracle of ease and delight in movement. The style clearly owes a great deal to Egyptian painting but has a freedom of treatment, a gaiety and a lack of formality not found in Egyptian paintings.

Clay Figure: Snake Goddess (*c.* 1600 B.C.). *Palace of Knossos, Crete* (Fig. 16). This little clay figure, which may be a queen or a

Fig. 16

princess, but is more likely a snake goddess, has an elegant Victorian-style slim waist, full bosom and flounced, almost bustled, skirt. Part naked, part voluminously draped, she stands superbly erect with a snake in each hand. These figures are in black and white, with added colours of blue-green, brown and yellow and are most naturalistic, bearing a strong resemblance to the Cretans of today.

Colossal cyclopian walls of rough-hewn boulders mark the entrance to Mycenae. Some of them are nearly 20 feet long, raised we know not how to form an entrance with, as lintel, a stone block 14 feet long, 6 feet thick and 3 feet high, supporting the triangular slab of rock on which the famous lionesses are carved. Too strong to be destroyed by warring tribes, they guard the rubble and debris piled above the beehive tombs and shaft graves. Here the nineteenth-century archaeologists found goblets and jewellery—necklets of golden rosettes, golden ear-rings worked with exquisite care for detail and finish, masks which may have been attempts at portraits with curious stylized eyes and ears of beaten gold.

THE ORDERS OF GREEK ARCHITECTURE

Classical Greece set the standard for architecture and had the greatest single influence on the development of European art. It was the Greeks who laid down the rules of proportion and who constructed their buildings according to scientific formulas. They

Fig. 17

translated these rules into 'living' buildings—buildings which have a timelessness and immortality. They still live and seem to move and almost breathe, for their lines swell and shrink, their size and shape and height are slightly varied, but so subtly that it cannot be noticed by the ordinary observer. Every line, every shape fulfils a function and contributes to the flow of the building and the astonishing sense of perfection it imparts.

The Greek orders were Doric, Ionic, and Corinthian, named after the three regions of Greece from which they originated (Fig. 17).

The Doric is the oldest of the three and has a very sturdy fluted column without a base, but with a simple capital beneath a plain architrave. Above this the frieze is divided into panels and surmounted by a cornice.

The Ionic order has a more slender column set on a base, and a capital with volutes supporting the plain entablative (architrave, frieze, and cornice).

The Corinthian order, which was not very popular with the Greeks, had an even lighter column with a much more elaborate capital of acanthus leaves. The Romans modified these orders and added two of their own: the Tuscan, even simpler than the Greek Doric, and the composite, a rather ungainly combination of Ionic and Corinthian.

Vitruvius, a Roman architect of the first century B.C., produced a manual of architecture which gave details of Roman buildings and of Greek architecture which he had studied. It explained the orders and provided rules for architectural design according to Greek traditions. Although this book fell into disuse in the Middle Ages, it was rediscovered in the fifteenth century and is still consulted today.

Any student of architecture must have seen hundreds of photographs of the Parthenon in Athens, diagrams and photographs of its details and plan: but once he is actually face to face with this masterpiece, in ruins as it is, he realizes he is seeing something he could never possibly imagine. Its impact is colossal; it lives, it breathes, and its very stones change their colour with the changing weather and the changing light. It takes on an ethereal beauty on a moonlight night; against a purple velvet sky and drenched with rain, the marble turns a pale grey-violet, softening the outlines against the blue. Magnificently sited, like all Greek temples, it is inseparable from the rock on which it stands high above the town, with the old Byzantine city crowding at its feet (Plate 24). Since the word 'building' implies piling one thing on another, and raising height as a child builds bricks or card castles, I prefer to describe the Parthenon as a great sculptured monument rather than a building.

The lovely temple of Athena Aphaea (Fig. 18) on the island of Aegina stands on golden sand among pine trees high above the sea, and the temples and theatre and stadium at Delphi are terraced on the awe-inspiring slopes of Mount Parnassus among wild thyme and flowers, with the towering rocks above and the contrast of cooing doves and swooping eagles. But not all Greek temples are high; those at Agrigento in Sicily lie in the Valley of the Temples and are picked out in the floodlighting of the rising sun; the temple at Paestum, south of Naples, stands by the sea.

It is hard to realize that these buildings were originally coloured and gilded and might have seemed almost garish to modern taste, for the beautiful tones of the weathered marble enhances their lovely proportions. It is hard also to visualize the Acropolis in Athens with all its statues and reliefs when we know it and appreciate it in its present desecrated state.

The sacred hill at Delphi would have seemed crowded to our eyes with the hundreds of statues lining the way to the temples; and the famous temple of Zeus at Olympia, despite its magnificent sculpture, must have looked as brilliant as a Byzantine mosaic, with gold and ivory and paint and precious stones.

Fig. 18

We value the peace and tranquillity of these ancient monuments and their perfection of form and proportion which is stressed by the absence of positive colour.

GREEK SCULPTURE

Greek statues exemplify the perfection of the ideal human form; the beautiful bodies of their gods are visualized as possessing the ideal athletic figure in splendid health.

Bronze: Apollo (*c.* 530 B.C.). *National Museum, Athens* (Plate 25). This sculpture is not just a copy of the ideal human form, it is a re-creation of a living, breathing, but impersonal body in bronze.

For centuries the superiority of Greek architecture and sculpture has been recognized, but to modern taste the less idealized work of other periods is sometimes more acceptable. Clearly such a highly developed civilization as the Greek, with its tremendous achievements in architecture and sculpture, made its influence felt in other parts of Europe. Greek artists travelled abroad to help in some of the great artistic projects in other countries or to furnish objects for rich patrons.

THE ETRUSCANS

According to varying views the Etruscans arrived in Italy either from Asia Minor after the Trojan War, or were already established there at that time. What *is* certain is that they were inspired by the Greeks. Their history and their language is full of mystery, and their architecture, being largely of wood, has disappeared. Their temples followed the Greek tradition, so did their vases and their figures; but in all these there is a particular Etruscan flavour and there are enough differences for it to be worth considering Etruscan art separately, even in this brief survey, especially in respect of the grave paintings and sarcophagi.

We have already looked at the terracotta horses in the museum at Tarquinia, but close to the town there are graves with mural paintings which are more sophisticated conceptions than those of the prehistoric hunter. Some represent animals and birds, but in contact with man. Religious rites, dancing, music, and sport are favourite subjects revealing the Etruscans to be a gay, active people who loved life and liked to surround their dead with paintings and models of the familiar things of their world. Horses painted in black, brown, and red step out with controlled power, their heads held high and their tails sweeping the ground; priest-like figures are engaged in some religious rite, the whole design being divided into sections by formal trees bearing flat, dark-green leaves.

Tomb of the Triclinion Musicians (detail). *Tarquinia, Italy* (Plate 26). The most remarkable thing about this painting is the flowing movement conveyed with extreme economy of line. The figures are outlined in the oriental style, their heads are in profile while the eyes look to the front, and the movement of their arms and legs is formal. All of this might well make them stiff and lifeless, yet their vitality is very strongly felt and the rhythm of the music is almost discernible. The variety of pose in which some figures seem to turn back and others go eagerly forward controls the onward surge and contains it within the walls. The drawing of the hands is particularly sensitive, and so is the sweep of the drapery as it swings away from the body. Here, too, decorative trees separate the figures.

Etruscan jewellery was coarse and overcrowded and the workmanship unremarkable compared with Minoan or Mycenaean. The Etruscan civilization, which began in the seventh or eighth century B.C., lasted until the third century B.C. when the Romans overcame the Etruscans and looted their works of art.

ROMAN GRANDEUR

It is generally agreed that Roman art is far inferior to Greek art. The Romans copied the Greeks but modified the orders of architecture, which lost their simple perfection and became almost clumsy; they overloaded their sculpture and they lost the idealized proportions of Greek art. As a generalization, the reliefs on Roman triumphal arches and columns are crowded and lacking in dignity compared with the sculptured Greek reliefs. Although they debased

PLATES

1. *Top left*. **Bronze cult chariot from Strettweg, Austria.**
Landesfremdenverkehrsamtes für Steiermark.

2. *Top centre*. **Bronze head of a Queen Mother, Benin, Nigeria.**
Reproduced by courtesy of the Trustees of the British Museum.

5. **The Birth of Aphrodite. Museo delle Terme, Rome.**
Mansell Collection.

3. *Top right*. **Winged horses from an Etruscan Temple, Tarquinia.**
Mansell Collection.

4. *Left.* **The Madonna Enthroned. Giorgione. Castelfranco, Italy.**
Italian Institute.

6. *Top.* **Château de Steen. Peter Paul Rubens.**
Reproduced by courtesy of the Trustees, The National Gallery, London.

8. *Right.* **The Finding o Christ in the Temple. Simone Martini.**
Walker Art Gallery, Liverpo

9. *Above left.* **St. Ansanus. Francesco d'Antonio di Bartolommeo. Church of San Nicholò, Florence.**
Uffizi—Florence.

9a. *Above right.* **Sinopia.**
Uffizi—Florence.

10. *Top.* **Crucifixion. Church of San Domenico, Pistoia.**
Uffizi—Florence.

10a. Sinopia.
Uffizi—Florence.

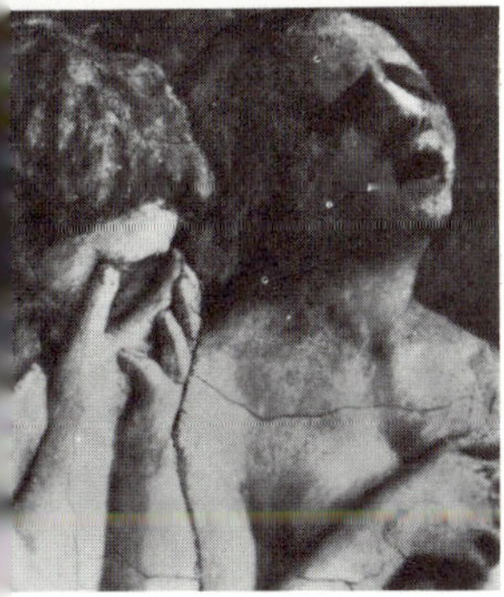

5. *Top left*. **Expulsion from he Garden of Eden. Masaccio. hurch of the Carmine, lorence.**
Aansell Collection.

5a. Detail of 15.
talian Institute.

7. *Top*. **Goat's Skull, Bottle and Candle. Pablo Picasso.**
The Tate Gallery, London.© by S.P.A.D.E.M., Paris.

16. Don Balthazar Carlos. Velasquez.
Museo del Prado, Madrid.

11. West Frieze of the Parthenon, Athens.
Reproduced by courtesy of the Trustees of the British Museum.

13. Reclining Figure. Henry Moore.
City Art Gallery, Leeds.

21. Two daughters of Akhenaton, painting on plaster Ashmolean Museum, Oxford.
Photograph Ashmolean Museum.

12. Portrait of Christ. Book of Kells. Trinity College Library Dublin.
The Irish Tourist Board.

18. *Top*. **Sumerian Relief of Imugud from Ubaid.**
Reproduced by courtesy of the Trustees of the British Museum.

19. *Centre*. **Assyrian Lion Hunt of King Assurnasirpal.**
Reproduced by courtesy of the Trustees of the British Museum.

20. *Right*. **Queen Nefertiti, fourteenth century B.C. Egyptian. Berlin.**
Mansell Collection.

14. *Left*. **The Circus. Georges Seurat. The Louvre.**
Archives Photographiques—Paris.

22. *Top*. **Radha and Krishna. North Indian, eighteenth century.**
Victoria and Albert Museum. Crown Copyright.

17. *Right*. **Girl Sleeping. Rembrandt.**
Reproduced by courtesy of the Trustees of the British Museum.

30. *Top.* **Tassilo Chalice. Kremsmünster, Austria.**
Landesfremdenverkehrsamt Oberösterreich.

30a. *Centre left.* **Ardagh Chalice. Dublin.**
Irish Tourist Board.

30b. *Above left.* **Christ in Majesty. Carolingian ivory plaque.**
Reproduced by permission of the Syndics of the Fitzwilliam Museum, Cambridge.

23. *Above.* **Landscape painting on silk. Ch'ing Dynasty.**
The property of the Gulbenkian Museum of Oriental Art, University of Durham, Great Britain.

25. *Above.* **Bronze Apollo from Piraeus. National Museum, Athens.**
V. & N. Tombazi, Psychico-Athens.

24. *Top right.* **The Acropolis with Temple of Zeus in foreground. Athens.**
Dimitri photo: Greek Tourist Office.

26. *Right.* **Tomb of the Triclinion Musicians (detail), Tarquinia.**
Italian State Tourist Office.

28. *Top.* **The Good Shepherd. Mausoleum of Galla Placidia. Ravenna.**
Mansell Collection.

29. The Empress Theodora. Mosaic. Ravenna.
Mansell Collection.

33. *Above*. **Chartres cathedral, France.**
French National Tourist Office.

31. *Top right*. **Christ in Glory. Tympanum, Abbey Church of Vézelay.**
French National Tourist Office.

31a. *Right*. **Interior of church, Vézelay.**
French National Tourist Office.

32. *Left.* **Twelfth century portal of St. Trophime at Arles.**
French National Tourist Office.

35. *Right.* **Jerónimos Monastery. Lisbon.**
Portuguese State Office.

36. *Top.* **Jerónimos Monastery, cloisters.**
Portuguese State Office.

37. Manueline window at Tomar, Portugal.
Portuguese State Office.

34. Chartres cathedral, portal.
French National Tourist Office.

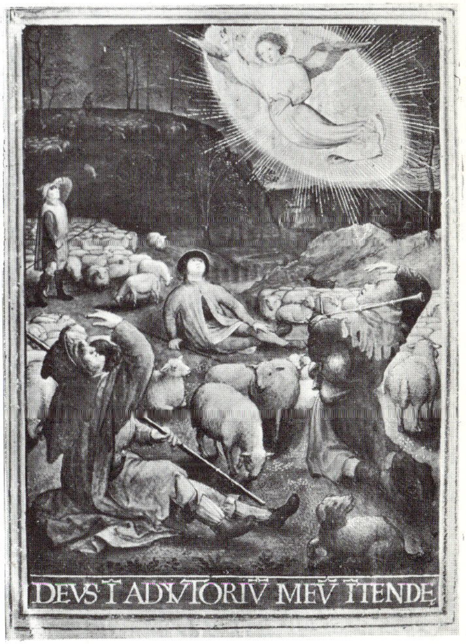

39. ***Left*** **The Marriage of Giovanni Arnolfini and Giovanna Cenami. Jan Van Eyck.**

Reproduced by courtesy of the Trustees, The National Gallery, London.

38. ***Right.*** **The Shepherds at Bethlehem. Sforza Book of Hours.**

Reproduced by courtesy of the Trustees of the British Museum.

40. ***Top.*** **Altarpiece of St. Vincent (detail). Lisbon Museum.**

Portuguese State Office.

41. Maestà, Duccio.
Siena Cathedral Museum.
Mansell Collection.

42. *Top.*
Guidoriccio da Fogliano.
Simone Martini. Siena.
Mansell Collection.

much that they took from Greece, they also made contributions of their own in sculpture, architecture, and mosaic and above all, in engineering and town planning. Their portrait busts of emperors and generals have a certain nobility, and their triumphal arches and great monumental engineering achievements have splendour. They conceived everything on a grand scale: roads, stadiums, arenas, hippodromes, and aquaducts—and these aquaducts sweep magnificently across the landscape like the Pont du Gard at Nîmes.

No one can deny the tremendous impact of the equestrian statue of Marcus Aurelius (Plate 27) cast in the second century A.D. It now stands in the Square of the Campidoglio (the Capitol) in Rome, where it was placed by Michelangelo. No one would dispute the beauty of the mosaic pavements which have been brought to light all over the Roman Empire; in particular those in the baths at Ostia, once the port of Rome, where Neptune sweeps across the floor in his chariot. It was of course the Romans who produced the round arch which was used all over Europe in the Middle Ages in the Romanesque style of architecture (termed Norman in the British Isles, since it was brought across the Channel by the Normans).

Linguistically the Roman Empire was divided between the peoples of the west who became Romanized and spoke Latin, irrespective of their race, and those who continued to speak Greek in spite of the Roman conquest. This applied not only to the inhabitants of Greece and to the coastal regions of Asia Minor, but also to many of the countries occupied by Alexander in the fourth century B.C., including Syria, Palestine, and Egypt. Cleopatra's native language was Greek and so was St. Paul's, although he was a Jew and a Roman citizen. So, in the Near East, the superior civilization remained dominant.

When the Roman Empire was split into two parts by the Emperor Constantine, it happened that these two parts were already divided linguistically. The Empire of the East had its capital at Byzantium (now Istanbul). Its art, known as Byzantine, had a definitely eastern flavour, but its influence was to be felt further west, in Sicily, in Venice, and in Ravenna.

THE EARLY CHRISTIANS

With the coming of Christianity, the main flow of European art was gradually dedicated to the Church; and the tremendous European heritage of medieval, Renaissance, and even baroque art is mainly religious in its function, even if not produced for the Church. The main exceptions are, of course, the art of the Court, portraiture, and the recording of historical events.

Since all previous art was concerned largely with magic or with placating the gods, we can imagine what a tremendous impact Christianity must have had on the artists' subject-matter as it became accepted by country after country. To begin with, in places, the new faith inspired only some artists, while others kept to the old source of inspiration; thus in Rome we have early Christian art alongside pagan art, with both subjects being treated in more or less the same manner. During the persecution, the Christians could only express themselves crudely in the darkness of the catacombs, and the qualification for decorating the walls was to be a Christian rather than an artist. But these early painters thought of themselves as working in the service of their faith rather than as artists and, indeed, it is only comparatively recently that 'craftsmen' have become consciously 'artists'.

In the catacombs many symbols were used which continued to be employed in later centuries in Byzantine art (Fig. 19). The fish became

Fig. 19

the symbol of Christ, since the initial letters of the Greek words *I*esous *CH*ristos *TH*eou *U*ios *S*oter (Jesus Christ, Son of God, Saviour) spell *ichthus*, Greek for fish. The anchor, too was an ancient symbol of hope. The Good Shepherd and the Fisherman are obvious in their significance, and instead of representing God the Father, He was often symbolized by a hand reaching from the skies. Gradually painting and mosaics began to have much greater spiritual significance: the soul became more important than the body. This was largely due to stress being laid on spiritual rather than material values by the Christian faith, but was also due to the more 'spiritual' style of portraiture introduced from the Middle East.

THE BASILICA

It followed that the inside of a church—where God was to be found—became more important than the outside, which could remain quite plain. To begin with, the early Christians made use of the existing basilicas, or halls of justice, and modified them into churches; and when they did build new churches as specifically Christian places of worship, they were in the form of the old basilicas. They had a forecourt or atrium for those who were not yet baptized (also, in the east, a second chamber for pilgrims and penitents), and then a long rectangular building dividing lengthwise into three by columns supporting either arches or a straight beam. The central section had a roof raised higher than the sides, in which were windows.

In the centre of the main aisle at the eastern end was the priests' section, entered through an arch; the altar, often raised and reached by steps, was situated in the centre of the semicircular extension of the nave or apse. Here the priests sat on benches on either side of a throne for the bishop.

These buildings were curious structures assembled to provide for new needs.

EARLY CHURCH ARCHITECTURE

The temple had been the dwelling of the god, where only priests were allowed to enter; it was indeed rather more of a monument and the exterior was of great importance. The Christian church, on the other hand, had to make room for a large congregation and so it was developed to give space for assembly and was decorated within. Since most of the people of the Middle Ages had no means of measuring time or, for that matter, dates, it was found necessary to introduce bells to summon the congregation to worship. Bell towers

Fig. 20

were added separately, often even a short distance away from the main building, with the result that the church looked like a group of buildings with no real cohesion. But the interior was decorated with gleaming mosaics which gave a brilliance to the gloom and set the often windowless apse glittering in the mysterious shadows. Churches of this type can be seen today in Rome, where the campaniles are always square, and in Ravenna where they are round and just as bare and even rather shabby-looking in dusty red ochre (Fig. 20). Even though they are not very well articulated, they attract by their simplicity and by the tiers of arcades of varying sizes.

Nevertheless, compared with a Greek or Roman temple, the earliest 'compromise' churches were certainly neither monumental nor imposing, though Byzantine churches built specifically for

Christian worship had an oriental splendour. With certain modifications, these first churches served as a pattern for all subsequent churches, although later builders and architects gradually conceived them as a unified whole instead of a kind of patchwork.

The baptisteries followed the pattern of Roman rotundas and were also extremely bare outside and very simple in design inside. They were mainly single domed rooms or, on occasion, more elaborate with a perististyle (that is, an inner circle of columns) supporting the dome. Later, many of these baptisteries were built on an octagonal plan. Both types were brilliantly decorated with mosaics, and some of the capitals were intricately carved.

BYZANTINE SPLENDOUR

Byzantine art is, of course, splendidly exemplified in the city of Byzantium (later Constantinople and now Istanbul) where Justinian commissioned the building of St. Sophia with the intention that it should surpass in size and splendour every monument in the world. There are very beautiful early churches to be seen in Kastoria, Thessaloniki (Salonica) and other cities in the north of Greece. The superb monasteries in Greece have richly decorated chapels of this type, and churches in the same style can be found in Ravenna, Venice, and the islands of the lagoon. All these places have excellent examples of Byzantine art and architecture in small and large buildings decorated with superb mosaics and with carved capitals to the marble columns. It is even possible to get some idea of the style from Westminster Cathedral, London, though of course the mosaics and sculpture there are modern and have none of the impact of early work.

MOSAICS OF RAVENNA

The art of mosaic was a favourite form of decoration with the early Christians and the Byzantines. At first, black-and-white or coloured pebbles were used for pavements and courts; very lovely designs were made naturalistically with a stress on the third dimension. By the first century A.D. this rather austere material with its limited range of colour was replaced by coloured marble, mother-of-pearl, and gold laid on a firm base with a thin layer of glass on top. The use of colour may have been responsible for a rather different attitude towards mosaic and a much more fanciful and imaginative style, decorative rather than strictly realistic or pictorial. The brilliant medium of coloured-glass tessarae (obviously unsuitable for floors) was probably not used for wall decoration until the fourth century.

The subjects chosen were the same as for frescoes, and the two techniques ran concurrently, mosaic being much more costly and luxurious than painting.

The Good Shepherd. *Mausoleum of Galla Placidia, Ravenna, Italy* (Plate 28). In this mid-fifth century mosaic, Christ is seated in a pose much like that used to depict the classical Apollo. He is shown among sheep in naturalistic attitudes, standing and lying on uneven ground with trees silhouetted against a blue sky. Apart from the golden halo and the cross in Christ's hand, it would be difficult to attribute any Christian message in this three-dimensional composition. It is, nevertheless one of the most lovely mosaics in existence.

Executed in a small range of subtle blues, greens, and gold, it expresses, in the compact arrangement of the figure and animals, a monumental splendour. The composition is perfectly balanced and conveys an atmosphere of complete tranquillity. Externally the mausoleum is almost crude in its rough simplicity: it is in the shape of a Greek cross, with spare uncompromising lines and very small windows—it gives no hint of the exquisite loveliness of the interior. The plant motifs inside are interwoven into delicate designs in the roof, and all the mosaics are lighted by a golden glow from the slabs of amber, of a later date, set into the windows.

The Empress Theodora and Her Suite. *Church of San Vitale, Ravenna, Italy* (Plate 29). This mosaic of the mid-sixth century expresses sumptuousness and majesty. The tesserae are of the most gorgeous deep purple, green, blue, gold, yellow, and white with the gleam of gold and jewels and satiny sheen of mother-of-pearl. Theodora is the personification of majesty, austere and splendid, slightly larger than the members of her suite, with diadem, necklaces, and ear-rings in which the pieces of glass have been set at angles with special subtlety to shimmer with light. She stares straight ahead with huge wide eyes, and the artist has managed to convey dignity and character in the face, but there is little variety in the faces or figures of her suite. The impression of majesty is stressed by the long vertical lines of the draperies with only occasional subtle curves, and variety in the general design is supplied by the arch under which the Empress stands and by the reversed arch of the draped curtain. The effect of this glittering sheen of colour and gold in the church is unbelievable; especially when seen amid the other mosaics—of which the group of the Emperor Justinian and his court is equally gorgeous—and the lace-like carved capitals of the pink and white marble pillars.

In some ways more lovely than either of these, is the decoration of the apse of Sant' Apollinare in Classe, a few miles outside the city of Ravenna and, until a few years ago, standing forlorn in the fields. Although it is obviously essential for these buildings to be properly looked after, the impact of the interior of this basilica is weakened now that it stands, well tended, off the main road instead of neglected and weed-grown across a marsh when the astonishing revelation of the interior was overwhelming to any visitor.

St. Apollinare. *Church of Sant' Apollinare in Classe, Ravenna* (Fig. 21). St. Apollinare stands erect in the dome of the apse, with arms outstretched, majestic and remote from the delightful, imaginative landscape of decorative trees and plants. The stylized sheep on either side of him, disposed between lovely little flowering plants, symbolize the souls of the saints. Above his head, a huge cross is seen in the sky in a circle of stars, and God's hand appears through the clouds. Stylized this may be, but it is a satisfying composition

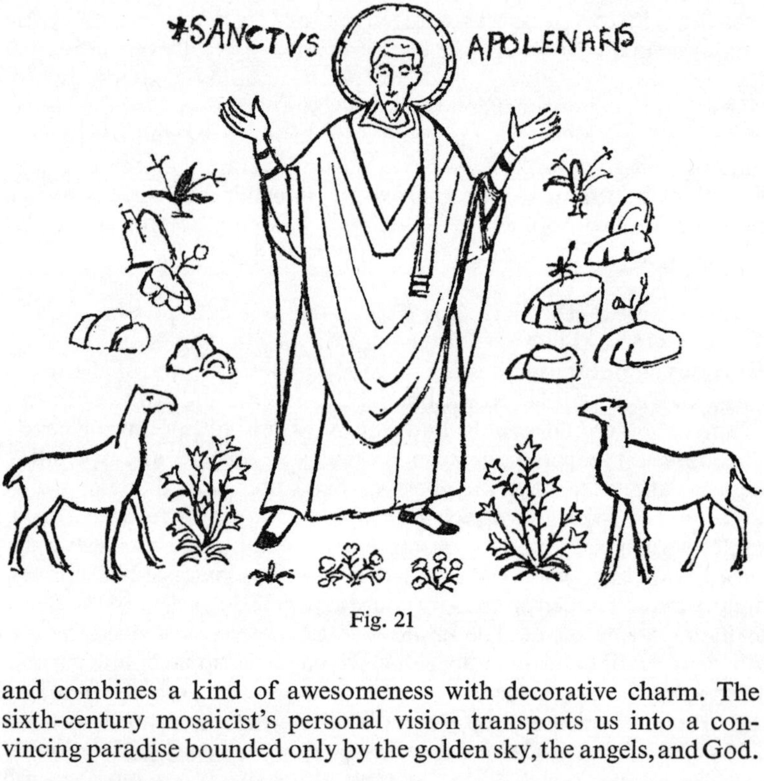

Fig. 21

and combines a kind of awesomeness with decorative charm. The sixth-century mosaicist's personal vision transports us into a convincing paradise bounded only by the golden sky, the angels, and God.

MANUSCRIPTS

As well as being masters of the art of mosaic, these early artists could carve lace-like capitals with incredible delicacy and grace, piercing designs of acanthus leaves in pale coloured marbles.

The Christians produced illuminated manuscripts as early as the sixth century. Of particular beauty is the *Rossano Codex*, executed on purple parchment and now in the cathedral treasury at Rossano, southern Italy.

Another manuscript of perhaps the same date and again on purple parchment is the *Vienna Genesis*. This manuscript of Eliezer and

Rebecca, shows Rebecca at the spring giving water to Jacob's messenger. Her camels stand in the most lively attitudes of expectation, and are depicted together in a solid decorative group (Fig. 22). This is again a continuous treatment, for Rebecca is also seen leaving a walled and turretted town with the pitcher over her shoulder.

As a very broad generalization, from the death of Justinian in A.D. 565 until the eighth century, artistic expression in western Europe gradually weakened and disappeared because the whole area fell under wave after wave of Barbarian attacks and invasions. The Franks controlled Gaul; Spain was in the hands of the Visigoths (though in the seventh century they were ousted by the Moors).

Fig. 22

The Angles and Saxons conquered Britain; Lombard hordes occupied Italy. Consequently it is easy to understand why there was a period of artistic darkness in these lands.

Oddly enough it was in Britain that some of the finest manuscripts of any age were produced towards the end of this period. Among these were the *Lindisfarne Gospels*, the *Book of Yarrow* and the *Book of Kells* (Plate 12). To these must be added the *Anglo-Saxon Psalter* and the *Winchester Bible*.

EARLY CHRISTIAN CHALICES

It was during the eighth century, the approximate date of the *Book of Kells*, that the famous Ardagh Chalice (Plate 30*a*), a fine example of the art of Ireland's Golden Age, was fashioned from a variety of metals including gold, silver, and lead, and decorated with filigree, enamel, amber, crystal, and glass.

The Tassilo Chalice (eighth *century*). *Monastery of Kremsmünster, Austria* (Plate 30). Like so much monastic art of the period, this superb vessel has some of the qualities of Irish art. Of gilded copper inlaid with silver, it is in the shape of an egg-cup on an oval silver panel. Christ is depicted with a halo and robe of gold, and the saints decorate the base in the style of the *Book of Kells*. There is a kind of barbaric splendour akin to the Irish, but also something of Byzantine sophistication. At this period and a little later some of the arrestingly beautiful royal crowns of Europe were wrought, among them that of Charlemagne now in Vienna.

POSSIBLE ESSAYS, DISCUSSION AND RESEARCH

1 Compare the *Toreadors* or any other wall painting at Knossos with the *Etruscan Musicians* at Tarquinia or with any other wall painting at Tarquinia.

2 Describe three Ionic or Doric Greek temples and refer each to its setting.

3 Look at the Elgin marbles in the British Museum; describe and give an appreciation of one of them.

4 Do you personally find you have enlarged your experience when looking at a Greek statue (the Elgin Marbles for instance) or do you get a greater stimulus from Henry Moore?

5 Compare a mosaic decoration with stained glass (but only if you have actually seen examples of both).

6 Do you think that the inside and the outside of a church are equally important?

7 Do pages of the *Book of Kells* impress you as much as an easel painting?

Suggested Further Reading

Baynes, N. H., and Moss, H. St. L. B.: *Byzantium: An Introduction to East Roman Civilization*. Oxford University Press: London, 1961.

Cottrell, Leonard: *The Bull of Minos*. Pan Books: London, 1955.

Higgins, Reynold: *Minoan and Mycenaean Art*. Thames & Hudson: London, 1967.

Lassus, Jean: *The Early Christian and Byzantine World*. Paul Hamlyn: London, 1967.

Rice, David Talbot: *Byzantine Art*. Penguin: London, 1954.

Roper, Hugh Trevor: *The Rise of Christian Europe*. Thames & Hudson: London, 1965.

Strong, Donald: *The Classical World*. Paul Hamlyn: London, 1965.

Vryonis, Speros: *Byzantium and Europe*. Thames & Hudson: London, 1967.

Wheeler, Mortimer: *Roman Art and Architecture*. Thames & Hudson: London, 1964.

Chapter Six

THE MIDDLE AGES

CAROLINGIAN ART

Carolingian art, is art of the period of Charlemagne (768–814) and of his descendants. It was being produced from the late eighth century until the beginning of the tenth century and is exemplified especially in the art of France, Germany, Northern Italy, and the Netherlands. The style was modelled on the Byzantine, but Charlemagne inaugurated a 'Carolingian Renaissance' inspired by Roman Christian art. This, modified by the individual regions, links Byzantine and Romanesque art, but much of the Romanesque, especially in Britain, developed independently.

Naturally enough, the palace chapel at Aachen, the centre of Charlemagne's empire, is the most often cited existing building of this style. It is usually taken to be a copy of San Vitale in Ravenna, but the planning of the palace and its precincts re-created many features of the Rome of Constantine.

In comparison with the splendour and spaciousness of Byzantine architecture it seems a little pedestrian and clumsy, falling between the two styles of Roman and Byzantine. Nevertheless some vigorous wall paintings subsist, and illuminated manuscripts, ivories, and jewellery of a very high standard were produced in abundance. I have already mentioned the magnificent crowns.

Christ in Majesty. *Fitzwilliam Museum, Cambridge* (Plate 30*b*). The Roman influence in this Carolingian ivory plaque is evident in the surrounding laurel wreath, in the formalized drapery which rather unhappily encircles the knees, and in the curled hair. The treatment of the face as a portrait is Roman, but gentler in style, and, whereas the heavy head on the small body is far removed from the elongated Byzantine figures of the Ravenna mosaics, the sense of majesty is Byzantine.

ROMANESQUE SCULPTURE AND ARCHITECTURE

We now turn to the main stream of Romanesque architecture and sculpture which developed in Europe during the tenth and eleventh centuries from the mystical, and in some ways hesitant, Byzantine and early-Christian styles. Romanesque was not entirely a natural outcome of early-Christian: it owed a good deal to Rome and even indirectly to Greece and to Egypt, for even though the builders, sculptors, and painters may never have seen Greek or Roman art, some of these traditions were inevitably handed on through succeeding centuries.

The dome, the rounded arch of the Romans and the columns which they modified from the Greeks were still employed in the Romanesque style (referred to in Britain as Norman). This style of building was in use in Europe from the tenth century onwards, and in every region had almost identical characteristics of strength, protection, power, and mass. Huge piers support rounded arches and a great round arch leads into the choir. Buttresses give added strength to the massive walls, especially when they are high. There is a kind of

Fig. 23

restful, permanent feeling of an architectural whole: a living structure with organized space and complete unity. There is always satisfaction in the finality of a rounded arch on solid supports, succeeded by others which repeat the curves and verticals. It is a definite statement which does not lend itself to much modification, though in Germany and Austria there are examples of existing Romanesque being married very successfully at a later time with the exuberant baroque or rococo styles.

Early British architecture is exemplified by the Saxon churches which almost always favoured the square rather than the Continental circular apse, and this remained the favourite form throughout the Middle Ages and to the end of the Gothic period.

Saxon architecture had the conglomeration of boxes of the Byzantine basilica, but none of its grandeur and feeling for space. So it is to Norman architecture that we look for the first flowering of the great cathedrals and churches in Britain: Durham cathedral, Iffley church near Oxford, Barfreston in Kent, St. Bartholomew's the Great in London, the beautiful little St. John's chapel in the Tower of London and a host of others. The use of the round arch and barrel vaulting, massive piers, flat buttresses, and solid masonry, were the most obvious characteristics of Norman and Romanesque architecture.

The semicircular arch of the portal or chancel entrance was often made up of multiple arches resting on several pillars which receded towards the doorway and had carved capitals; the concentric arches were decorated with crude but vigorous, more or less geometric, patterns in low relief. Some of the carvings of the capitals and even round the doors were delightfully imaginative, as for example at Barfreston (Fig. 23), and many portals had carved tympanums depicting Biblical themes.

The massive piers, as at Durham and in the Norman crypt at Canterbury, were often incised with patterns to lessen their heavy appearance.

VÉZELAY

One of the most impressive Romanesque buildings in Europe is the Burgundian abbey church at Vézelay, which is not only a miracle of building but also of carved capitals and sculpture. Although a reconstruction, the abbey façade is the most noble of its kind to be seen in Burgundy. The carving in the tympanum over the central doorway represents Christ in glory, surrounded by apostles, all strangely elongated like Himself and each with flowing robes which accentuate this effect (Plate 31). Full of movement and a certain agitation, these figures strive and strain and thrust but, even so, are contained within the framework. The composition is so well knit as to make a completely satisfying whole, held in control within the decorations of the rounded arch. The figures seem to be surging from the stone and yet confined within it. Across the lintel are the people who have been converted by the apostles. A delightful touch is given by the group of pygmies characterized by the fact that they are climbing on to their horses by means of ladders. In the voussoirs (wedge-shaped segments in an arch) more groups symbolize converted nations and there are also signs of the zodiac and the occupations of each month.

Quite apart from the dramatic force of this wonderful carving, it provides a description of a whole Christian world and is as easily readable as a book—more so to the bulk of the early congregations. Beyond the doorway, the two rows of nine columns and the black-and-white vaulting not only lift the gaze to the vast expanse above, but draw it along and to the altar through a kind of tunnel of light (Plate 31*a*).

The world of the grand portal is contrasted with the world depicted in the capitals of the columns carved by Cluniac craftsmen who varied their subjects by using legendary themes. Not only do they present an entire cavalcade of contemporary life, of prelates, priests, monks, knights, ladies, peasants, children, and animals, but these are contrasted with a fantastic procession of imps, apes, monsters, and all kinds of grotesques which might have been taken from medieval bestiaries.

If you walk from pillar to pillar, interest in this fantastic world increases and admiration for the strength of inventiveness and imagination of these brilliant craftsmen. Each pillar is a work in itself, but also contributes materially to the whole effect of the building. Just how these medieval craftsmen co-ordinated their effects so successfully we do not know. There must have been 'master' craftsmen and there were, of course, the unifying requirements of a religious building as laid down by the Church. Probably, too, the tremendous responsibility of making this house of God, this centre of life, a place worthy of its purpose, and the stimulus given by the interest taken by everyone, rich and poor, in its completion, helped to make this possible.

The vaulting of the nave is stressed by immense curved ribbing of black and white stone, while the masonry of the choir and of the transept is of uniform colouring. Everywhere in the abbey there is a skilful balance of strains and stresses. Even the columns seem to march solemnly but purposefully towards the altar. Nothing is cramped, yet even the loftiest of the arches keeps the building within compass, for, unlike a pointed arch which leads away into the sky, the downward curve of an arch or barrel vault girdles in the building and gives a feeling of protection and great strength when resting on massive pillars.

In Styria, the south-eastern province of Austria, the imposing abbey church of Sechau stands austere in contrast to Vézelay, though it was actually built a little later. A portal of golden stone is supported upon ancient lions and flanked by twin towers. The whole length of the nave is flanked by great round pillars with flat capitals sparingly decorated with geometric designs. They form an arcade to support the huge roof and give a vista, a kind of telescopic view, to the very simple wooden figures set in the altar recess. All three were carved at the end of the twelfth century and are Romanesque. They have been carefully restored, though originally there was much more colour. The wood is now mainly creamy white with traces of darker colour on the hair, and pale pink and green on the drapery of the saints.

Here, too, is astonishing unity obtained by rather simpler means than at Vézelay, for the weight of the huge pillars and arches is offset by the delicate ribbed vaulting sweeping from the capitals to the roof, and the very simplicity and tragedy of the three figures of the altar makes it a focal point. Many of these types of crucifixes and saints are to be seen all over Austria, carved in wood and with a graceful curve of the body and a tragic droop of the head, often elongated both in body and slender arms, with hair flowing decoratively over the shoulders.

PROCESSIONAL CROSSES AND ALTARPIECES

Even modern craftsmen in Austria, with no pretensions to being great artists, will carve a traditional crucifix or saint or an altar rail which blends extremely well with the original building. Crucifixes in the wayside chapels are renewed when the ravages of the weather destroys them, by contemporary carvers who carry on the medieval tradition much as primitive peoples continue to work in the style of their prehistoric ancestors. Austrian craftsmen, too, wrought miraculous crucifixes in gold and silver and bronze. They decorated the cross with precious stones and sometimes, in a remote church in Bavaria or Austria, a precious Romanesque crucifix of incalculable value will be brought out from its locked chest and used in a procession, on a saint's day. But these crosses are not, of course, peculiar to Austria.

Very rich church decorations were wrought by goldsmiths during this period. In 1189, Nicholas of Verdun designed 51 scenes from the Bible in champlevé enamel to cover the front of a pulpit, but this is now known as the Verdun Altar and preserved in the Monastery of Klosterneuberg near Vienna. The effect is of gleaming gold and blue with the exquisite attention to detail of an illuminated manuscript. Each episode is dramatically and simply expressed and set in a frame of gold.

Simple Romanesque chapels are scattered all over Europe. Many of these have wall paintings and each year more and more early frescoes are being uncovered. In Spain, particularly in Catalonia, many remote churches and chapels were splendidly decorated in deep earth colours, but as the paintings were deteriorating from neglect and damp, a number have been stripped from the walls and can be seen in a reconstructed setting in Barcelona. Excellent facsimiles of early French frescoes can be seen in the Musée des Monuments in Paris.

Romanesque architects had developed vaulting and buttressing beyond Roman practice and had also developed cross-vaulting. We have seen how the Roman columns became massive piers, as being more able to bear a heavy vertical load or the thrust of an arch. The tower, which in the early Christian churches had been separate from the main building, was moved up against the church and this feature often became twin towers, one on either side of the façade as at Sechau. To begin with, they still gave the appearance of being a separate section of the church, whereas later they were incorporated into the façade and often flush with it.

During the period of Romanesque building, the basilica had developed into a monumental structure with great attention paid to proportion, unity, and strength. With the Gothic builders this quality was to be modified into the desire for height, lightness of effect, delicacy, and decoration, with a great deal of attention given to the adornment of the outside of the building. In early Romanesque works, by contrast, massiveness with restrained exterior decoration was usual; decoration was often confined to the portal and rose window (as at Barfreston) although by the twelfth century splendid portals were being carved in anticipation of the even more elaborate manifestations of the Gothic style which followed.

ST. TROPHIME

The twelfth-century portal of St. Trophime, at Arles in the South of France, is a magnificent example of a Romanesque carved entrance (Plate 32). In the tympanum, Christ sits enthroned amid symbols of the four evangelists. The lintel is decorated with the 12 seated apostles. The frieze to the left depicts the blessed being welcomed to heavenly bliss and to the right the wicked are condemned to the flames of hell.

Even more fascinating, perhaps because of their tranquil setting away from the trafficky street, are the reliefs on pillars and capitals in the cloisters (Fig. 24).

Fig. 24

The long period of Gothic building began during the twelfth century: the actual word 'Gothic' was not applied to this style until the seventeenth century when it was used as a term of derision, for the style was considered to be barbarous—like that of the Goths and Vandals.

THE POINTED ARCH

The introduction of the pointed arch solved the problems of vaulting. It was probably brought to Europe by the crusaders, since it had been in use in the Middle East as early as the sixth century A.D. Now that arches were no longer unalterably semicircular, but could be made more or less sharply pointed to suit the different heights of aisles and nave, stone ribs could take the weight of the vaulting, and buttresses could counteract the outward thrust of ribs. The thick Romanesque walls, with their small windows, could be replaced by lighter walls which could be pierced with large windows. It is easy to see how this led to the development of huge traceried windows filled with coloured glass and, since wall space was reduced, to the disappearance of wall paintings. Just as mosaics gave a richer effect than frescoes, so did stained glass give a much more sumptuous effect than frescoes which in small Romanesque churches, at any rate, were not very well lighted.

No doubt the main reason for the change of 'direction' in building in the thirteenth century was due to the pointed arch and the flying buttress. These did not add to the massive bulk of the building, but rather seemed to give it wings as a second arch was formed outside the building.

The early Christian builder, as we have seen, filled his church with mystery—a kind of trembling brilliance—with God depicted as remote in majesty. The Romanesque architects produced a great confident monument enclosing in its vast spaciousness a world of Biblical images and saints: a world of art dedicated to Christianity. The Gothic architects built a fantasy of carved and pinnacled stone-work soaring to heaven in towers and spires, always growing, always moving forward to the altar and upwards through the slender pillars to incredible heights of vaulting. Everywhere were vertical lines, never cut off but continuing into ribs and fans, spreading up and out like the branches of a tree; vertical panels of glowing glass told the Bible stories more vividly than the Romanesque frescoes or the Gothic paintings. The side aisles were filled with statues and monuments, the pillars rising sometimes in simple clusters to the roof, sometimes with saints decorating their length. Everything in the great Gothic cathedrals gives the semblance of hosts of worshippers, saints, and angels, and all were originally brightly coloured.

In the Middle Ages the church or the cathedral was the centre of existence for the throngs of worshippers and pilgrims, and it provided the colour in their lives: the gorgeous robes, the ceremony, the incense, the singing, and the gathering together, not to mention the brilliant 'colour strips' of the windows or the painted walls. The processional crosses and the jewelled robes with which statues of the saints were bedecked on occasion, enlivened a constantly repeated gala day.

Compared with the massive solemnity of Romanesque, Gothic was almost a lyric poem of lightness and grace, in which it is hardly possible to say one expression was a major art and another a minor, for the treasuries were filled with exceedingly beautiful and precious objects. In most cathedrals today, the treasuries are museums where everything exhibited is of a very high order.

Gothic architecture reached its most splendid achievements in England and in northern France; it was a heavier-handed expression in Germany, the Netherlands, and in Spain. In Italy, Gothic architecture never attained the grace of the French and English. This was largely due to the very strong Roman tradition in that country and the popularity of frescoes, which needed plenty of wall space, compared with glass.

CHARTRES CATHEDRAL

I have taken Chartres (Plates 33 and 34) as the example for all Gothic cathedrals despite the fact that there are many superb examples in Britain, and even in France there are others with equal or better claims to first place. But Chartres was basically completed in the incredibly short time of twenty-six years and it was the result of the inspired effort of all Christendom. The cathedral suffered repeated disasters; in the crypt you can see evidence of earlier sanctuaries but there is no trace of the first Christian church built in the fourth century, nor of the second destroyed by the Normans in the middle of the ninth century. The subsequent building was destroyed by lightning in 1020, but the crypt still subsists and on it Bishop Fulbert rebuilt the church. Two steeples added to the Romanesque façade in the twelfth century escaped the fire of 1194 and form one of the wonders of Romanesque art. In the main, the astonishing marvel of architecture we can see today was completed by 1220.

There must have been a single mind of great genius directing such a work, but his name is unknown to us. We do know, though, that he was supported by a tremendous enthusiasm. Kings and princes gave splendid gifts; men, women, and young children worked on the project. It is even alleged that the Virgin wrought miracles to speed the building, and it is certain that the participants worked in an atmosphere of miracles. One cannot overestimate the work of the masons, but it was the direction which produced this building, governed by logic and revealing perfect proportions, with every detail playing an essential part but subservient to the whole.

That the left spire was destroyed by lightning at the beginning of the sixteenth century is, to me, not a disaster but a piece of good fortune, for the 'flamboyant' sixteenth-century replacement designed by Jehan de Beauce is incredibly beautiful and gives just the right contrast with the sober right spire, breaking the symmetry in an imaginative and wholly satisfying way. Added to this marvellous conception of the building as a whole, must be the superb carvings of the portals where statues are individual works of art, where elongated figures are at the same time part of the stone pillars and yet rising out of them, and where the smaller figures and scenes are wonderfully executed.

STAINED GLASS IN EUROPE

The interior of Chartres cathedral is a miracle of lightness and grace, exemplifying all that is best in Gothic architecture; it is raised to a crescendo of glory by the brilliance and design of the stained-glass windows.

In the twelfth-century window of the Annunciation the artist shows complete mastery over the technique of stained glass and has miraculously trapped the light in the deep glowing green, blue, red, and yellow glass and disposed these colours so that the angel and Mary stand out dramatically. The angel is separated from Mary, who is given an earthy background, by a great green wing.

The early statues on Gothic buildings were still Romanesque in character. They were often rather stiff in body and heavy in the head, and definitely part of the column or stonework which gave them vigour and architectural unity. They did not become separate entities like later Gothic statues.

THE MADONNA AND CHILD IN THE MIDDLE AGES

The Romanesque and Gothic periods produced carvings of the Madonna and Child all over Europe, and they had considerable similarity and strong traditional characteristics. It is often said that the peculiar grace of the Gothic Madonnas was due to the fact that so many were carved in ivory and followed the naturally graceful curve of the tusk, but sculptors of genius were surely too sensitive and creative to be enslaved by this when they used stone or wood as a medium. We shall be looking at various types of madonnas in a later chapter.

THE SAINTE CHAPELLE

One of the most perfect small Gothic monuments in existence, even in its restored state, is the Sainte Chapelle in Paris, a fantastic two-storey church with spires and pinnacles built in soaring lances of lace. Like a goldsmith's elaborate reliquary set with jewels, this was designed to hold the sacred relics of St. Louis. It is an elaborate stone setting for the brilliance of the slender glass windows: deep shining blues and greens and reds, all shimmering and holding the light; a monument perfect within and without.

The Gothic period lasted from the twelfth to the sixteenth centuries and of course there were many changes in outlook and style during that time, but the same miraculous harmony between mason, builder, architect, and stained-glass worker prevailed throughout.

PORTUGUESE ARCHITECTURE

In the early sixteenth century in Portugal the Gothic style of building reached its climax in the extraordinarily exuberant flowering of the Manueline style named after King Manuel I (1495–1521). Like a parallel movement in Spain, this was the result of the enormous wealth pouring into the country from overseas and was a kind of immortalizing of Portuguese maritime strength and of her great discoveries. The motifs in this elaborate style were twisted ropes, anchors, shells, pineapples, and exotic fruits in superabundance. At times this exuberance was overstated and flamboyant; at others it has a marvellous decorative quality and sense of grandeur.

The Jerónimos Monastery in Lisbon (Plate 35) has a deep serenity despite the elaborate carving, and the cloisters (Plate 36) are a marvel of harmonious proportion and elegance.

Opinions differ about the famous window at Tomar (Plate 37). Although it is often criticized as being very much overdone and far too weighty, I find it a riot of delight and marvellously inventive. Admittedly the whole building in which it figures is far too heavily encrusted with decoration and this elaboration detracts from its architectural value.

TAPESTRY

Obviously building in the Middle Ages was not exclusively ecclesiastical, for there were splendid town halls, castles, and palaces in many parts of Europe; but for our purpose, the greatest skill was

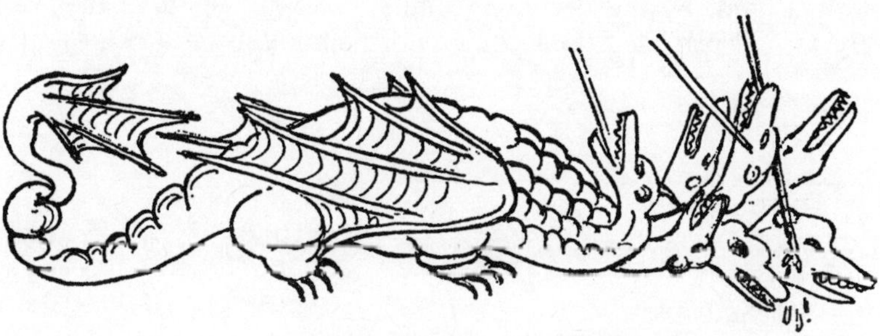

Fig. 25

lavished on the church in painting, sculpture, stained glass, and the 'minor' arts. Tapestry, though used in churches, was largely commissioned to warm the cold stone walls of castles and dwellings and often even to form partitions dividing the vast draughty halls.

It was during the fourteenth century that the wonderful series of tapestries of the Apocalypse was woven at Angers. Jean Lurçat, a foremost French tapestry designer of our times, has described them enthusiastically as 'a monumental example of French art which equalled in importance a Vézelay or a Poussin among the glories of France', and of 'extraordinary lyrical power' obtained by the greatest economy of means (Fig. 25). Even from the rough diagram you can see the astonishing mastery of design, and be impressed by the drama of the angels so vigorously slaying the many-headed dragon.

ILLUMINATED MANUSCRIPTS

At this time when great works of architecture were being achieved, when huge stained-glass windows, immense cathedral portals, large-scale wall paintings, and large tapestries were being carried out, there were also countless artists engaged in the minute detail of illuminated manuscripts such as the *Très Riches Heures du Duc de Berry*, at Chantilly in France, and the sixteenth-century *Sforza Book of Hours*.

The Shepherds at Bethlehem. *British Museum, London* (Plate 38). A lovely example of the international Gothic style depicting a scene on a small scale dramatically and often naïvely, with natural details rendered with exquisite care and grace. Here, despite the wealth of detail, the utter bewilderment of the shepherds is very convincing, and an unearthly radiance emanates from the angels to transfigure the onlookers and the sheep.

While England and France were devoting all their artistic energy to architecture, sculpture, stained glass, and manuscripts, Flanders was also expending a great deal of energy in Gothic buildings, following the French style. They were also producing beautiful manuscripts, and, by the beginning of the fifteenth century, the Van Eycks had perfected the technique of painting in oils.

POSSIBLE ESSAYS, DISCUSSION AND RESEARCH

1 What are the qualities peculiar to (*a*) stained glass, (*b*) mosaic, (*c*) fresco?

2 How do Romanesque reliefs compare with classical Greek?

3 Do you find Romanesque architecture more or less impressive than Gothic? Do either of them have anything in common with Greek architecture?

4 Compare a Romanesque carved Madonna with a Gothic.

5 Study one of the English cathedrals or abbeys. How does it compare with Chartres or Vézelay?

6 Look at a Norman church and study the capitals, the doorways, the windows and the frescoes, if any.

7 How important was landscape in illuminated manuscripts?

Suggested Further Reading

Beckwith, John: *Early Medieval Art.* Thames & Hudson: London, 1964.

Bony, J. and Hürlmann, M.: *French Cathedrals.* Thames & Hudson: London, 1967.

Clapham. A. W.: *English Romanesque Architecture.* (2 Vols.) Clarendon Press: Oxford, 1934.

Dos Santos, Reynaldo: *L'Art Portugais.* Librairie Plon: Paris 1953.

Evans, Joan (ed.): *The Middle Ages.* Thames & Hudson: London, 1966.

Kidson, Peter: *The Medieval World.* Paul Hamlyn: London, 1967.

Martindale, Andrew: *Gothic Art.* Thames & Hudson: London, 1967.

Porcher, J.: *French Miniatures from Illuminated MSS.* Collins: London, 1960.

Webb, G. F.: *Architecture in Britain: The Middle Ages.* Penguin: London, 1956.

Chapter Seven

EARLY PAINTINGS, MOSAICS AND SCULPTURE IN EUROPE

FLEMISH PAINTING

The Flemish painters Hubert and Jan Van Eyck produced oil paintings of astonishing accomplishment in the early fifteenth century. It is often said that they invented the technique of oil painting, but this is not strictly true. Nevertheless, Jan Van Eyck certainly employed a technique which gave him complete command of handling, and his works have endured undimmed to the present day. He completed the famous altarpiece at Ghent (Plate 49) begun by his brother, and is himself perhaps more famous for the portrait of Giovanni Arnolfini and his wife.

The Marriage of Giovanni Arnolfini and Giovanna Cenani. *Jan Van Eyck* (*c.* 1390–1441). *National Gallery, London* (Plate 39). Even setting aside its greatness as a work of art this is a painting of such skill and genius that it must have an appeal for everyone. It is carried out in tempera with superimposed oil glazes (transparent layers of oil paint). The obvious delight with which Van Eyck shows us the detail of everything in the room, his incredible powers of observation and his keen perception of the different textures of wood, fur, metal, skin, hair, orange peel, and wool, and above all his ability to render them convincingly, make a close study imperative. It is well worth while analysing this picture which, though at first impact may represent two stiff and formal figures in a background much like that of a miniature painting, has great subtleties and a basically monumental composition.

Arnolfini in dark clothes is silhouetted against the lighter half of the room, while his wife, in lighter clothes, stands out from the red draperies of the bed. Their hands are linked, but they are also bound together by the lines of the composition. Look at the dog in the foreground and soon your eyes will be drawn up the zigzag of the white edging of the woman's robe and then across to the man. Try any point in the picture and you will be led on to find more and more of interest, such as the light bathing the oranges on the sill, the reflection in the mirror, the hard shining metal of the chandelier and the writing on the wall proclaiming that Jan Van Eyck was here —he actually saw it with his own eyes and makes sure that we can see it too. Now forget about the details, half-close your eyes and get the impact of the marvellously co-ordinated architectural whole of the painting.

Jan Van Eyck's best-known successors were Rogier Van der Weyden (*c.* 1400–64) who was less a genius but more emotional and dramatic in his rendering of religious subjects, and Hans Memlinc (*c.* 1430–94) whose works will be familiar to anyone who has visited Bruges in Belgium. These cannot fail to appeal, with their jewel-like colouring, characteristic of the Flemish school, and their gentle serene rendering of religious subjects and portraits.

PORTUGUESE PAINTING

Nuno Gonçalves (active 1450–72) was painting great religious works in Portugal during the same period as Van der Weyden and Memlinc, and he was working somewhat in the Flemish style. Here it must be noted that Flanders had many contacts both economically and artistically with Portugal (Jan Van Eyck spent some time there in 1428) and it was natural that Portuguese painting should be influenced by the northern school.

Altarpiece of St. Vincent (detail). *Nuno Gonçalves. Lisbon Museum* (Plate 40). There was no great painting in Portugal before the sudden appearance of Gonçalves, although several artists are known to us by name. Gonçalves certainly has Flemish characteristics in his rendering of detail and texture, and his modelling of heads shows the northern influence of wood-carving; but no Flemish painter arranged his figures quite so austerely or had this feeling for the monumental grouping of a large number of people in a relatively small space without any feeling of crowding. Like Michelangelo nearly a century later, he dispensed with landscape and relied on the human figure for his effects, though his figures are clothed and it was not the human *form* which interested him so much as the relationship of characters.

You will notice what splendid searching portraits Gonçalves gives of these different types of men and how the saint stands separately, emphasized by his rich and elaborate cope and by the unworldly look on his pale face. All the other personages are indentifiable types and all are very devout and solemn. Gonçalves has an unusual sense of colour, using muted tones, especially of green and red.

This single painter who stands out in the history of Portuguese art can certainly rank with the great European artists of the fifteenth century.

In the sixteenth century in Flanders Pieter Brueghel the Elder (*c.* 1520–69) popularized Biblical, historical, and legendary subjects, translating them into contemporary terms and putting them in lovely natural settings. Since he was one of the first real landscape artists, Brueghel's painting will be described in a later section.

LANDSCAPE AS A BACKGROUND

It is of course true that landscape was used in illuminated manuscripts and, as we have seen, in the *Books of Hours*, but in large easel paintings it was a background to a figure composition illustrating a great event or even to a portrait.

From early times the Italians used landscape where necessary in illustrating Bible stories, and, later, the Flemish influenced them to make these backgrounds a fascinating part of the design.

SCHOOLS OF ITALIAN PAINTING

From approximately the fourteenth century onwards, Italy contributed a continuous flow of painting, sculpture, and architecture of the highest order until, towards the end of the sixteenth century, decadence set in. There was to be another great period in the eighteenth century in Venice, and today contemporary Italians are internationally established among the foremost painters, sculptors, and architects. The greatest works of art were produced when Italy was made up of a number of principalities, republics, and kingdoms, each producing its own particular style of painting, architecture, and sculpture. These schools were, however, interrelated to one another and were often in the service of patrons, in Florence, Rome, and Venice, each of which had its own artistic tradition.

For our purpose we can divide the Italian schools arbitrarily into two main sections: those of Florence, Tuscany, and Umbria; and those of Venice, Verona, and Padua. We can even make the broader generalization of Florence on the one hand and Venice on the other, since these two cities and the regions around them either gave birth to or patronized at one time or another the greatest Italian artists. Rome had her own early artists, but for the great painting and sculpture produced during the Renaissance she drew from the genius that was abundant in Florence.

MOSAICS IN ROME

In the thirteenth century in Rome, Pietro Cavallini (active 1273–1308) was pre-eminent as a mosaic worker, the art inherited from the Romans. His compositions had all the vigour of the Roman feeling for the monumental, and his geometric patterns are a reminder of the ordered design of Roman art and architecture. He is little known to the general public and has only recently been recognized, but he was sufficiently well thought of to be invited to contribute to the decoration of Assisi and it is just conceivable that he had some influence on Giotto. He links the classical style of Rome with Giotto's new vision of the world around him. Giotto (1266–1337), with his predecessor Cimabue (1240–1302) about whom very little is known, is generally considered to be the 'father' of European painting.

PAINTING IN SIENA

We have seen some examples of the work of the Byzantine artists and the early Christians, including the rich mosaics of Ravenna with which the Sienese School had some points in common. We have seen how Byzantine art was majestic, cold, aloof; how Christ, the Virgin, and even the angels were at first represented by symbols and then by formalized figures, never human in themselves, although the works of art in which they figure have their own vitality. Now Siena kept the decorative arrangement of Byzantine painting and their brilliant jewel-like colours had some of the luxury of mosaic.The Sienese also show the influence of the courtly art of the north.

Duccio (*c.* 1260–1318) and Simone Martini (*c.* 1284–1344) were the most important members of the Sienese School. The *Maestà* is of infinite interest and one of the outstanding works of art of Europe.

Maestà. *Duccio. Cathedral Museum, Siena* (Plate 41). A large two-sided altarpiece with predella (a shallow horizontal strip along the bottom of the frame) painted in 1308–11. This huge picture was originally designed to stand in the middle of Siena Cathedral on the high altar. The Madonna sits in majesty, surrounded by saints and angels. Above her are scenes from the life of the Virgin and below, in the predella, scenes from the infancy of Christ. On the back, narrative scenes tell the story of the life of Christ from his manhood to the resurrection. This narrative style is an obvious reminder of early manuscripts, such as the *Rossano Codex*, and of Byzantine frescoes, but Duccio is not a fresco painter. He has the qualities of a miniature painter: elegance and refinement, the delicate handling of feet and hands, a jewel-like quality and glowing colour. He handles decorative detail with consummate skill, and the figures have gentle controlled gestures and move as befits a company of saints and angels; the drapery flows gracefully in soft, but defined folds. The heads are given variety by being set each at a slightly different angle. Notice the controlled flow forward towards the Virgin of the standing and kneeling figures. There is still the majesty of Byzantine art, but the Virgin has a look of tenderness as she gently lays her hand on the Child, and the angels leaning over the back of the throne gaze at Him. The colours of the robes are the colours of an illuminated manuscript, not the deep earths and ochres of early Spanish wall paintings or of the hunters' caves; the rows of flat golden haloes proceed towards the throne, and there are subtle touches of violet, blue, sage, crimson, scarlet, pink, cream, and pale blues. The Virgin is isolated in her majesty, but there is a human link with the saints. Here Duccio shows himself to be a master of design and colour. The faces are types rather than individuals but, despite their affinity with miniature painting, they have a monumental dignity and the subtle forward movement is accentuated by the skilful disposition of the colours which help the forward flow. The blue robe of the Virgin is not repeated elsewhere and the depth of colour focuses attention upon her; but the touches of red where her dress is exposed, and the wonderful looping of the drapery on either side of her over the arms of the throne, link her to the advancing procession. The figures themselves are impersonal.

Look for the intricate and beautifully flowing lines of the drapery and the dignified figure of St. Agnes, and note how these are echoed in the Virgin's robes. See the sinuous curves of the Virgin's head-dress and mantle and the hugging folds of the head-dress of St. Agnes. Trace the wonderful pattern of the wings between the haloes, the decorative curves and curls of the hair and the decisive outline of the flat golden halo. It is just such a delicate interlacing of pattern and detail used in a manuscript but modified to fit the grandeur of scale. Although these people are all so completely calm and serene, one can enter into the flow of movement and experience the wonderful world that Duccio has created: a world of people with their gaze on heaven and their thoughts concentrated on the next world rather than this one.

On the back of the altarpiece scenes from the Passion include a marvellously designed Crucifixion, depicted with great dramatic force and occupying twice the space of the other incidents. The Entry into Jerusalem is also a large panel in which there is the same appearance of movement and a good deal of characterization. One is impelled to enter into this picture. In some mysterious way the flow of figures coming out from the gate towards Christ, draws one *into* the town, to mingle with the group who are waiting while two men have climbed to the tops of trees and are breaking off and distributing the branches. There is a subtle contrast in the one figure leaning down towards the upraised arms of those below, and the second, smaller figure clambering upwards. Christ, in a red robe and dusky blue mantle, bestrides a gentle donkey who plods forward purposefully while her offspring presses along behind. A crescendo of greys and greens and blues culminates in the deep colours of Christ's robes and is echoed in the crowd surging to meet Him.

Simone Martini (1282–1344) is usually presumed to have been Duccio's pupil, though there is no proof that he was. He painted many pictures in tempera and some large altarpieces, but he was also a fresco worker, a medium which Duccio never used. Perhaps his most attractive work is the equestrian portrait of a general in Siena.

Guidoriccio da Fogliano. *Simone Martini. Palazzo Publico, Siena* (Plate 42). This masterly painting of the solitary rider in his orange costume patterned in black is to me one of the most satisfying and arresting frescoes of the Sienese school and full of inventive genius. Here again are the qualities of miniature painting carried out with grandeur: the rider is confident, victorious, isolated in his importance on his grey charger and silhouetted against the deep sky. His steed treads the dusty ground, the undulating rather arid soil around Siena. The artist represents the two towns the condottiere had captured, the military encampments in delicate detail, pale and almost ghostly, the bristling spears and pennants appearing over the side of the hill, the towers and battlements of the walled castle with its flags flying. This is a kind of composite of the hill towns of Tuscany. The winding roads tempt one to enter into the streets and castles, to climb the slope of the hill to peer into the tents with their flaps invitingly open—a kind of backcloth, but a very enticing one.

GIOTTO'S FRESCOES

Giotto, who was more or less contemporary with these Sienese painters, was a Florentine and came under Roman influence rather than Byzantine. His style is almost Romanesque in the grandeur of his forms and their sculpturesque quality but, for me, he always reaches forward to the inquiring, boldly inventive, spirit of the Renaissance in his approach to painting. He abandoned Byzantine austerity and he cannot be said to have much in common with the International Gothic style nor to have been influenced by illuminated manuscripts. He has little in common with the Sienese in the matter of technique, but he does bring to his monumental art a new humanity akin to theirs, an inkling of which we have seen in Siena and also in the works of Cavallini. In fact he brought his characters down to earth. They are recognizable human beings, individuals who could be identified with the types walking about the streets of Florence or with the monks at Assisi. In the famous fresco of *St. Francis and the Birds* at Assisi the saint is a contemporary monk talking to the birds and there is nothing particularly saint-like about him except his halo. The monk behind him shows the human emotion of astonishment at the fact that the birds are listening. Even more remarkable, at that time, was the fact that Giotto placed his characters in a familiar world, but a world explained and broadened by his own observation and nature. He abandoned the use of the golden sky (technically known as a *fond d'or*) symbolizing heaven and focusing attention on a spiritual world. He is more interested in showing us how delicately the sky lightens as it touches the horizon of this world. He does not use the shapes of leaves and flowers as flat pattern and design, detailing every section diagramatically, but he notices that leaves group together and make larger forms, that the branches of the trees are lost behind them and then emerge again, and he accentuates the third dimension by light and shade instead of relying on outline for his effect. His drapery, though simplified reveals the solidity of the form beneath.

This is why Giotto seems to me to belong to the Renaissance, the great awakening which spread over Europe in the fourteenth and fifteenth centuries, since he really does express an intense interest in the world and in mankind—a world where men no longer fix their eyes upon the next life, but are deeply curious about their own. Such men were not necessarily less religious than their predecessors but they brought their religion down to earth. The Sienese and Cavallini had glimmerings of this attitude but they still clung, the one to the jewel-like decorative and remote rendering of the Byzantine, the other to the Roman world. Giotto was entirely liberated and absorbed in the world of thirteenth- and fourteenth-century Florence.

The Flight into Egypt. *Giotto* (1266–1337). *Scrovegni Chapel, Padua, Italy* (Plate 43). With extreme economy and detail Giotto forcefully and simply tells the story so that the humblest in any congregation could understand it. Mary holds the Child protectively as she is seated in a curiously noble pose on the realistic and rather lovable donkey. This is the focal group and is given pre-eminence over the other figures. Joseph leads the way and his cloak links him to the donkey and stresses the animal's forward plodding; above, an angel in a rhythmic flight protects the route and encourages them on. The figures move across a landscape that is merely indicated enough to show they are on a cross-country journey. Giotto has observed the rocky hills and the growth of the miniature trees, but he has not been concerned with distance or aerial perspective.

SCULPTURE AND THE PISANO FAMILY

Nicola Pisano (*c.* 1206–78), who was considerably earlier than Giotto, achieved for sculpture what Giotto achieved for painting. Renowned for his pulpits in Pisa and in Siena, he is also responsible for a wonderful relief over the west door of the cathedral at Lucca. The whole effect of the pulpit at Pisa is a marvel of construction. Pisano lifts the octagonal form of the pulpit on columns rising from the backs of lions; these alternate with columns on plain bases with decorative leafy capitals. The panels are separated by columns and statues.

Crucifixion. *Nicola Pisano. Panel of pulpit in the Baptistery, Pisa.* In this panel it is clear that Nicola Pisano is inspired by classical art. His figures are formally posed and noble and not very much involved with each other emotionally. Each individual seems to be suffering alone, but the figures are massed together architecturally in a most satisfying way: the tragic Figure on the Cross rises from the midst of them and yet is separate. The figures are part of the panel and contained within it in relatively low relief. The marble has not been forced beyond its function and no irrelevant detail is included. To me this is the most moving and restrained rendering of the crucifixion and far more satisfying than some of the later compositions which express a frenzied religious fervour. In the crucifixion panel of the pulpit at Pistoia, near Florence, Giovanni Pisano, Nicola's son, has produced a design which is basically the same, but the figure on the cross has no nobility and seems to be jostled by those around him. The effect is of a crowded restless scene where the forms are forcing their way free from the stone in deep relief.

Giovanni Pisano (*c.* 1240–1328) was at the time considered to be the greater artist. It is simply a matter of whether you find deeper satisfaction in the monumental simplicity and classical severity of Nicola's almost Romanesque work and with his rather touching sobriety, or whether you are more stimulated by the excited expressive movements of Giovanni's figures which are almost free from the background and clearly show the influence of Northern Gothic art in the freely flowing graceful drapery.

Nino Pisano (*d.* 1368) was the son of Giovanni and was responsible for much of the decoration on Orvieto cathedral, but the extremely gifted and likeable Andrea Pisano (1270–1348) is only assumed to be a member of the family and his early years are wrapped in mystery. We do know, however, that Andrea worked on the reliefs of Giotto's Tower in Florence and produced panels of great distinction. Giovanni goes perhaps too far in naturalism and at times overcrowds his panels, but Andrea cleared the background of detail and made far more dramatic effects.

THE BAPTISTERY DOORS IN FLORENCE

Twenty years after Duccio painted his *Maestà*, Andrea Pisano was entrusted with the design for one of the three Baptistery doors in Florence. He designed these exceedingly quickly, but there were difficulties about casting and the work was held up until he himself undertook to do it and completed them by 1336. He designed 28 panels, 20 of which deal with the Baptist's life and eight with the Virtues. Lions' heads are set at the corners of these panels. His genius lies in the manner in which he depicts dramatic scenes with the minimum of figures and, in most cases, without a background. He is not only determined to convey a scene with the simplest possible means, but he is fully aware of the limitations of his medium and does not attempt to force a relief to do what is best done in painting. He also stresses the graceful lines of the drapery with great skill. There is no superfluous detail in most of the panels, though in a few, where he has introduced landscape backgrounds, some of the dramatic force is lost. It is rare for perspective and deep recession to be convincingly or beautifully conveyed in bronze, but there is an exception to this in the eastern doors to the Baptistery by Lorenzo Ghiberti (1378–1455). Michelangelo described these doors as 'fit to serve as the Gates of Paradise'. The northern and eastern doors were commissioned from Ghiberti as the result of a competition held in 1402. Both Lorenzo Ghiberti and Filippo Brunelleschi (1377–1446) produced designs of great accomplishment but it was finally decided that Ghiberti's was the more suitable.

The two panels submitted for the competition have been preserved in the National Museum in Florence, and it is interesting to consider them in the light of fifteenth-century expert opinion. Competitors had to design a 'sample' panel illustrating the sacrifice of Isaac.

The Sacrifice of Isaac: (*a*) *Lorenzo Ghiberti:* (*b*) *Filippo Brunelleschi. Bargello, Florence* (Plates 44 and 45). Both competitors had the same means at their disposal, but obviously the judges appreciated Ghiberti's sober classical design combined with the grace and skill of Gothic rendering of form. Only a glance is needed to reveal the restless complexity of Brunelleschi's effort and the restrained dignity of Ghiberti's. Note the rather obvious handling of the dramatic moment in Brunelleschi's conception: Isaac's twisted head and awkwardly crouched body, Abraham's turbulent cloak entangled with the tree, the unfortunate shapes created by the ram's neck and Isaac's knee just touching. Notice also that two scenes are being enacted here and separated horizontally. The attendants with the donkey are not architecturally linked with the sacrifice. Turn the panel upside down; forget what the shapes represent and you will be confronted by a series of distracting curves and lines and masses without any unity. Do the same with Ghiberti's panel; you have a well-knit, satisfying design where lines, curves, and masses are co-ordinated but a little heavy at the top. This is obviously so that the weight gives stability when the panel is the right way up.

Now enjoy the grace, restraint, and unity of Ghiberti's relief. There is rhythm instead of turbulence in the draperies and movement of the figures. The dramatic moment is made more dramatic since the chief characters are not entangled. The figures with the donkey are knit into the design but of secondary importance in telling the story. The donkey is partly obscured by the standing figure whose drapery echoes Abraham's; he is looking into the design and so leads us towards Abraham and the superbly modelled body of Isaac.

When Ghiberti had completed the northern doors he was immediately commissioned to carry out those on the east of the Baptistery. These have a far greater popular appeal, largely because they are so extraordinarily skilfully handled, though many of the panels are crowded and their design is more fitted for a painting than for a panel. Nevertheless no one can deny their grace and their charm, and certain panels have succeeded, especially one showing the *Queen of Sheba and Solomon.* Here there is no confusion and no crowding, for the figures are grouped monumentally, and the sobering vertical lines of the architecture have a unifying effect. Yet it is not because some of the panels are successful works of art in themselves that the Baptistery doors are so famous as much as for the enchanting surrounding detail, especially now that they have been cleaned and partly gilded. The row of five panels on each door is enclosed in a framework of figures in niches, alternating with portrait heads divided by panels of foliage motifs, the whole surrounded by a framework revealing all the delicacy of the goldsmith's art in which Ghiberti, the son of a goldsmith, excelled. Leaves and flowers and small animals, wrought in minutest detail, show his sympathetic understanding of nature and the questing spirit of the

Renaissance, which made him study them and handle them so meticulously.

Yet, even though deeply impressed by the grace and brilliant accomplishment shown in these doors, there is a sense of relief and deep satisfaction in turning to Ghiberti's earlier effort with its absolute mastery of the problem of restrained design, its perfect balance and architectural dignity, softened by the detailed and continuously flowing decoration of the framework.

GOTHIC PAINTING

In other parts of Italy, the Gothic spirit lingered longer, particularly in the more easterly states. In Verona, Gentile da Fabriano was still painting in a courtly Gothic style a century after Giotto was leading the way to the Renaissance.

The Adoration of the Magi. *Gentile da Fabriano* (*c.* 1370–1427) *Uffizi, Florence* (Plate 46). Gentile was possibly partly inspired by French manuscripts or the *Books of Hours* in this gorgeous, lovingly delineated pageant; he may, too, have been remembering the processions in which he himself had taken part on many a feast day. Yet even though he has such a strong decorative sense and applies his touches of gold with such beautiful precision and obvious delight, this is more than a large-scale illumination and is far greater than a detailed description of a scene. The balance of texture against texture—silk, brocade, velvet, fur, rocks, and animals' pelts—the continuous but not crowded movement of the procession, the keen observation revealed in the natural poses of the animals and figures and the control over the theme of the picture, all show him to be a painter of genius. Note the arrival of the three meticulously painted, gorgeously dressed kings in different attitudes, culminating in the figure in red brocade kneeling before the Virgin and Child (these so simply portrayed in contrast to the yellow-clad Joseph behind), and the ox and the ass peering into the manger. The meandering procession so arranged as to fill the three arches of the frame is a skilful touch; and so is the treatment of the predella of the *Flight into Egypt*, where his delight in the observation of nature is obvious and links him with the inquiring minds of the Renaissance.

POSSIBLE ESSAYS, DISCUSSION AND RESEARCH

1 Do you look upon Jan Van Eyck's *Marriage of Giovanni Arnolfini and Giovanna Cenani* as a large-scale illuminated manuscript?

2 What are the characteristics of the International Gothic style?

3 What is so revolutionary about Giotto's style?

4 Do you prefer the simple nobility of Romanesque carving or the flowing grace of Gothic?

5 Do you agree with the decision of the judges to accept Lorenzo Ghiberti's panel and reject Brunelleschi's?

6 Plates *A–J* are unnamed and have not been discussed. Give your opinion of them.

Suggested Further Reading

Alazard, Jean: *L'Art Italien* (*Des Origines du XIVe Siècle*). Henri Laurens: Paris, 1949.

Cammaerts, Emile: *Flemish Painting*. Avalon Press: London, 1945.

Holmes, Charles: *The National Gallery* (*The Netherlands, Germany and Spain*). G. Bell & Sons: London, 1930.

Vasari, Giorgio: *Lives of the Painters*. Everyman: London, 1927.

Venturi, Arnolfo: *A Short History of Italian Art* (translated by Edward Hutton). Macmillan: London, 1926.

44. The Sacrifice of Isaac. Ghiberti. Baptistery doors, Florence.
Mansell Collection.

47. *Top.* **The Rout of San Romano. Paolo Uccello.**
Reproduced by courtesy of the Trustees, The National Gallery, London.

45. The Sacrifice of Isaac. Filippo Brunelleschi. Baptistery doors, Florence.
Mansell Collection.

43. *Top*. **The Flight into Egypt. Giotto. Padua.**
Mansell Collection.

46. Adoration of the Magi. Gentile da Fabriano.
Mansell Collection.

46a. Adoration (detail)
Italian Institute.

49. *Top*. **Adoration of the Lamb. Hubert and Jan Van Eyck. Ghent.**
Mansell Collection.

50. Ophelia. Sir John Millais.
The Tate Gallery, London.

48. The Vision of St. Eustace.
Antonio Pisanello.
Reproduced by courtesy of the Trustees, The National Gallery, London.

51a. *Top left.* **Madonna. Joanneum, Graz, Austria.**
Landesfremdenverkehrsamtes für Steiermark.

51b. *Top centre.* **Madonna. Amiens Cathedral.**
French National Tourist Office.

51c. *Top right.* **Madonna. Northern France.**
Courtauld Institute Galleries, London.

27. *Top left.* Equestrian statue of Marcus Aurelius, Rome.
Italian State Tourist Office.

53. *Above.* David (bronze). Donatello. Bargello Museum, Florence.
Italian Institute.

54. *Top right.* Colleoni. Verrocchio. Venice.
Italian Institute.

52. Pazzi Chapel, Florence.
Italian Institute.

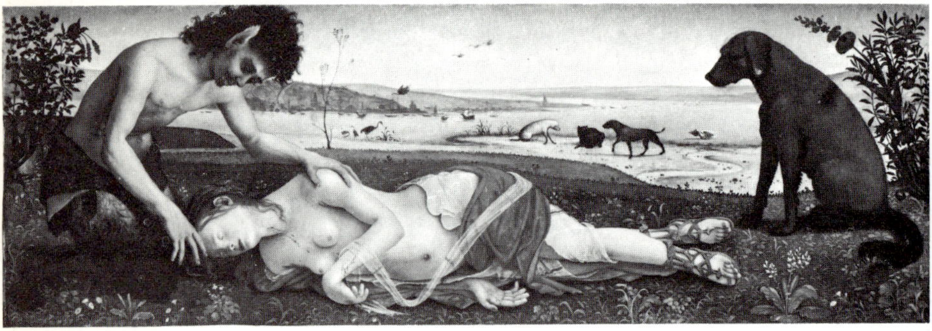

55. *Top left.* **The Flight into Egypt. Fra Angelico. Florence.**
Mansell Collection.

56. Death of Procris. Peiro di Cosimo.
Reproduced by courtesy of the Trustees, The National Gallery London.

57a. *Top right.* **The Resurrection of Christ. Piero della Francesca. Sansepolcro.**
Mansell Collection.

58. *Top left.* **The Nativity. Sandro Botticelli.**
Reproduced by courtesy of the Trustees, The National Gallery, London.

59. *Top right.* **The Adoration of the Shepherds. Rembrandt.**
Reproduced by courtesy of the Trustees, The National Gallery, London.

57. The Nativity. Piera della Francesca.
Reproduced by courtesy of the Trustees, The National Gallery, London.

60. Cartoon for Virgin and Child with St. Anne and St. John. Leonardo da Vinci
Reproduced by courtesy of the Trustees, The National Gallery, London.

61. Virgin and Child with St. Anne. The Louvre.
Archives Photographiques—Paris.

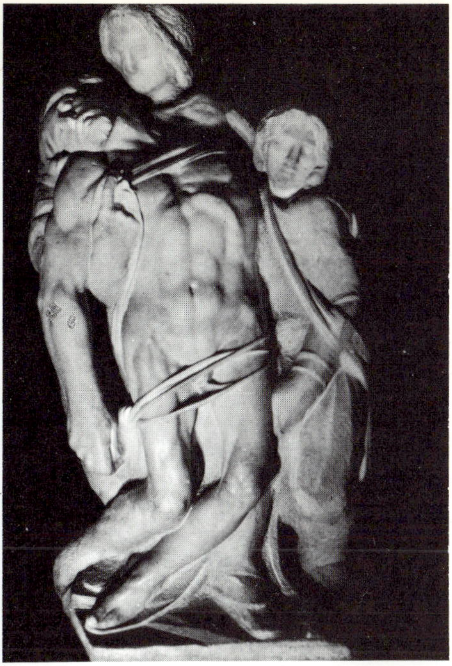

63. *Top left.* **Pietà. Michelangelo. Florence Cathedral.**
Italian Institute.

63a. *Top right.* **Pietà. Michelangelo. St. Peter's Rome.**
Italian Institute.

64. Madonna, Child, St. John and Angels. Michelangelo.
Reproduced by courtesy of the Trustees, The National Gallery, London.

62. Drawing. Michelangelo.
Reproduced by courtesy of the Trustees of the British Museum.

65. The Madonna of the Meadow. Raphael.
Kunsthistorischen Museum, Vienna.

65a. La Belle Jardinière. Raphael. The Louvre.
Archives Photographiques—Paris.

66. The Knight's Dream.
Raphael.
Reproduced by courtesy of the Trustees, The National Gallery, London.

66a. Cartoon for 66.
Reproduced by courtesy of the Trustees, The National Gallery, London.

67. The Agony in the Garden. Giovanni Bellini.
Reproduced by courtesy of the Trustees, The National Gallery, London.

68. The Agony in the Garden. Mantegna.
Reproduced by courtesy of the Trustees, The National Gallery, London.

69. The Agony in the Garden. El Greco.
Reproduced by courtesy of the Trustees, The National Gallery, London.

70. *Above left.* **Beato Serretti. Carlo Crivelli.**
Reproduced by courtesy of the Trustees, The National Gallery, London.

71. *Above right.* **The Tempest. Giorgione. Accademia, Venice.**
Mansell Collection.

72. Bacchus and Ariadne. Titian.
Reproduced by courtesy of the Trustees, The National Gallery, London.

73. St. George and the Dragon. Tintoretto.

Reproduced by courtesy of the Trustees, The National Gallery, London.

74. The Adoration of the Magi. Paolo Veronese.

Reproduced by courtesy of the Trustees, The National Gallery, London.

75. *Top.* **St. George. Albrecht Altdorfer.**
Pinakothek, Munich.

75a. Charon Crossing the Styx. Joachim Patinir.
Museo del Prado, Madrid.

76. The Four Horsemen of the Apocalypse. Albrecht Dürer. Vienna.
Mansell Collection.

77. Mountain Landscape. Dürer. The Louvre.
Mansell Collection.

Chapter Eight

THE EARLY YEARS OF THE RENAISSANCE

MASACCIO

With the death of Giotto there was a period of near stagnation in Florence as he had no worthy followers; but in 1401, the year art historians often take as marking the beginning of the Renaissance, Masaccio was born. His real name was Tommaso di Giovanni di Guidi, and it is thought that he came to Florence when he was young. We know nothing about his early childhood, nor do we know where he was born. His tragically short life ended in Rome when he was about 27 years old. Despite the shortness of his working life, Masaccio is one of the most important influences of the Renaissance and he contributed materially to the development of European art. Masaccio ignored or found distasteful the rather facile decorative style which was popular at that time and also, though he worked with Masolino, a much older man, he had little in common with him and seems to have modelled himself more closely on Giotto. But he did not, like his predecessor, have to free himself from the Byzantine yoke of cold formality and remoteness. This had already been achieved by Giotto.

Masaccio benefited by Giotto's discoveries and successes and he developed along the same lines, stressing Giotto's innovations and employing them more gracefully and with more confidence. By a much stronger chiaroscuro (the use of light and shade) he makes his figures absolutely solid and monumental and indeed almost sculptural in their third-dimensional power.

Expulsion from the Garden of Eden. *Masaccio* (1401–28). *Fresco in the Church of S. Maria del Carmine, Florence* (Plate 15). Astonishing dramatic force is achieved in this fresco, with the greatest economy of detail. The athletic young limbs of Adam and Eve, although they tread firmly, sag with despair as we gaze at them, the unbroken arabesque of their bodies expresses deep tragedy and desolation. No one could fail to be moved by the utter agonized despair of these human beings, cast into the unknown horrors outside the protection of the garden of Eden—itself suggested only by two simple verticals and an arch guarded by the angel with a sword, hastening them from their haven. Nothing else is needed to emphasize this event told with such complete mastery of form and composition and treated with such bold conviction.

This fresco of Adam and Eve is the first Italian painting to express the nobility of the naked human body. Magnificently simplified, though of no great elegance, Masaccio's figures are fundamentally noble: he painted the world he saw; he did not idealize it. He observed, studied, and understood form so well that he could simplify to give the effect of grandeur. Look again at Plate 15 and you will see that it has a kind of youthful lack of compromise, the confident conviction of a young painter. Masaccio gives it such tremendous force and direct communication. This is a perfectly realized composition which does not falter. He seems to have assimilated the growing contemporary knowledge of perspective, anatomy, and form and translated it into this nobility.

At the same time Masaccio's contemporaries were concentrating on technical problems. This was far from being laborious scientific research, nor was it allowed to detract from the artist's creative expression. First, these men were artists and they were deeply enthusiastic in their research because they considered it would enable them to express what they wanted more effectively. They had a burning enthusiasm for increased knowledge of the world around them which they found so exciting. Most of them interpreted religious themes in terms of this world, which they loved passionately, not in terms of the next world which the Gothic artists look at with such fervour.

UCCELLO

Though Uccello (1396–1475) worked late into the night over problems of perspective, his pictures, far from being dreary geometric excercises are a delight. True, his work has not the monumental force and nobility of Masaccio's, but it is certainly of a very high order and he manages to communicate to us some of the fascinations he felt in solving his problems and in incorporating his discoveries into his paintings with a certain naïveté.

The Rout of San Romano. *Paolo Uccello. National Gallery, London* (Plate 47). This is a painting to sit and gaze at for a long time. Looked at superficially, apart from its striking colour, it could be described as an essay in perspective. The man in armour is laid carefully on the ground leading straight into the picture so that Uccello could try out some of the rules of perspective he had established. The broken lance also demonstrates this new knowledge, and the little men in the distance, dashing about over the hills, seem to be cut out of felt, but they grow smaller in perspective.

To dismiss the painting as a rather naïve excuse for the display of new-found knowledge, is to miss its subtleties of colour, composition, and decorative design within a fine composition. It also has pictorial dramatic force, although the horses and riders are toy-like. Nothing of the rush of battle has been missed; the light and dark horses on the right clash fiercely and one can almost hear the clang of steel on steel. The horses are rocking-horses, but how powerful they are and how decorative. They are solid too, as the light catches the receding plane of the forelegs.

Everything in the picture is perfectly balanced, but with plenty of variety so that there is no monotonous repetition, The two light horses facing each other do not clash together because the right-hand one is engaged in combat with the dark horse and the thrust of the rider holds back the onslaught of his rival. Broken lances and pieces of armour are scattered on the ground in a kind of controlled confusion. They are exercises in perspective, but they also convey the tumult of battle. The large figures in the foreground in the splendid heraldic costumes and brilliant colours have their counterpart in the scurrying small figures against rather bare slopes, which are none the less very solidly conceived.

A beautifully painted decorative hedge of flowers and fruit against shiny dark green leaves divides the scene of battle, but they are subtly linked by the decisive lines of the lances on the left, the flutter of pennons against the deep sky and the decorative helmets and head-dresses which break into the barrenness of the hills. A delightful touch is given by the placing of the light hooves on small patches of dark grass which show them up admirably.

Try an experiment. Put your hand over the lances and you will find that the picture loses its cohesion. Then look at it as a design, forgetting the figures and animals, and see how marvellously conceived it is as a series of shapes.

It is worth while spending a whole half-hour seated in front of this picture and experiencing what Uccello has to say. Climb into the picture and follow the incredibly well-arranged forward rush of the combatants as the composition gathers force to culminate in a crescendo with the gorgeously attired figure on the central horse balanced by the serene boy in attendance who carries his helmet. See how the long, simple lines of the lances contrast with the detailed foliage and the less purposeful bustle in the background of the right-hand side of the picture. Climb out of the painting and admire it as a miracle of decoration of colour against colour and a rising intensity of colour skilfully interwoven to lead up to the focal points. Look at it through half-closed eyes, through your eyelashes, and take in the whole immense conception of a man, who though intensely concerned with perspective and its pictorial potentialities was, above all, a very great artist and was interested in expressing his ideas through paint.

PISANELLO (VERONA)

It is interesting to compare this picture by a Florentine with the *Vision of St. Eustace* by Pisanello. The latter has not the same dramatic force and architectural unity, but is nevertheless one of the most important pictures in the National Gallery.

The Vision of St. Eustace *Antonio Pisanello* (*c.* 1395–1455). *National Gallery, London* (Plate 48). Pisanello was a contemporary of

Uccello, but had a very different outlook. Like Gentile da Fabriano he was still working in the late Gothic style and his painting brings to mind the painstaking detail of the miniaturists; but he was absorbed in the quality of paint, and his outline, instead of being decisive like the miniaturists, softly merges with the background. Although not very much concerned with any scientific problems of perspective, he is obviously delighted with the world around him: the world of the illuminated manuscripts where flowers and birds and foliage and every detail of nature is of absorbing interest. But there is no interest in the anatomy of the human figure. St. Eustace is a gorgeously attired nobleman, and it is the richness of his dress, the sheen of brocade, the sparkle of gold and jewels, the softness of fur and the decorative flow of the garments, rather than any curiosity about the human frame beneath, which absorbs the artist. He is obviously not interested in the relative scale of the animals and birds, nor in aerial perspective, but this in no way detracts from his imaginative approach, nor from the fascination of the painting and its sympathetic portrayal of nature.

This is still 'Court Art' and has all the imaginative delight of the medieval world, enriched by the depth of colour and the handling of paint to make it a glowing panel with depths of shadow and light. Light plays over the animals' skin and fur to make them exist in space; yet, although the rabbit scurries out of the picture into the woods at the dog's approach and a bear crouches in a cave and birds flutter in the trees, there is a great stillness and calm. Even Eustace shows his surprise in the most gentle, controlled manner. The intricacies of the patterning and the preoccupation with the natural forms give this the aspect of a tapestry, for it is some time before the dramatic force of the story is conveyed to us. We are lost in admiration of the trappings of the horse and of the rider, the delicate painting of the groups of dogs, the grass spangled with flowers and the forest trees scarcely larger than the rabbit. Prominence is given to the stag with the crucifix on his head by raising him right above the diminutive woods, although his feet seem to be firmly planted in a thicket. Attention is distracted by the stag beyond him, with his back to us, the fawn in a group of trees and another stag facing the main animal and making a perfect foil for him. There is not a sound in this velvety painting, even the horse's hard hooves are silenced by the mossy grass he is standing on, and the whole conception is in direct contrast to the *Rout of San Romano* with its triumphant movement. This is not a monumental painting but a lyric of delight.

HUBERT AND JAN VAN EYCK

We find the International Gothic style in Pisanello combined with his own love of the richness of the medium of paint, but his is not a grand conception of painting such as the Florentines showed —a conception which was even evident in the Netherlands with

Hubert and Jan Van Eyck. We have already considered Jan Van Eyck's *Arnolfini*; his brother Hubert was initially responsible for the famous altarpiece of the *Adoration of the Lamb* although Jan completed it after his death. They conceived their painting on a huge scale and, although the treatment of detail is as refined and minute as that of a miniature, it is conceived massively and forms a complete architectural unity.

The Adoration of the Lamb. *Hubert and Jan Van Eyck. Central panel of Altarpiece, St. Bavon, Ghent* (Plate 49). The scenes from this vast conception can be read continuously and the colour is organized in masses. Each panel is a perfect composition and yet takes its place in the whole scheme of the altarpiece. In the main panel several processions stream across the landscape from different directions, and it is given perfect unity by an undulating green sward dappled with flowers and minute plants. Woods and groups of trees divide the separate concourses as they approach the Lamb, surrounded by adoring winged angels. A delicate varied skyline is provided by celestial towered and pinnacled cities on the slopes of gently rounded hills, partially obscured by woods; beyond again is an infinity of blue ranges of hills.

No other painter has ever been able to combine such a grandiose scheme embracing such a vast assembly of peoples, all depicted in minute detail and yet all subservient to the great dramatic force of the theme of adoration. The Van Eycks draw us into the landscape, show us the hard texture of rock, the down on the underside of a leaf in the meadow, the glint of light on an old man's beard and the glitter of golden ornament on the trappings of a horse. Even the fountain delicately sprays a thin stream of shining water which we can look upon without losing the impact of the picture as a whole. There are no banal, obvious comments; every statement is revealing and significant.

NINETEENTH-CENTURY RETURN TO 'BEFORE RAPHAEL'

Let us take a leap over the years, and look at another painting presented in great detail and presumably, in its own smaller scale, meant to produce an effect of drama or at least emotion.

Ophelia. *Sir John Millais* (1829–96). *Tate Gallery, London* (Plate 50). This painting could hardly be more detailed, nor more banal. It is as though Millais had set out to make an inventory of everything that grows in a hedge by a stream, without any selection: the dog roses, the foxgloves, the weeds; they are massed together in maddeningly minute detail and the willow, with all its tortured twigs and leaves, has to offer the final insult to the imagination by harbouring a very red-breasted robin on one of the branches. A pretty, wax-like Ophelia floats gently down the water, bestrewn with garishly bright flowers and duckweed caught up in the reeds.

Despite the cloying effects that this picture creates, no one can deny that Millais has skill of hand, but he copies nature and does not interpret it; he slavishly renders every detail without selection and without delight in its growth or form. In this picture he has not enriched our experience of nature in the slightest degree, rather does he make it commonplace. He certainly had a great enthusiasm for accuracy and he had the passion of the Renaissance artists for research, taking the utmost trouble to authenticate his backgrounds. But never was enthusiasm more misplaced, nor did real technical skill result in such a failure. Yet he made a contribution to English art. He revolted against the rather pompous, grand manner of the period, and with all his preoccupation with detail there is a certain freshness of outlook: an outlook which was sufficiently attractive to the more receptive painters of his time to inspire them to form the pre-Raphaelite Brotherhood.

SIXTEENTH-CENTURY FRENCH TAPESTRY

In Chapter 2 we examined the tapestry of *La Vie Seigneuriale*, an example of Court Art. Let us now look at another example, a tapestry woven in about A.D. 1500 on the banks of the Loire. The whole series of *La Dame à la Licorne* ('The Lady and the Unicorn'), displayed in a room built especially for the purpose in the Cluny Museum in Paris, is a revelation of subtle, aristocratic grace. It is possible that these hangings were commissioned by a nobleman for his betrothed, 'the most beautiful girl in the whole of France', chosen as 'the most precious jewel from a jewel case'. Designed and woven with infinite sympathy and imagination, they take us into a magical world of woods and flowers and animals. The white unicorn, symbol of chastity, is always on guard and in the enchanted circle of flowers, the beautiful, elegant 'beloved' stands, protected from evil. A deep rose background and a thousand flowers and birds and animals make this a delight. Of the six panels, five are allegories of the senses: sight, smell, hearing, touch, and taste. The sixth panel is entitled *à mon seul désir*, where *La Dame à la Licorne* stands before the entrance to the tent and chooses a jewel from a little casket—a subtle compliment from her lover, who chooses her from all the women of sixteenth-century France.

In *à mon seul désir*, the lady stands in graceful elegance at the entrance to her tent, in the enchantment circle of flowers. A small figure hands her the casket from which to choose the jewel; a little lap-dog, griffin-like, sits on a brocade cushion at her side. The lion holds back the tent flap and supports the unfurled standard, while the pale unicorn holds another on her left. Exquisite trees grow within the circle, and the background is a decorative delight of flowers and birds and beasts. No attempt is made at distant perspective since this is a hanging and unsuitable for such treatment: the birds fly in the air, the rabbits scurry through the undergrowth, yet all is arranged in a miraculous flow of design completely appropriate for the medium of tapestry (Fig. 26).

This lovely hanging never for a moment loses the quality of a woven tapestry. It falls vertically and the vertical lines are accentuated. It is designed to clothe and warm the cold stone walls, and it brings a world of fantasy into the castle. We are not drawn into

Fig. 26

depth, but we can delight in the creatures, in the flowers and the trees so ingeniously wrought into a perfectly satisfying design. This delicate 'Lady and the Unicorn' has something in common with the elegance and gentle calm of the many Madonnas carved in stone and wood during the Middle Ages.

THREE FOURTEENTH-CENTURY CARVED MADONNAS

Madonna (14th century). *Joanneum, Graz, Austria* (Plate 51*a*). This charming Madonna was originally in the monastery at Admont. White-robed, the figure sways slightly backwards as she takes the weight of the Child on her hip, supporting the Baby with her slender hand and inclining her head towards Him as He holds a bird to His shoulder. A long green robe, edged with gold, flows in folds from her shoulders, its straight lines emphasizing the curve of her body.

Madonna (14th century). *Amiens Cathedral, France* (Plate 51*b*). Carved in stone and adorning the cathedral portal, this figure is even more graceful in its subtle, scarcely perceptible swing, just sufficient to keep it balanced. There is a marvellous flow in the mantle continuous with the crown and shoulders and swinging round to loop over her arm and down again in a beautiful sinuous line which seems to envelop and contain the composition of the two figures.

Madonna (14*th century*). *Courtauld Institute*, *London* (Plate 51*c*). This statue from northern France combines Romanesque and Gothic characteristics. The figure sways only slightly and is massive and not elongated, but the drapery is elaborate and reveals the form beneath; curved lines contrast with long verticals falling gracefully to the feet. The Child is held rather stiffly, but He does caress his mother's neck. She has a rather remote smile but does not show the tenderness of so many of these Gothic Madonnas.

POSSIBLE ESSAYS, DISCUSSION AND RESEARCH

1 Does *The Expulsion of Adam and Eve* impress you more or less than Giotto's *Flight into Egypt*?

2 Do you think that Uccello's insistence on perspective detracts from the value of the *Rout of San Romano*?

3 Find three more medieval Madonnas and discuss them.

4 In what way does Pisanello's treatment of animals differ from that of Uccello and Giotto?

5 What, in your opinion, are the essentials of good tapestry designing?

6 Do you find any painting by members of the pre-Raphaelites stimulating?

Suggested Further Reading

Alazard, Jean: *L'Art Italien au XVe Siècle*. Henri Laurens: Paris, 1951.

Berenson, Bernhard: *Italian Painters of the Renaissance*. Collins, Fontana Library: London, 1930.

Burkhardt, Jacob: *The Civilizations of the Renaissance*. Allen & Unwin: London, 1944.

Howe, William Norton: *Animal Life in Italian Painting*. George Allen: London, 1912.

Martindale, Andrew: *Man and the Renaissance*. Paul Hamlyn: London, 1966.

Waters, W. G.: *Italian Sculptors*. Methuen: London, 1911.

Chapter Nine

THE RENAISSANCE IN FLORENCE

Young artists in Florence were apprenticed to goldsmiths and sculptors and they learnt to respect form above colour. Colour was secondary in importance to most of the Florentines.

PATRONS OF THE ARTS

Florence produced the greatest artists of the fifteenth century, and their services were sought by patrons in Rome, Milan, and even Venice. The great prosperity of the individual states of Italy stimulated art, and Florence was particularly fortunate in having Lorenzo de Medici as a discerning patron of the arts. Lorenzo encouraged every kind of artistic expression, with the result that Florence became the centre of art in Europe.

At the same time, there was a tremendous enthusiasm for learning, for discovery, for experimenting with techniques and, above all, a great curiosity about the world in general. Artists studied anatomy, perspective, effects of light and shade; they passionately desired to represent the world around them, to recreate mankind, to paint or carve the individual rather than an idealized type, though they looked for classic beauty in the human body. They were no longer wholly absorbed in religion, though the Church was still their chief patron. Their main job, which had been to illustrate the Bible for an illiterate congregation, was now to produce great altarpieces to enrich the church, and to carve and model the saints and the Holy Family.

ITALIAN GOTHIC ARCHITECTURE

Churches and palaces were still being built, but not in the old Gothic style, for architects were looking back to the sculptors and architects of Greece and Rome and were creating a new style which made use of the rules of proportion and the simple classic lines of temples. This was not just a revival, for this architecture was an entirely new interpretation. Since Italian Gothic never had the significance of English or French Gothic, and did not produce the inspiring upward surge of a cathedral nor its unity of purpose, I shall only touch on it in this book.

The Gothic cathedral of Milan certainly has pinnacles and spires, but it lacks a magical upward thrust. The beautiful little church of della Spina in Pisa has a rare quality and complete architectural unity, though it is very firmly planted on the ground and has nothing of the lacy elegance of the Sainte Chapelle in Paris.

RENAISSANCE ARCHITECTURE AND BRUNELLESCHI

It is in the superbly proportioned building of the Renaissance that we find the height of Italian achievement in architecture. It was as if the Romanesque style had been lightened and made elegant with the perfect proportions of Greek art. Round-arched arcades with slender pillars and Corinthian capitals flanked entrance portals, and these could be decorated with medallions or reliefs. The buildings were always dignified and always harmonious and the Florentine architects were just as inventive and just as anxious to solve problems of technique as the painters and sculptors.

Filippo Brunelleschi (1377–1446) was the great architect of the Renaissance. He turned to architecture when his panel for the bronze doors of the Baptistery was rejected. He overcame all the difficulties of placing a large dome on the octagonal base of Santa Maria della Fiore (the cathedral) in Florence, and has left us the lovely graceful pink brick structure with its slender white ribs rising up in splendour beside Giotto's Gothic tower and enclosing the vast spaciousness of the cathedral. He was also responsible for the original and lovely churches of Santo Spirito, and San Lorenzo where Michelangelo's splendid sculpture can be seen in the chapel.

Perhaps the most delightful of all Brunelleschi's achievements is the small Pazzi Chapel in the Basilica of Santa Croce in Florence. This chapel (Plate 52) is a building of absolute perfection, with its round-arched entrance portal flanked by slender columns supporting a simple decorated entablature on Corinthian columns. No single detail of this building could be removed without spoiling the whole completely co-ordinated design. Remove the dome, and the chapel becomes just a loggia; take away the arch between the columns, and the design is monotonously horizontal and vertical. Take away the panelling on either side of the arch, and this portion of the building would appear bare; the decoration on the frieze relieves the horizontal lines; the lunettes in the drum of the dome not only let in light, they emphasize the round of the arch and counteract the straight lines as well as accentuating the roundness of the drum. When I look at the Pazzi Chapel I feel convinced that this is the only possible way it could have been designed: that this is perfection —it is so perfect that perhaps it may lose a little in astringency.

SCULPTURE AND DONATELLO

Architects, sculptors, goldsmiths, painters were all caught up in the tremendous enthusiasm for perfection. Sculptors were often also painters, and a man such as Verrocchio might begin his career as a goldsmith, then become a painter and then a sculptor.

One of the foremost of Florentine sculptors was Donatello (*c.* 1386–1466), famous as the greatest Italian sculptor before Michelangelo, and responsible for many superb statues in Florence and elsewhere. Both his famous *St. George*, designed to stand in a niche, and the free-standing bronze *David* are in the National Museum in the Bargello, Florence. His tall, superbly posed figure of St. George compels attention by the very conviction with which it is carved and by its restrained dignity.

David. *Donatello. Bargello, Florence* (Plate 53). This bronze is perhaps more appealing than *St. George* in its miraculous subtlety of form. The boy's body is so superbly modelled that one can only marvel at the economy of means with which it is presented. Though standing firmly, it is full of rhythmic movement, the easy slant of the hip and the taut thigh taking the weight. Note the graceful slackness of the relaxed leg, the twist of pelvis and thorax, the slender upper arm and the lovely sweep forward of the forearm and the bend of the wrist. It is a creation in bronze of a superbly formed youth and its grace and touch of elegance hark back slightly to the Gothic.

The equestrian statue of *Gattamelata* is another wonderful bronze by Donatello, set up in the Piazza del Santo in Padua. A perfectly controlled figure of a warrior on a powerful horse, it is always interesting to compare this with the *Colleoni* Statue by Verrocchio in Venice, in some ways even more splendid, and to be dealt with later (Plate 54).

PAINTING

Of the painters, Fra Angelico (1387–1455) was not only fervently religious but a great technician who experimented with colours and produced lovely tones of olive green, dusky blue, petunia, saffron, and violet which he orchestrated subtly. He was also a superb draughtsman.

FRA ANGELICO

The Flight into Egypt. *Fra Angelico. Fresco. Convent of St. Mark, Florence* (Plate 55). Compare this fresco with Giotto's of the same subject and you will see at once that it is not so monumental and has not the same well-knit design, but it has a tenderness and grace and a delight in nature not evident in the earlier work. In Giotto's conception the solid figure of Joseph holds the donkey within the picture but Fra Angelico's rather unfortunately-placed tree emphasizes the fact that the Virgin is riding out of the painting. Fra Angelico's Madonna sits gracefully as she tenderly clasps the Child and a very humble Joseph, dressed in tones of yellow, trudges behind. The group is set in a fascinating decorative landscape with slender groups of trees adding to the sculptured hills. Delicately painted flowers flank the route.

PIERO DI COSIMO

If Fra Angelico is one of the most deeply religious painters of the Renaissance, Piero di Cosimo (*c.* 1462–1521) is one of the most magical for his wonderful inventive powers. He painted classical legends and made them take place in idyllic landscapes.

The Death of Procris. *Piero di Cosimo. National Gallery, London* (Plate 56). This painting is an utter delight, but just what it illustrates remains a mystery. Although the prone body of the dead women fills the breadth of the panel and the mourning faun and a huge dog fill the rest, there is a feeling of vast space and quietness in the decorative landscape. Cosimo obviously found great pleasure in painting a landscape where each delicate flower and plant is lovingly described and displayed to reveal all its structure almost diagrammatically and combining to make a kind of tapestry meadow for Procris to lie on. In the distance, strange animals and birds walk about on the shores of a lake where slender rushes grow and a single fragile tree is silhouetted against the water and the sky. The curve of the back of the sad and lovable dog is echoed in the exotic plant which grows behind him. There seems no end to Cosimo's imagination and re-creation of a strange legendary world.

PIERO DELLA FRANCESCA

Usually these early Italians present the scenes they paint arranged directly in front of the spectator. They follow a tradition of frontality and we do not look at the characters from the side or get a three-quarters view. The Madonna and Christ are nearly always depicted facing us, while lesser figures may be in profile, looking towards them, as necessitated for instance in the Annunciation. This frontality becomes almost an obsession with Piero della Francesca (*c.* 1410–92), whose figures are entirely statuesque, motionless, and serene, their feet very firmly on the ground and foreshortened as they point towards us. His characters stand in space, vast space with never a breath of a wind, where everything is hushed, waiting motionless. His paintings have the same architectural perfection as is found in Brunelleschi's Pazzi Chapel; nothing, not a leaf of the tree, not a cloud, not a fold of drapery, can be altered without upsetting the perfect balance of the painting. Any effect of lifelessness which this might give is compensated for by the exquisite harmony of colour and the delicate play of light with clear-cut shadows over the decorative backcloth landscape.

The Nativity. *Piero della Francesca. National Gallery, London* (Plate 57). One has only to look at the miraculous cadence of blues in this painting to recognize della Francesca as one of the greatest of colourists. The robes of the angels and of the Madonna shade from dusky violet to grey blue, sea blue, and soft ultramarine, and the background is a pattern of brown shrubs and trees on a creamy-white sandy ground. The group of angel musicians stands behind the infant Christ on a carpet of flowers and plants, and Mary spreads her mantle for the Child to lie on. To the right, a touch of clear scarlet in a robe accentuates the delicacy of the range of blue.

The Resurrection of Christ. *Piero della Francesca. Sansepolcro, near Arezzo, Italy* (Plate 57*a*). Christ steps out of the tomb which is painted to look like an altar. He is monumentally calm, utterly majestic but not entirely remote as in Byzantine painting, though His gaze is fixed on another world. Deeply relaxed soldiers sleep in the foreground and form a perfectly knit composition of solid figures, further bound together by the inter-relation of dusky greens, browns, and reds. Christ rises, His body pale, the drapery catching the pearly morning light; the landscape of trees and hills is unearthly in the sunrise. The sky is clear and chill, and on one side the trees pattern it with their branches; on the other, evergreens make a soft contrast. The impact of this painting is very powerful; as the great drama takes place, everything but the figure of Christ is only just about to stir into life.

BOTTICELLI

As Sandro Botticelli (1444–1510) was active throughout the period of the Renaissance, his work passed through a number of different phases. His early paintings are religious but, like most of the progressive painters of his time, he turned to illustrating mythological subjects of Greece and Rome. To these themes he brought a particularly delightful sense of rhythm and joyousness combined with a certain melancholy.

Caught with enthusiasm for the preaching of Savonarola, he turned from pagan to religious subjects, which he then depicted with an almost fanatical fervour and a rather pathetic sadness.

Botticelli developed the lyrical quality of outline to perfection. His figures are entirely enclosed within a rhythmic but constantly moving line suggesting movement even in repose. Within this outline scarcely perceptible modelling is indicated with exquisite sensitivity. Hands and feet are meticulously drawn; even the features of the faces are decisively outlined, and he shows a miraculous gift for facial expression without more than hinting at form. He manages to convey a kind of sweet melancholy which gives a lyrical beauty to his figures and to his landscape background. In the *Primavera* ('Spring'), in the Uffizi, Florence, his figures tread lightly on the flowers and grasses. The flowers here are in perspective, not diagrammatic as in works by earlier artists; the petals and leaves are foreshortened and the grass spreads flat beneath the dancing feet. Drapery not only reveals the form of the limbs, but continues the flow of line of the bodies; the fruit on the trees, although clinging to the branches, might have been blown across the panel by a breeze. Light breaks through the rather gloomy tree trunks and, in the centre, a dark patch of foliage is fringed with delightful patterning of leaves against the sky.

The Nativity. *Sandro Botticelli. National Gallery, London* (Plate 58). This is a complete contrast in mood from the *Primavera* and the *Birth of Venus*. It was painted at the end of Botticelli's life, after he had come under the influence of Savonarola's austere teaching and was again concentrating on religious themes. Even so, it has less of the melancholy of the mythological subjects and is infused with a certain gaiety and rejoicing, and a circle of angels dances rhythmically in the sky against a realm of gold. The Virgin and Child and Joseph are grouped together, watched over by the ox and ass. Through an opening in the rocky shelter with its incongruous thatched roof, slender trunks of trees let through a gleam of light. It is this group with the angels on either side which is so completely satisfying in its unity, its lovely muted colour and the natural attitudes of the figures and animals.

Personally, I find the three angels on the roof most distracting, and so are the dancers in the sky. They form too many horizontal lines across the top of the painting, drawing attention away from the focal point instead of towards it, and they overcome the picture. The exuberant turbulent effect of all these figures makes a kind of baroque frame surrounding a tranquil scene of the Nativity—baroque in that it has all the glow and energy and tendency to overstate of later painters and sculptors.

NATIVITY SCENES COMPARED

Since the Nativity and the Adoration of the Shepherds and Magi has always been one of the favourite themes of painters and sculptors, let us look at a completely different interpretation of this subject.

The Adoration of the Shepherds. *Rembrandt* (1606–69). *National Gallery, London* (Plate 59). Like Piero della Francesca's *Nativity* which we have already considered, Rembrandt's interpretation also produces a silence, but this is a hushed silence in the shadows of a spacious barn, an enclosed and almost cosy space, a far cry from Francesca's limitless expanse in a petrified but noble world. The Italian's *Nativity* is a scene which is arranged frontally before us; Rembrandt has placed his people in a group and we feel we are looking down on the scene from a crack in the rafters. We are not really invited inside this picture; we are spectators of a completely conceived scene, given dramatic force by the light emanating from the Virgin and Child, yet there is nothing in the least cloying about this light, even though the scene is a homely one. The awe and wonder expressed even by the poses of the onlookers give it dynamic power. This small painting is so perfectly composed to illustrate the event and give architectural unity that it has as much impact as a much larger picture. There is also an impression of deep glowing colour, warm flesh, and gleaming light, but if you examine the painting closely, you will find that very few colours have been used. Notice the wonderfully rendered child with the dog, both creeping forward, hardly daring to breathe in case they might break the spell.

With these two pictures, we have two masters depicting the same scene in entirely different ways, but each has a tremendous impact.

GREAT MASTERS OF THE RENAISSANCE

I have mentioned only a few of the Italian Renaissance masters, but others will be discussed in comparisons later on, and it now remains to make some assessment of the three undisputed giants of the High Renaissance: Leonardo da Vinci (1452–1519), Michelangelo (1475–1564) and Raphael (1483–1520). All three were men of outstanding genius with a breadth of vision and an astonishing mastery of technique in several fields. Leonardo was centuries ahead of the thought of his day; he was engineer, inventor, writer, anatomist, scientist, architect, musician, sculptor and, as a kind of afterthought, he himself said that he could 'paint as well as any man'. Michelangelo was architect, sculptor, and poet and did not consider painting to be his real profession even though important commissions such as the Sistine Chapel prove otherwise. Raphael, besides being popular and handsome, was both architect and painter and had the other normal accomplishments of the times, of making verse and music.

So much has been written about these three men and they have been so heavily romanticized by popular novelists that there is no lack of general information about their personal lives and even their emotional lives. Of all such accounts the most enlightening are by Giorgio Vasari (1511–74), a painter and architect working in Rome and Florence but famous as the author of *The Lives of the Italian Architects, Painters and Sculptors*, first published in 1550. Though it has inaccuracies, this book does reflect the atmosphere of Renaissance Italy and the reaction of the sixteenth century to the works of Italian artists. Vasari says of Leonardo:

> 'This marvellous and divine Leonardo . . . would have made great profit in learning, had he not been so capricious and so fickle, for he began to learn many things and then gave them up. . . . He devoted some time to music and soon learned to play the lyre, and being filled with lofty and delicate spirit, he could sing and improvise divinely with it . . . he made designs for mill filling machines and other engines to go by water and, as painting was to be his profession, he studied drawing from life. . . .
>
> His charming conversation won all hearts . . .'

Of his contemporary, Michelangelo Buonarroti, for whom he had almost an obsession, Vasari wrote:

> 'The great Ruler of Heaven . . . resolved . . . to send to earth a genius universal in each art, to show, single handed, the perfection of line and shadow, and who should give relief to his paintings, show a sound judgement in sculpture, and in architecture should render habitations convenient, safe, healthy, pleasant, well-proportioned, and enriched with various ornaments'.

of Raphael he wrote:

> 'Raphael Sanzio of Urbino . . . was as excellent as gracious, and endowed with a natural modesty and goodness. . . . Thus Nature created Michelangelo Buonarroti to excel and conquer in art, but Raphael to excel in art and in manners also.'

Vasari may have let his enthusiasm run away with him in his writings and some of his statements were based on very flimsy evidence, but he does convey the tremendous respect in which artists were held and the way in which their new works were acclaimed at the time.

Of the three, it is Leonardo who appeals to us most by his imagination and inventiveness, Michelangelo by his tremendous power, and Raphael by his charm (though Raphael is a taste which often comes rather late in life). All three mark the height of the Renaissance in Florence, and after their time a decline set in although Venice was still producing great men.

If we examine works by each of the three, we can see not only how widely they differ in their personal approach to a subject but also to what degree they are all of the same period of civilization.

Leonardo and Michelangelo were both Tuscans, but Michelangelo worked a great deal in Rome and Leonardo in Milan. Raphael was from the gentle countryside of Umbria in central Italy, and this shows in his landscape backgrounds and in the gentle faces of his Madonnas and saints. Leonardo was the personification of Renaissance Florence in the astonishing range of his knowledge and in his unending curiosity about the world around him, a curiosity which led him to diffuse his genius and express it in a hundred different ways. Though extremely versatile, Michelangelo was single-minded in the conviction with which he carried through a project; he was the highlight of Florentine art because his genius lay in his miraculous grasp of form, in his unrivalled draughtsmanship and in his ability to perform incredible feats of endurance without losing his original inspiration.

LEONARDO DA VINCI

Cartoon for the Virgin and Child with St. Anne and St. John the Baptist. *Leonardo da Vinci. National Gallery, London* (Plate 60). This exquisite drawing, full of freshness and charm, was not strictly adhered to in the finished painting which hangs in the Louvre (Plate 61); the composition of the painting is much more compact and follows the widely used convention of arranging figures to form a pyramid, giving stability by the weight at the base and the lightness by the tapering to the apex. In the cartoon, the two women's heads are level, and the Child leans out of the composition but is skilfully linked to it by St. John, though the upward pointing hand of St. Anne rather breaks the unity. In the painting, Leonardo changed the position of the heads and made the group more compact by keeping more closely to the basic triangle. In the background are the mysterious rock formations in which Leonardo was so much interested. The figures no longer have the definite outline which Botticelli favoured: the contours are softened and often merge into the background with a stressed chiaroscuro that had not been used in this way in Florence since Masaccio.

Leonardo's forms are gently modelled in light and shade, so subtly that the figures seem to be enveloped in atmosphere. The characters are no longer superimposed against a background: they have become part of it. Leonardo could produce this effect whatever his medium: chalk, pencil, ink or paint. Notice the delicately graded modelling of the Virgin's head and shoulders; her truly beautiful features, lighted by a gentle radiance. Look down on the children, and the exquisite drawing of the heads is echoed in the folds of drapery which reveal the form beneath. There is almost as much individual character in the modelling of the robes as in the heads. The swing of the material falling from St. Anne's left knee to her right foot flows with the line of her hand and every fold is searched out and convincingly rendered, yet subservient to the design as a whole. Nothing is overstated, yet one feels that no one could have discovered more about the effect of light and shade on material nor just how it could reveal or hide a form beneath it.

No one before the time of Leonardo had been able to express so much in a drawing or to convey so much subtlety of form in so limited a medium as line, chalk, and wash. Some may think that this drawing is too perfect to warrant analysis, yet Leonardo himself took the deepest scientific interest in everything he painted or drew, and searched out forms with great precision.

There is something wonderfully alive and free about the cartoon —a conception freshly recorded though not completely realized— whereas the finished painting in the Louvre loses the spontaneity and some of the appeal of the cartoon, though it gains in its perfection as a finished composition and an accomplished work of art.

MICHELANGELO

Michelangelo's drawings are the vigorous work of a sculptor in which the exploration of form and the body in action is of paramount importance. Every line is essential and explains a shape or a movement or a strain (Plate 62). The figures are alive, and glorying in their vitality, for Michelangelo's passion was to re-create the human body in marble: his painting was a secondary interest. It was form that he could shape with his hands, form that he could describe with his pencil, form that could be realized in architecture and then, too, in the human forms on the ceiling and walls of the Sistine Chapel in Rome—a commission which he accepted unwillingly at first as he considered himself 'no painter'.

Everyone is familiar with the superb figure of David in the Accademia in Florence and its replicas in the city a *tour de force* of complete perfection; but much more moving is the *Pietà* now in Florence Cathedral.

Pietà. *Michelangelo. (a) Florence Cathedral. (b) St. Peter's, Rome* (Plate 63). This sculpture expresses unbearable intensity of sadness, yet reveals tremendous power in its execution. Three figures occupy little more than the space of one, but they are so perfectly disposed as not to look crowded or confined. The depth of suffering expressed in the faces, the loving care with which the body is gently lowered, the emaciated and very dead body of Christ, and the superb modelling of the loosely hanging arm and the crumpled legs make this one of Michelangelo's most human achievements.

Compare this with the Pietà in St. Peter's, of an earlier date, when Michelangelo was still rendering the classical ideal of beauty in the human figure. Here the Mother is sorrowing over her dead Son, quietly and alone: in the later carvings Michelangelo expresses far deeper emotion and twists the figures in torment. Let me remind you here, too, of his genius for showing life just beginning as well as life just over; his *Creation of Adam* in the Sistine Chapel in Rome, or even the drawing for it, shows Adam the second before he comes to life at the touch of the finger of God.

Madonna, Child, St. John and Angels. *Michelangelo. National Gallery, London* (Plate 64). This painting is only 'ascribed' to Michelangelo since the rather clumsy modelling of the feet leads some experts to think it is not entirely his. It has the sculptural and monumental qualities of a Michelangelo: the compact composition in which seven figures are tightly grouped together without crowding, filling the whole space, and with only the merest indication of a landscape background in which this artist was not interested.

RAPHAEL

Many people find it difficult to enjoy Raphael's paintings fully, mainly because of the rather cloying sweetness of expression on the faces of his women, whose eyes turn heavenwards and who have an over-sweet smile. Yet Leonardo could do this without being irritating: the Mona Lisa's smile is only hackneyed by constant cheap reproductions and by overpraise and romanticism in literature. My advice is to accept Raphael as one of the greatest painters, as everyone accepts Milton or Shakespeare as great poets, and then ease your way along to understanding him, when you will gradually come to appreciate him.

In some instances we have to accept the judgment of time and experience. Raphael was an Umbrian, a man of great charm and good looks, admired by everyone both for himself and for his paintings, some of which were carried in triumphant procession to their resting place. He studied and assimilated the styles of the greatest painters of his time and added his own special interpretation and genius. Perhaps it is best to approach him first through his Madonnas, for their very charm and sweetness is the stumbling-block. He painted a number of Madonnas, exploring the possibilities of triangular composition and setting them in the magical soft countryside of Umbria, bathed in a shimmering light with feathery trees just trembling in the air.

The Madonna of the Meadow. *Alte Pinakothek, Munich* (Plate 65). **La Belle Jardinière.** *Louvre, Paris* (Plate 65*a*). **The Madonna of the Bullfinch.** *Uffizi, Florence.* Each is a perfection of composition of warm, glowing colour; a complete statement radiating charm in the best meaning of the word. If you relax and let yourself into these paintings, you will gradually feel the warmth, the humanity and the wonder which Raphael felt as he set his gracious group in the idyllic countryside that he loved, and you will come to love, too, the gentle turn of a wrist, the soft contour of a cheek, the astringent perfection of the composition and the softly undulating landscape.

The Knight's Dream. *Raphael. National Gallery, London* (Plate 66). Look now at this picture painted when Raphael was only 17, with the cartoon which hangs beside it. See the assurance with which the cartoon is carried out, pricked ready for transfer. (Detailed drawings or even preliminary paintings were made before the final work: the design was then pricked and laid on the new surface; coloured chalk rubbed over the cartoon came out as a tracing.) Note amidst the melodious background of the painting, the soft colours and extreme gentleness. What a master of design Raphael is, even at this early age and before he had come to Florence to study the powerful draughtsmanship and construction of Leonardo and Michelangelo. Then look at the brilliant designing of his frescoes, his great compositions in the Vatican. Raphael was not just a charming and suave painter of Madonnas, nor merely of pleasing countryside, he was a splendid designer and had grand conceptions on a monumental scale. To appreciate them to the full, you must go to the Vatican.

POSSIBLE ESSAYS, DISCUSSION AND RESEARCH

1 Take one painting, other than described here, (*a*) by a Venetian and (*b*) by a Florentine and discuss them.

2 How does Fra Angelico's *Flight into Egypt* compare with Giotto's?

3 Do you prefer the religious or mythological paintings of the Florentines?

4 Do you think that subject-matter is important in a work of art?

5 Try to forget all you have read or heard about Leonardo's *Mona Lisa* and give your own appreciation of it.

6 What strikes you most about (*a*) Michelangelo's *David* and (*b*) Donatello's?

7 Do you consider Renaissance architecture an advance on Romanesque and Gothic?

Suggested Further Reading

Berenson, Bernhard: *Italian Pictures of the Renaissance: The Florentine School*. Phaidon: London, 1963.

Bode, Wilhelm: *Florentine Sculptors of the Renaissance*. Methuen: London, 1928.

Borenius. Tancred: *Italian Painting* (Vol. I). Avalon: London, 1946.

Brion, Marcel: *Lumière de la Renaissance*. Robert Laffont: Paris, 1946.

Clarke, Kenneth: *Leonardo da Vinci*. Cambridge University Press, 1939.

Cox, Trenchard: *The Renaissance in Europe*. Methuen, London, 1933.

Henessy, J. Pope: *Italian Renaissance Sculptors*. Phaidon: London, 1958.

Murray, P.: *The Architecture of the Italian Renaissance*. Batsford: London, 1963.

Chapter Ten

VENETIAN PAINTING

VENETIAN LOVE OF COLOUR

The early Venetian painters differ from the Florentines mainly in that they worshipped colour. In Venice and the near-by town of Ravenna, mosaics adorned the churches in all their richness. We have already discussed those in Ravenna, and those in Venice were mainly executed between the eleventh and thirteenth centuries. Gold was used as a background to paintings long after Florentine artists were using a realistic sky, and Biblical figures tended to be dressed in the most gorgeous robes (it was still a Courtly Art); we have seen in Pisanello's *Vision of St. Eustace* (Plate 48) how much importance was still given to princely garments, golden trappings, and the noble way of life, Venice had all this gold and richness emphasized by her contact with the East, by the fact that the island was crowded with merchants and that every day her citizens could see silks and brocades and Eastern finery. They loved the glittering mosaics in the Basilica of San Marco; they loved colour just as passionately as the Florentines loved form and, indeed, when they wanted to erect a statue to Colleoni, it was the Florentine Verrocchio who got the commission since Venetians scarcely practised the art of sculpture. While the Florentines favoured frescoes and painting in tempera, the Venetians liked glowing panel paintings, even before the oil technique came to Venice in the fifteenth century. They loved display, and processions were part of the pageantry of their lives. The Florentines also loved processions and feast days, and they, too, portrayed contemporary notabilities in their crowd scenes, even in the Adoration of the Magi, but they found delight in the pattern of beautiful clothes and draperies, superbly executed in detail and form, with almost transparent colour as an added embellishment.

The Venetians too made the Bible stories an excuse for the most splendid processions, and they used the sheen of oil paint to bring out the glow and texture of rich clothes.

THE BELLINI FAMILY

As we have seen, Gentile da Fabriano was one of the most delightful exponents of the International Gothic style. He is believed to have been the master of Jacopo Bellini (*c.* 1400–70), the first of a remarkable family of painters. There are very few of Jacopo's paintings left, but two of his sketch-books have been preserved: one in the British Museum and one in the Louvre. In them we find his ideas for compositions which he handed down to his sons, Gentile (1429–1507) and Giovanni (*c.* 1430–1516). One depicts in a few lines all the tragedy and dramatic intensity of the Crucifixion; the crosses are empty against the sky and a ladder lies stretched across the ground. The utter simplicity of this design and the economy of means employed, combined with a sensitive line, make it extraordinarily moving.

Both of Jacopo's sons were distinguished painters, but Giovanni is of greater interest to us as he produced more than his brother, and he was more closely associated with Giorgione.

The Agony in the Garden. *Giovanni Bellini. National Gallery, London* (Plate 67). We can compare this with Plate 68 showing the same subject by Andrea Mantegna (*c.* 1431–1506), who had married Giovanni's sister and was steeped in the Bellini tradition. Giovanni's composition is simpler and less crowded, but Mantegna's has a wealth of detail combined with a power expressed in the very strongly three-dimensional and sculptured figures which is not apparent in Giovanni's.

MANTEGNA (PADUA)

Mantegna was not a Venetian; he was the foremost painter of the neighbouring school of Padua and had been trained in a studio which specialized in painting from the antique. His great knowledge of archaeology is evident in much of his work. Giovanni's sleeping disciples are not so well grouped together as those in Mantegna's picture, but they are naturally and deeply asleep. The rather sturdy figure of Christ is flooded with a theatrical light which also picks out the disciples in relief. This is not from the light of the setting sun, but comes from a different direction and some third source of light illumines the castle on the hill and the soldiers in the middle distance. The masses of light and shade, the pale pathways and foreground draw the composition together, and the isolated kneeling figure of Christ accentuates His loneliness at this moment. With what miraculous skill Giovanni has painted the feet of Christ—soles towards us and toes just touching the ground—to cast a clearly defined shadow over the rock. The keenly observed sunset sky, with the clouds edged with light, poignantly silhouettes Christ's head.

Mantegna's composition is more closely-knit but it is, to me, less moving since more stress is laid on the configuration of the peculiar rocky landscape and its decorative quality than upon the 'agony'; the superbly drawn figure of Christ merges with the background detail although it is depicted as dark against light, and the beautifully rendered sleeping disciples draw our attention away from the central figure by virtue of the sensitive harmony of colour and the grouping together in profound sleep. Skilful handling of the curves of the roadway draw us right into the landscape, and make us want to explore the countryside, the walled town with its towers, and the decorative rock formation beyond. The minute details of rabbits, birds, and even pebbles and tiny plants lend charm to this picture which combines keenly observed natural forms with a powerful step-by-step building up of a picture to form an architectural unit. A little crowded, we have to admit, and there is too much to take in, so that the drama of the moment is lost, but who would want to remove that wonderful menacing bird on the delicately drawn tree, or the furry rabbits trying to pass on the rocky ledge?

EL GRECO COMPARED WITH THE VENETIANS

One hundred years later, El Greco, who lived in Spain, produced his version of the story.

The Agony in the Garden. *El Greco* (1541–1614). *National Gallery, London.* (Plate 69). Considering that this Greek who was born in Crete (at that time a Venetian colony) had studied in Venice under Titian, one might imagine that he would have a good deal in common with Mantegna and Bellini. But El Greco does not fit into any century or any school; he is completely individual and a mystic. He was reared in the Byzantine tradition and he obviously felt something of Byzantine majesty, splendour, and mysticism. Although he belongs in date to the early baroque period, he also had all the fervour of the Gothic architects whose spires soared into the sky. El Greco's brilliant patches of light rise up like tongues of fire as they caress the mountains; the angels' wings point upwards and Christ's robe catches the light so that these folds, too, lift upwards in a blaze of light. The picture is disquietening, mystical, and stimulating; in the strange barren landscape, flowers come to life under the radiance of a shaft of light from the clouds which illuminates Christ's face. The sky, the rocks, the angel, and Christ are linked together in an experience which is going on in a different mystical world from that of the cave in which the diminutive disciples sleep.

CRIVELLI

Carlo Crivelli was also painting in Venice in the fifteenth century and, like Mantegna and Giovanni Bellini, he shows intense interest in nature and in the minute detail of birds and small animals. He was definitely a Venetian painter, but he left the city when he was about 28 years old to live in the Marches. Much of his work has a Paduan flavour reflected in his attention to architectural detail, to marble and stone used in the background and to the festoons of fruit and flowers, all of which were favoured by the Paduan school reared in the study of the antique. Crivelli's type of the infant Christ is of a strange little old man with almost gnarled limbs and wrinkled face; the hair is painted as though it were carved out of stone, and landscape backgrounds are painted with infinite care for detail and design.

Beato Serretti. *Carlo Crivelli* (*active* 1468–93). *National Gallery, London* (Plate 70). This composition shows a kneeling monk to whom a vision of the Madonna appears in the sky in the form of a rather heavily carved medallion. From the sky, too, hang swags of fruit in sharp relief. The saint, with his wrinkled face, the sharp, hard folds of his gown, kneels in adoration, his hands painted with the utmost delicacy as fingers and palms hardly touch. The rather harsh treatment of the robe is in strong contrast to the gentle, though precise handling of the background. Naïvely the painter cuts down the tops of the foremost trees on the right, so that they do not obscure the road which leads through more trees to a small town, or perhaps a large walled monastery. One fragile bare tree cuts across the horizon and a superbly placed flight of swallows soars upwards, breaking the monotony of the vertical clouds. Fissures in the meticulously recorded structure of the rocks behind the saint allow all manner of plants and creepers to take growth, and one tree, with branches which make a living pattern against the sky, has the spiral of a creeper entwining the very straight trunk until it festoons its foliage over the branches. Following its lines we see the beautifully observed goldfinch, with his back to us, looking into the distance, foreshortened, and the bright colour of the head just showing over his back. Notice how entirely different is the effect of this bird, treated with such restraint, from the robin in Millais' painting of *Ophelia* (Plate 50). In the left-hand foreground is a pond hewn out of the hard rocky ground: the transparency of the water is just disturbed by two ducks very gently swimming.

One may well ask why this painting should be so infinitely superior to Millais' *Ophelia*. It is infinitely moving and stimulating: the detail is almost a re-creation of natural forms recorded with intense interest and enjoyment and drawing us into a landscape of endless discovery. Subservient to the main drama of the saint and his vision, it is essential to the composition as a whole and every line adds to to unity of the design.

The pictures by the pre-Raphaelites were an attempt to get back to the outlook of the early Italian painters but, being of the nineteenth century, they do not show the same wonder of excitement: they merely make details look commonplace and show us little that we did not already know. Carlo Crivelli, although he does not rank with the great epic Venetians like Titian and Tintoretto, certainly produces works of art which add much to the sum total of man's achievement.

VENETIAN PAGEANTRY AND CARPACCIO

Apart from those who turned religious themes into pageants, there were a number of Venetians who recorded pageantry. Gentile

Bellini, mentioned earlier, was the elder brother of Giovanni and was held to be the foremost Venetian painter during the last part of the fifteenth century. He was commissioned to paint great events abroad as well as being much in demand as a portrait painter, depicting character with almost brutal frankness. His works were nevertheless rather formal and stiff without the magical detail of painters like Fabriano or Crivelli, but he did just hint at the softer, subtler handling practised by Giovanni Bellini and Giorgione. There is certainly much to delight us in Gentile's paintings, above all in the play of light on the clearly defined planes of the building, in his exploitation of perspective, in his recordings of the events of the fifteenth century in settings which can largely be recognized today, and in the recording of the features of people of great importance and interest.

If Gentile Bellini gives us the rigid formality of great events, his younger contemporary, Vittore Carpaccio (active 1490–1520) painted the everyday life of Venice, the pageant of the street scene in a homely, but delightfully decorative and often amusing way. After wandering round the section devoted to his paintings in the Accademia in Venice, you will walk back into the city with a new vision and a sharpened interest, for although Carpaccio does not reach Gentile Bellini's heights of monumental composition, nor has he his genius for giving atmospheric conditions, his painting is always lively, always spontaneous and colourful, showing great decorative qualities.

Giovanni Bellini carried Gentile's efforts at atmospheric envelopment much further and this was made easier by the fact that Antonello da Messina had brought to Venice the highly accomplished technique of oil painting of the Van Eycks. It is probable that he learnt this from Van Eyck's pupil, Petrus Christus, who was working in Milan. This technique found great favour with the Venetians for its richness and warmth and for its inherent 'painterly' quality unlike the dryer, stiffer tempera. It had its own beauty *as paint* which could be revealed in its handling. A certain 'sketchiness' and atmospheric effect could be created, and the voluptuous quality of its warmth and richness influenced the lines along which Venetian painting developed in the sixteenth century.

Although Gentile Bellini had many pupils, they were not of the first rank as painters. The most promising students studied with Giovanni, whose influence upon the great painters of his time cannot be overstressed. He was the master of Giorgione (1477–1510) and possibly of Titian (1418–1576).

GREAT VENETIANS

GIORGIONE

Had it not been for Giorgione's early death from the plague, he might well have been in Titian's position of pre-eminence. He was the earliest Venetian painter to give landscape not only atmosphere and aerial perspective, but to treat it three-dimensionally, to envelope his characters within it, instead of leaving it more or less as a backcloth.

The Tempest. *Giorgione* (*c.* 1477–1510). *Accademia, Venice* (Plate 71). You have only to compare *The Tempest* with the background in Giovanni Bellini's *Agony in the Garden* (Plate 67) to realize that great changes had come about in the treatment of landscape. We have already seen indications of it in Gentile and Giovanni Bellini and, in Umbria, Piero della Francesca showed a feeling for space. Leonardo da Vinci was already enveloping his figures in atmosphere, but even so, the landscape was definitely of secondary importance to the main theme, and was a kind of stage for it. Now with Giorgione we do not even know what the theme is, for the relationship of the 'gypsy' and the mother and child is not explained, and the very title 'The Tempest' shows that the landscape is the main entity in the picture.

It is an almost impressionistic painting, with the foliage treated as a mass, the outlines of house or buildings sometimes lost in a soft glow of light, a curious stillness in the foreground, though the trees in the middle distance are just ruffling as the wind catches them and the menacing storm in the background draws nearer. You can walk into this background as you can into the *Château de Steen* by Rubens (Plate 6) and you can feel the atmosphere all round you.

TITIAN

This kind of landscape was developed by Titian and formed an integral part of his composition. In his early works he appears to be strongly under the influence of Giorgione. It was inevitable that he should take on Giorgione's work at his death, and he was soon to become the foremost painter of the Venetian school, if not of all Italian schools. Whereas Giorgione was at times even a little indecisive, and his *Tempest* lacks a firm architectural unity, Titian has a sure grasp of structure in everything he paints, and a strongly-marked dramatic sense makes his pictures epics in contrast to Giorgione's lyrics. Titian had tremendous power over his technique, a certainty of touch and an intensity of feeling which makes other pictures look tentative beside his tremendous *tours de force*. This power increased over the long years of his life, so that his final achievements are staggering.

Bacchus and Ariadne. *Titian. National Gallery, London* (Plate 72). If we look at this comparatively early work we can see that, unlike Giorgione's *Tempest*, there is no nostalgia, but a tremendous burst of joy combined with poetic imagination. This whole glorious composition is one of surging rush of celebration: not a restless writhing of bodies, but a forward surge, held pictorially in check by a dozen subtle means. Bacchus leaps forward, but his shining cloak flows into the picture, and Ariadne stands upright as a barrier to his rushing headlong out of the frame; the docile, lovable leopards wait quietly arrested in their movement. The sheer weight of the grouped revelling figures on the right and the noble trees gives added stability to the composition; a delightful touch is added by the little faun with the delicate shining flowers in his hair. The landscape bathed in changing light sweeps back beyond the horizon and Theseus' ship can be seen disappearing into the distance as, high above, in the darkening sky appears the crown of stars for Ariadne. Here Titian not only gives us the unbounded joy of revelry, but the impact of his genius in one of the world's greatest masterpieces. Note particularly the richness of texture and colour, the softness of the velvet skins of the leopards, the columbines and irises thrusting through the ground, the whole luminous countryside. You can almost hear the crashing of cymbals and the bark of the dog. Titian was to stress light more and more in his later pictures until everything in them was held together by the same pulsing glowing light. We are apt to hand all the laurels to the Impressionists for representing light, but Titian and, later, Turner—to mention only two—were certainly absorbed in the study of its effects on their subjects.

If the four outstanding painters of Tuscany and Umbria are Botticelli, Leonardo, Michelangelo, and Raphael, the four greatest figures in Venetian art are Giorgione (even though he left so few works), Titian, Tintoretto, and Veronese.

With the increased knowledge of perspective acquired throughout the Renaissance, the law of 'frontality' no longer applied; during the sixteenth century painters were departing from the practice of posing their figures to face the spectator and then began to arrange them at different angles from below or above. Figures twist and turn away, and whole groups are involved with themselves in space rather than being disposed as for a group photograph. Figures were now arranged three-dimensionally, reaching back into the new-found depths of the picture.

TINTORETTO

This new style was exemplified sensationally by Tintoretto (1518–94) who liked to make even his main characters recede into the composition. He achieved this largely by intensifying the chiaroscuro, by softening the contours and by abandoning the kind of outline Botticelli used. We have seen that Titian bathed his paintings in atmosphere, dispensed with outlines and heightened the lights, but Tintoretto intensified the shadow and silhouetted his figures. He seldom presents a character full-face but turning away, or with head and shoulders foreshortened.

St. George and the Dragon. *Tintoretto. National Gallery, London* (Plate 73). The importance of the characters and the rhythm of the composition depends on Tintoretto's capacity for rendering light and shade, and the effect is enhanced by delicate yet rich colour: the sheen of silk and satin, the glow of flesh and the play of light on flesh and material and the jewelled crown. Everything has accentuated drama and movement. The foreshortened figure of the princess comes fleeing towards us, the depth of shadow from the waist thrusts her shoulders forward, her head turns away, one side being deeply in shadow, and a golden light playing over the other side where it caresses the skin and hair and jewelled crown. The flowing silken robe swirls back towards the dead man, again silhouetted against the dark earth, and the folds of the coastline succeed each other. St. George further plunges us into the composition; the pale hindquarters of the horse stand out from the darkness of the trees and its forequarters are in shadow, dark against the sparkling sea. His forward thrust is checked by the firm dark shape of the dragon's wings, and the sky is a vision of glory illuminating the battlements of the castle, catching the knight's armour, drenching the sea with light.

VERONESE

Paolo Veronese (*c.* 1528–88) was a much less dramatic painter who does not seem to have felt the drama of great events but to have taken a great delight in the material side of life. He is clearly entranced with pageantry, but the pageantry of a worldy paradise where all is well, all is luxury, colour, and delight. His is a world of splendour, a world of silken clothes and brocades worn by personalities calmly taking their place among stately buildings or in marble halls: a material world, but what a magnificent one!

The Adoration of the Magi. *Paolo Veronese. National Gallery, London* (Plate 74). Veronese convincingly creates a larger-than-life materialistic world of gorgeously attired figures. How far removed this world is from the one Giotto interpreted, or even from the pageantry of International Gothic! Veronese's people are sophisticated and are painted in depth, voluminously clad in rich brocade and satin and arranged in theatrical poses: they are nevertheless designed to make an imposing and satisfying composition with complete architectural unity.

What extraordinary inventiveness Veronese shows in his setting! Decorative plants grow in the broken pediment of the imposing marble arcade, which conveniently falls away to let through some perilously perched *putti*, and winged heads are hurled down on a great spotlight beam to the Madonna—the only figure seated to face us. Even she turns her head and shoulders to the side as she holds the Child to catch the full light. There is no religious fervour here, no piety. It is an entirely 'painterly' picture, an astonishing example of virtuosity in handling paint and colour, in balancing shapes and in silhouetting figures theatrically. How superbly this is done!

Look at the flow of figures and draperies and portrait profiles and three-quarter views. See how magnificently the composition flows from the white mane and ear of the horse on the left which throws the dark rich cloak and turban of the king into relief. See how the reversed satin of his cloak seems to pour over his arm down to the kneeling figure in a swirl of brocade, repeated in the foremost king with the flowing beard, and how the repetition of the two kneeling figures is relieved by the lightness of the boy twisting round in an entirely different position. How beautifully the dog on the right is painted! Note touches like the tilt of his master's proudly feathered hat, the peasant above with his hand on the beam of the unlikely thatched shelter.

Forget all these people, forget the theme, get right away from the painting and see what a splendid, exuberant, flamboyant composition it is, saved from turbulence by the stability of the foreground grouping, the weight of the architecture and the controlled flow of curved lines. Try to assess the importance of the strongly stated arch and the more-or-less horizontal clouds.

Here is the movement and flow of baroque. Frontality has gone and so has classical restraint.

There is no space here to go into details of the decline of Venetian art with the death of Veronese. Individual painters of significance did appear, and we must not omit mention of a brief reawakening in the eighteenth century with the appearance of Tiepolo, the brilliant rococo decorator, and of Canaletto, the distinguished topographical painter of the city of Venice and of the elaborate water festivals. Canaletto's younger contemporary, Guardi, painted luminous pictures of the Lagoon. Some of these eighteenth-century Italian paintings will be described later.

ITALIAN ART AS A CRITERION

I have devoted a large amount of space to Italian painting because the Italian schools made by far the greatest contribution to the development of painting in Europe over six centuries, and also because they produced so many men of outstanding genius. Masters whose superiority is recognized by everyone. Here is the yardstick we have been looking for; here is a standard of undisputed excellence. Hold on to this, and when in doubt, think back to these men and to the great painters of other schools that rank with them: Rembrandt, Velasquez, El Greco, Rubens, Watteau, Turner and a host of others. It is so easy to become bemused by Modern art and force oneself to accept trivial and even idiotic work in an effort not to be prejudiced. It is also easy to miss greatness presented in an unfamiliar form. Set your moderns—or your ancients—against the established great men. Do they, even in a small degree, add to what has already been achieved? Do they lift the spirit or are they merely obvious, repetitive or sensational?

POSSIBLE ESSAYS, DISCUSSION AND RESEARCH

1 Colour is more important than form. True or false?

2 How do early Venetian paintings compare with the mosaics of Ravenna?

3 Do you consider that an everyday Venetian scene by Carpaccio can compare with a composition by Titian?

4 How have various Italian painters interpreted groups of sleeping figures?

5 What are the comparative merits of Giorgione's *Tempest* and Tintoretto's *St. George*?

6 Do you prefer Venetian or Florentine landscape backgrounds?

Suggested Further Reading

Alazard, Jean: *L'Art Italien au XVIe Siècle*. Henri Laurens: Paris, 1955.

Borenius, Tancred: *Italian Painting* (Vol. II). Avalon: London, 1945.

Crowe and Cavalcaselli: *History of Painting in North Italy*. John Murray: London, 1914.

Honour, Hugh: *Companion Guide to Venice*. Collins: London, 1965.

Ruskin, John: *The Stones of Venice*. (Various editions)

Chapter Eleven

THE RISE OF LANDSCAPE PAINTING

THE NORTHERN SCHOOLS

We are apt to think of landscape painting—that is true landscape where it ceases to be a setting but is the main theme of the picture—as beginning in Holland in the seventeenth century, but several painters of distinction were concentrating on interpreting the countryside before that date. Admittedly they were mainly working in the more northerly countries, in the Netherlands, in Germany, and along the Danube. Dürer can be counted among them, but he, of course, did not confine himself to landscape although he was obviously very much interested in it and in plants and flowers and animals.

JOACHIM PATENIR

In the Netherlands in the early sixteenth century, Joachim Patenir (*c.* 1480–1524) was painting landscapes with only the smallest attention to the figures. These were often painted by another hand, while he devoted himself to the curious rocky landscape with milky, unscalable rocks, toylike cities, and blue mountains.

Charon Crossing the Styx. *Joachim Patenir. Prado, Madrid* (Plate 75*a*). This fascinating painting of Charon steering the soul of a passenger across the Styx, where the story is an integral part of the picture, is a combination of delicate and intricate design with breadth of composition and an atmosphere of great space. See how beautifully the shining tributary winds away through the wooded hills on the left and how this calm is contrasted with the roaring flames on the right. The whole painting is carried out in a subtle series of blues and greens which convey mystery and unearthly atmosphere. Patenir obviously had a number of disciples who painted much as he did, and the two pictures in the National Gallery, London, cannot be proved to be by him.

ALTDORFER

At the same time, the German, Albrecht Altdorfer (*c.* 1480–1538) was producing his wooded landscapes where dense romantic, but rather frightening, forests overwhelm the diminutive human beings.

St. George. *Albrecht Altdorfer. Alte Pinakothek, Munich* (Plate 75). A golden autumn light redeems this painting from utter gloom, though the impenetrable foliage of the trees continues to rise up against the sky and cut it off and also to imprison the knight on his fairy-tale steed which serves mainly as a welcome touch of light

78. *Top*. **The Fall of Icarus. Pieter Brueghel.**
A.C.L., Musées Royaux des Beaux-Arts, Brussels.

79. The Return of the Herd. Pieter Brueghel.
Kunsthistorischen Museum, Vienna.

80. Italian Landscape.
Claude Gellée.
Reproduced by courtesy of the Trustees, The National Gallery, London.

81. *Top*. **The Avenue, Middelharnis. Hobbema.**
Reproduced by courtesy of the Trustees, The National Gallery, London.

82. The Edge of the Village. Camille Pissarro. The Louvre.
Archives Photographiques—Paris.

84. *Top.* **Return from Haymaking. Louis le Nain. The Louvre.**
Archives Photographiques—Paris.

85. Embarkation for Cythera. Watteau. The Louvre.
Archives Photographiques—Paris.

86. *Top left*. **The Fountains, Caserta.**
Mansell Collection.

88. *Lower left*. **Church of Ottobeuren, Bavaria.**
German Tourist Information Bureau.

87. *Top right* **Melk Abbey. Jacob Prandtrauer.**
Amt der Niederösterreichischen Landesregierung.

89. Interior of Our Lady of Four Columns, Wilten, Innsbruck.
Herbert Knittl, Innsbruck.

90. Derby Day.
William Powell Frith.
The Tate Gallery, London.

91. Snowdon from
Llyn Nantlle. Richard Wilson.
Walker Art Gallery, Liverpool.

83. Old Man Seated.
Rembrandt.
Reproduced by courtesy of the Trustees, The National Gallery, London.

92. The Souvenir. Fragonard.
Reproduced by permission of the Trustees of the Wallace Collection.

93. The Wine Harvest. Francisco de Goya.
Museo del Prado, Madrid.

94. The Grand Canal. Canaletto.
Reproduced by courtesy of the Trustees, The National Gallery, London.

95. Santa Maria della Salute and the Dogana. Francesco Guardi.
Reproduced by courtesy of the Trustees, The National Gallery, London.

95a. The Wise and Foolish Virgins. William Blake.
The Tate Gallery, London.

96. Crossing the Brook. Turner.
Reproduced by courtesy of the Trustees, The National Gallery, London.

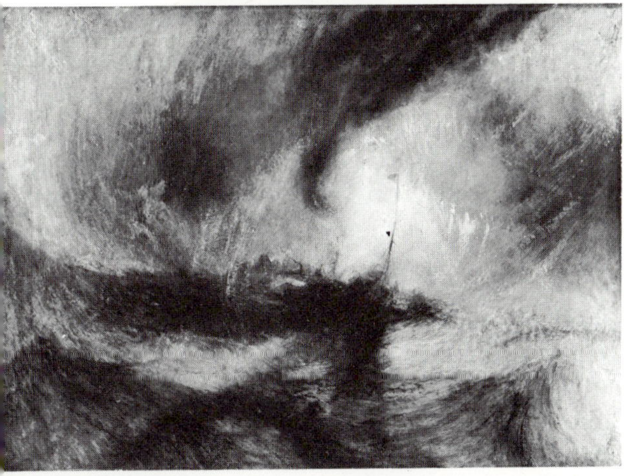

97. Snow Storm. Turner.
The Tate Gallery, London.

98. Hampstead Heath. John Constable.
Victoria and Albert Museum. Crown Copyright.

99. *Top.* **Yarmouth Jetty. John Crome.**
Castle Museum, Norwich.

100. *Centre.* **Durham Castle. John Sell Cotman.**
Castle Museum, Norwich.

105. Norfolk Wherries. Peter de Wint.
Southampton Art Gallery.

104. *Above.* **Landscape. Chang Jo-ch'êng. Ch'ien-lung period (1736-95) of Ch'ing Dynasty, China.**
The property of the Gulbenkian Museum of Oriental Art, University of Durham, Great Britain.

101. *Top left.* **The Journey of the Magi. Benozzo Gozzoli.**
Mansell Collection.

102. *Centre left.* **Italian Landscape. Claude Gellée.**
Reproduced by permission of the Birmingham Museum and Art Gallery.

103. *Left.* **An Extensive Landscape. Philipe Koninck.**
Southampton Art Gallery.

106. English Autumn Afternoon. Ford Madox Brown.
Reproduced by permission of the Birmingham Museum and Art Gallery.

107. *Top left* **Don Quixote and Sancho Panza. Daumier.**
Courtauld Institute Galleries, London.

109. Polo Player. T'ang Dynasty.
The property of the Gulbenkian Museum of Oriental Art, University of Durham, Great Britain.

108. *Top right.* **Mounted Warrior, Greek.**
Reproduced by courtesy of the Trustees of the British Museum.

110. Christ Riding upon an Ass. South German.
Victoria and Albert Museum. Crown Copyright.

111. Musique aux Tuileries.
Edouard Manet.
Reproduced by courtesy of the Trustees, The National Gallery, London.

111a. Déjeuner sur l'Herbe.
Edouard Manet.
Courtauld Institute Galleries, London

112. The Bathers.
Georges Seurat.
Reproduced by courtesy of the Trustees, The National Gallery, London.

113. Road at Honfleur.
Claude Monet. The Louvre.
Archives Photographiques—Paris.

114. La La at the
Cirque Fernando.
Edgar Degas.
Reproduced by courtesy of the Trustees, The National Gallery, London.

115. The Bed.
Henri de Toulouse-Lautrec.
The Louvre.
Archives Photographiques—Paris.

117. *Top left*. **Grande Arbres au Jas de Bouffon. Paul Cézanne.**
Courtauld Institute Galleries, London.

117a. *Top right*. **Jas de Bouffon. Paul Cézanne.**
Graves Art Gallery, Sheffield. Reproduced by permission of the Sheffield Corporation.

116. Snow at Louveciennes. Alfred Sisley.
Courtauld Institute Galleries, London.

colour. We can scarcely tell what the story is about but are more interested in the gleam of hope among the trunks of the trees where we can discern a faint glow in the sky and distant purple mountains.

DÜRER'S USE OF LANDSCAPE

Altdorfer was typically German, typically Northern, but Albrecht Dürer (1471–1528) was far too great a man to *typify* any school, although he had definite German characteristics. His conceptions are monumental; his paintings, and above all his superb drawings and woodcuts, are filled with intense vitality and even small woodcuts have the quality of great works of art. Everyone has seen reproductions of Dürer's drawings and water-colours of plants and animals which bear witness to his miraculous powers of observation.

Mountain Landscape. *Drawing. Dürer.* Louvre, Paris. (Plate 77). It is remarkable how in such a detailed wash drawing, Dürer has managed to convey such complete unity of composition. There is no overcrowding, no fussiness, but exquisitely delicate descriptions in line of the vegetation, verdant in the foreground and gradually merging into the rocky crag. The texture of the olives is extraordinarily well conveyed: the twisting hard black of the trunks and the silver, feathery softness of the foliage. How rhythmically the slopes in the foreground fold into each other and lead the eye on, winding across the country to discover farms, battlements, and towers and then to rise up the rocky ledges to the buildings silhouetted against the sky.

BRUEGHEL

Pieter Brueghel (*c.* 1525–69) of the Netherlands, certainly one of the greatest of landscape painters, often painted figure compositions and he normally included figures in his paintings, though landscape was never just a background and it often constituted the main interest.

Before we look at some of his paintings it would be as well to identify him clearly since there were several Brueghels and the name can be spelt in various ways. Pieter Brueghel (sometimes spelt Bruegel, Breughel) was born between 1525 and 1530 and died in 1569. He is also known as Pieter Brueghel the Elder, sometimes as 'peasant Brueghel'. He is by far the most important member of the family and he is responsible for the famous series of *The Months*. He had a son called Pieter (1564–1637) referred to as Pieter Brueghel the Younger or 'Hell Brueghel'. He showed great skill in copying his father's work. Hell Brueghel also had a painter son called Pieter.

Pieter Brueghel the Elder had a younger son Jan (1568–1625) called 'Velvet Brueghel', and he too had a painter son called Jan. In the short space of this book Pieter Brueghel the Elder is the only one of interest.

Most readers will be familiar with the painting of the *Hunters in the Snow* in the Vienna Gallery, with the marvellous tracery of the trees and the decisive patterning of dark figures against the crisp white snow, but there are others less well known such as the magical *Fall of Icarus*, a light-drenched scene of the coast of southern Italy with a peasant ploughing on the hillside and ships on a transparent sea. The story is only a pretext for the brilliant illumination of the sunset and no one could possibly guess the title of the picture (Plate 78).

The Return of the Herd. *Brueghel. Kunsthistorisches Museum, Vienna* (Plate 79). This painting makes no pretence at being anything but a landscape. It has Brueghel's characteristic trees etched against the sky, and the whole countryside sweeps back deeply into the picture. There is the obvious forward thrust of the beasts being urged on by peasants, but the trees, the cliffs, and the river seem to swing round and far into the distance where the hills merge with a horizontally designed sky. The balance is perfect throughout but there is a feeling of controlled movement and it is a movement in which the spectator joins through ravishingly lovely countryside.

Brueghel's love of the countryside was equalled by his love and understanding of the peasants, and he painted them at work, at play, on the land, and at the village *Kermesse* or fair. Many of his pictures were satirical and directed towards contemporary social abuses.

FLEMISH AND ITALIAN LOVE OF NATURE

We have already noted the fascinating landscapes used as the background by such artists as Pisanello, Piero della Francesca, Gentile da Fabriano, and Mantegna and we have seen the exquisitely detailed landscape background in the Flemish *Adoration of the Lamb* (Plate 49) as well as having a glance forward to the sophisticated seventeenth-century painting of Rubens. We have noticed that, as time went on, landscape was being treated more and more as an integral part of the composition and in some instances it was assuming even more importance than the alleged theme of the painting. Even so, many painters were inclined to take mythological or Biblical subject as an 'excuse' for landscape, even as late as the seventeenth century. Claude Lorraine *alias* Claude Gellée (1600–82), a French landscape painter who worked mainly in Rome, puts diminutive figures in the foreground illustrating a story rather perfunctorily. At other times figures form an integral part of Claude's compositions, as for instance in his sea port paintings, but his interest is always with the landscape.

If we look again at some of the paintings that we have already discussed, we shall find that in manuscripts whose function was fundamentally ornamental, landscape was a charming decoration and the plant and animal forms, the minute hill towns, the castles, and the trees lent themselves admirably to decorative schemes, and in many cases, they were essential to the story (Plate 38).

Frescoes did not really need landscape backgrounds; the story could often have been told as effectively without any background, but the Italians used it more and more as time went on.

Both Flemish and Italian artists, as we have seen, loved the countryside around them. Although rules were laid down by the patron—the Church—for the carrying out of the 'illustration', painters were presumably free to complete the scheme as they wished, and it is easy to detect the relaxation and delight they found in painting their background landscapes. They could not, however, seriously paint a landscape as such. The patron was in charge; it was he who ordered what he wanted. The artist, with no conscious thoughts of 'expressing' himself, carried out these orders, at first adhering very strictly to them. Gradually, and more especially in the enlightened thinking of the Renaissance, when, as well as the Church, the State and private individuals were competing for the artist's services, a great deal more laxity was given and painters slowly began to make their own terms.

SEVENTEENTH-CENTURY FRENCH LANDSCAPE

With the decline of painting in Italy, artists such as Salvator Rosa in the seventeenth century, and Zuccarelli in the eighteenth, took to painting landscapes, and artists of other countries still considered that a visit to Italy was essential to their careers.

POUSSIN AND CLAUDE

Both Poussin and Claude, the leading French landscape painters of the seventeenth century, were influenced by Italy and did a great deal of work in that country. Poussin (1594–1665) worked largely in Rome where he lived for the last years of his life. His style was in the classical vein and he became absorbed in re-creating a classical world. He was influenced by Claude, and Claude was influenced by his classical fervour, but it is Claude with whom we are concerned at this moment (1600–82). Claude's landscapes are imbued with a magical light streaming towards us across a dreamlike countryside: a pastoral land ennobled by his own personal vision of it, a land which is never real, but flooded with an almost mystical light, gentle and calm. This is a world we can enter into and relax in, a world of infinite horizons, completely undisturbed in its quiet beauty. Claude's ideal world of nature combines the perfection of the classical world with French elegance. His *Enchanted Castle*, immortalized a second time by Keats in 'faerylands forlorn' is certainly enchanted in its misty setting by the sea.

Italian Landscape. *Claude Gellée. National Gallery, London* (Plate 80). A wonderfully peaceful landscape, despite the slight urgency of the small figure of the angel, where the diminutive boat scarcely disturbs the tranquil water and the beasts drink in quiet confidence.

The trees are living and growing and so are the shrubs which crowd down to the water, but Claude has arranged them in beautiful patterns and not even a breeze must disturb their perfection as they frame the romantic castle on its crag. Note how perfectly the three birds in the left-hand corner carry the eye across the sky and complete the framework and how the diagonal flight of four or five others spans the space of the sky to the castle.

SEVENTEENTH-CENTURY PAINTING IN HOLLAND

It was the Dutch painters of the seventeenth century who finally popularized landscape as a subject in itself and abandoned any pretence of its being only a setting. The Dutch were in a good position to do so because they were, so to speak, starting again from scratch now that they were no longer under Spanish rule. They revelled in their new freedom and were particularly sensitive to the delights of their own everyday world which they could now enjoy to the full. It must be explained here that the provinces which we know today as Belgium and Holland were ruled by the Spanish until 1581, when the Dutch proclaimed that King Philip II of Spain had forfeited his sovereignty over them. The provinces of the future Kingdom of Belgium remained under Spanish (and later Austrian) rule since their populations were predominantly Catholic.

THE NEW PATRONS

At this time there arose new patrons among the rich Dutch merchants who had built themselves large, but not palatial, country houses and needed reasonably small, undramatic paintings as a background to their everyday life and to lighten the gloom of the heavily furnished dark interiors. Above all they wanted and were copiously supplied by painters with 'extra windows' into another house, another courtyard or a stretch of calm uneventful landscape. As a nation of sailors they loved the sea, and here they could appreciate more stimulus and drama in the paintings for they were, of course, accustomed to storms. But it was always the familiar theme and not flights of fancy that they wanted and, with few exceptions, Dutch art, which flowered for almost exactly a century, is homely and a little tame, one of its outstanding qualities being the expression of the lovely golden light and the wide horizons to be found in flat countries.

Most of the Dutch painters produced at least one masterpiece, but the school also gave birth to Vermeer, who raises the light and atmosphere, the countryside and the people of Holland high above the ordinary in his luminous paintings. And of course there was Rembrandt, who undoubtedly ranks with the greatest masters of any school.

I do not mean to infer that the lesser Dutch made no contribution to the art of Europe. They satisfied an awakening interest in landscape for its own sake and, although they often painted the trivial, they also often raised it to something of significance. They knew precisely how to give warmth and intimacy to an interior, the play of light on silver or satin or glass, and the fun and boisterous enjoyment at the village inn. Being Protestants they were not called upon to produce religious paintings, and having only just begun as an independent nation, there was no demand for historical scenes. So they concentrated on 'genre', the painting of everyday life. They cannot claim to have invented it, for it was used to a greater or lesser degree in the background of Italian and Flemish painting and in illuminated manuscripts and *Books of Hours*. However, it was the Dutch who developed genre painting and the bulk of Dutch painters produced little else. Yet many people, who could possess only one painting, would choose a Dutch picture largely because it would be companionable, easy to live with, easy to understand and would make no great demands on them. Some of these painters will be discussed in chapter 12. Let us look at one of their outstanding achievements in landscape.

DUTCH LANDSCAPE

The Avenue, Middelharnis. *Meindert Hobbema* (1638–1709). *National Gallery, London* (Plate 81). This is a most satisfying painting and a masterpiece of design, so perfectly constructed as to be utterly convincing. It has not the glancing shadows and changing light of the Impressionists, nor the noble conception of Claude, nor does it give one the breadth of vision of Rubens, but Hobbema has chosen an ordinary avenue and with unerring skill he has perfected it pictorially. The painting has balance and variety as it entices us to explore the countryside to left and right and to follow the road to the horizon. This is not a countryside to catch the breath; avenues like this are to be seen all over Holland, Belgium, and northern France, but Hobbema loved those slender stretching trees crowned with tufts and he varied their shapes without breaking the tunnel of the avenue. The foreground is weighty to support the verticals of the trees, but there is sufficient detailed interest in the man pruning trees on the right and in the foliage on the left to make one want to follow into the country and up to the little figure holding the interest as he walks towards us. The wideness of the sky accentuates the flatness of the land, but the clouds building up lend it interest. This is a simple statement of a simple subject which has produced a great painting. There is spaciousness within a small area, a mile or so of countryside. Now let us see how a nineteenth-century French painter treated the same type of subject.

PISSARRO COMPARED WITH HOBBEMA

The Edge of the Village. *Camille Pissarro* (1830–1903). *The Louvre, Paris* (Plate 82). How differently Pissarro treats his landscape 200 years later! On a country road with tall poplars on either side, a horse and cart and small figures are coming towards us. We are right in this painting whether we like it or not. We can sense the warmth of the sun and the coolness of the deep shadows and almost feel them cutting across us. The trees are just moving. We can see Hobbema's light, and enjoy it as it bathes the countryside, but we *feel* Pissarro's and we know it is changing; there is exquisite detail in Hobbema's foliage and one is fascinated by its patterning against the sky; there is none in Pissarro's, for it is the radiance of the light that is falling upon it that matters in his painting. Pissarro's handling of the trunks against the sunlit houses is a marvel of subtlety which would doubtless have seemed unfinished to the Dutchman, yet Hobbema's trunks have their own subtleties of changing tone as they twist upwards, but he has not tried to solve the same problems as Pissarro. With Hobbema we start from the foreground and walk into the picture; with Pissarro we are already there.

THE EIGHTEENTH-CENTURY ITALIANS

During the years which passed between the execution of these two landscapes, Venice had had a reawakening after a period of decline and produced three outstanding painters: Tiepolo, Canaletto, and Guardi.

Giovanni Battista Tiepolo (1669–1770) worked for several years in Spain, but he was much in demand in Germany and in his own country. He is considered by some to be the greatest master of the eighteenth century; to me, however, he is a magnificent decorator who possesses neither the subtlety nor the magic of Watteau.

While Tiepolo was covering the walls and ceilings of palaces with decorative figure compositions and great sweeps of landscape and sky, Antonio Canaletto (1697–1768) was painting with absolute fidelity and an almost enamel technique the city of Venice—the palaces, the gondolas, the canals, and the lagoon.

The Grand Canal. *Canaletto. National Gallery, London* (Plate 94). A meticulous, almost photographic technique describes every feature of the architecture and conveys the shining surface of the rippling water, where the light on the ripples is a kind of calligraphy. The vast expanse of sky, only lightly flecked with clouds, relieves the wealth of detail in the buildings, and the broad stretch of water is given interest by the skilful distribution of individual boats and groups of gondolas. It is well known that Canaletto made use of the camera obscura, a mechanical aid to accuracy invented in the sixteenth century. It consisted of a series of lenses arranged in a darkened box which could throw the image of a view on to a sheet of paper. The artist could then trace this image and later, by means of 'squaring up', transfer it to canvas, thus ensuring an accurate record of the buildings. 'Squaring up' was commonly used to transfer the lines of a sketch to a larger surface, and simply involved covering the sketch with a network of numbered squares while a similar network of larger numbered squares is ruled on the painting surface.

Why then, is Canaletto's painting in any way superior to a good colour photograph? It is very difficult to define what the difference is, and had colour photography been in current use, I doubt whether Canaletto would have painted in this way. This painting does, I believe give most people far more than a photograph. To begin with, it is full of Canaletto's comments, full of his choice of what to stress, his explanations. A camera cannot comment, but Canaletto could and did select from his camera obscura. The photographer can only, in a limited way, choose what to stress by arranging for the light that suits him and he could wait for 100 years to catch the composition that Canaletto has designed.

Note the way the full light on the left-hand buildings and barges descends the scale to the horizon, and how the reflected light in the shadow of the opposite bank is a perfect foil for it. See how the clarity and detail of the elaborate barge on the left sweeps the eye down the canal, and what interest is lent by the three gondolas and their gondoliers. The one with his back to us, leaning forward, is superbly painted as he tenses his arm to pull back the sweep. The real question is, would you rather have this painting or a first-class colour photograph?

A little later, Francesco Guardi (1712–93) was interpreting the same subjects with a freer, less meticulous technique and he was, until recently, considered to rank far below Canaletto as a painter. In the light of what the Impressionists produced, modern taste now assesses his work above Canaletto's for its play of light and more 'impressionistic' approach.

Santa Maria della Salute and the Dogana. *Francesco Guardi. Birmingham Art Gallery* (Plate 95). In a sense this is more photographic than Canaletto's rendering as it is less obviously 'composed'. The distribution of the various craft, though balanced pictorially, is more as it might look in a snapshot, more casual, but the actual handling of paint, the 'sketchiness' and the flicker of light is very far removed from the camera. There is a certain theatrical nonchalance and a romantic approach completely absent from Canaletto's pictures, and the painting does not progress from the foreground, through the middle distance to the background; it is all several miles away.

COMPARISON WITH RICHARD WILSON

In England, Richard Wilson (1714–82), who was almost exactly contemporary with Guardi, was creating his beautifully composed, calm paintings simplified into harmonies of gold, olive, and brown. He has elements of the great Italian masters, transmitted both directly and indirectly, for we can see something of the Italian manner of Poussin in the diffused light which envelops everything, something of Claude in the way it is directed towards us, casting some of the hills into sharp silhouettes, and we can see something of Tintoretto in the handling of those silhouettes so that they play an important part in the whole design. But there is more than this: there is a calm appraisal of nature and a very keen sense of observation which enables him to reduce landscape features to large, basic masses. He has the great qualities of selection and of eliminating unnecessary detail. His is a tranquil, noble countryside in which to relax and yet aesthetically it is stimulating.

Snowdon from Llyn Nantlle. *Richard Wilson. Walker Art Gallery, Liverpool* (Plate 91). Even a glance at this painting reveals its essential design in all its power. The mountain peak is finely and jaggedly outlined against a delicately painted sky, yet it also has a structural shape and, in that sense, is monumental. This third dimension is emphasized by the dark silhouettes of the lower row of peaks which partly frame it. Note how subtly Wilson lights the side of the left-hand slope and how this is reflected in the smooth water, and how the very decisive sharpness of the peaks is softened in reflection to give a reverse of the shape, but not a monotonous one. Across both sides, oblique tree trunks caught by the light, curve gracefully across the sharp edges. The three small figures give a focal point of interest to the foreground: without them, it would become vague and diffused, and interest would wander away towards the edge of the painting. There is oriental influence in the insignificance of the fishermen in the vast land of mountains, and an Eastern sense of design in the lovely patterning of the branches and foliage against the sky.

Wilson had no contemporaries of his stature in this field in England; he was born over 60 years before Turner and Constable, and over 50 before John Crome and his followers of the Norwich school.

POSSIBLE ESSAYS, DISCUSSION AND RESEARCH

1 If you could choose to have one painting, would it be a landscape?

2 Do you find that Brueghel's 'homeliness' detracts from the value of paintings?

3 What different worlds do the following painters show us in their landscapes: Hubert and Jan Van Eyck, Hobbema, Claude, Rubens?

4 Compare *Balthazar Carlos* by Velasquez with *Charles I on Horseback* by Van Dyck.

5 If you could abstract a landscape background from a Flemish or Italian painting, would it bear comparison with a landscape painted for its own sake?

6 Compare a painting by Wilson with one by Canaletto.

Suggested Further Reading

Canton, Sanchez: *The Prado*. Thames & Hudson: London, 1959.

Clark, Kenneth: *Landscape into Art*. Murray London, 1949.

Hendy, Philip: *Spanish Painting*. Avalon: London, 1964.

Holmes, Charles: *The National Gallery (Germany, Netherlands, Spain)*. Bell: London, 1930.

Konody and Lathom: *An Introduction to French Painting*. Cassell: London, 1932.

Levey, Michael: *Painting in 18th Century Venice*. Phaidon: London, 1959.

Manson, J. B.: *Dutch Painting*. Avalon: London, 1945.

Wilenski, R.: *Outline of Dutch Art*. Faber & Faber: London, 1945.

Chapter Twelve

THE SEVENTEENTH AND EIGHTEENTH CENTURIES IN EUROPE

Landscape was not by any means the only contribution made by seventeenth-century artists. Indeed, the great masters of the period, Rembrandt, Velasquez, El Greco, Rubens, and Van Dyck were chiefly concerned with portraits and figure compositions, though we have seen that Rubens painted landscapes when he retired to his country home. El Greco gave us a haunting landscape of Toledo, Van Dyck sketched the countryside and trees for his own delight, and Rembrandt produced an occasional landscape as well as a large number of wash and ink drawings and etchings.

GENRE IN HOLLAND

To such an extent did the seventeenth-century Dutch artists specialize in their chosen fields of genre, landscapes, flowers, animals or portraits that a landscape painter might employ another painter to fill in the figures; yet among these men were artists of a very high rank.

JAN VERMEER

Although Jan Vermeer of Delft (1632–75) shows unbelievable skill in the absence of brush strokes and an extraordinarily smooth surface, his work is never facile or slick. A restful calm pervades his airy interiors and spacious townscapes, which all have the inevitability of great art; nothing could possibly be altered. However, it must be agreed that his compositions, although not static, are not exciting in the way that, say, a cave painting is exciting. Vermeer does not express excitement, so we need not look for it. Instead, he expresses a deep contentment and an acceptance of the beauty of light: he casts a pearly radiance over his interiors, over the lacemaker at work, over the cook as she pours milk from a jug, a light which seems to knit the component part of a picture into a perfect unity.

How wonderful this light is, too, when he pours it over a landscape, or rather a townscape, for he painted his town of Delft and a street in it. He manages to make a stretch of water before the town interesting by placing small figures on the bank, and he manages to make a few houses very special as they stand timeless in the mellow light.

PIETER DE HOOCH

Pieter de Hooch (1629–83) was the greatest master of Dutch genre painting in which he specialized, though he did not reach Vermeer's heights and at times his work is pedestrian. At its best it has an easy naturalness of composition and he invites us to take 'pot luck' with the inhabitants of his cool, dank rooms and courtyards. The beautiful play of daylight which filters into his interiors gives the rather characterless figures importance as it picks out, say, a happy choice of a glowing red skirt contrasting with soft black velvet. There is no early Italian frontality here, for a figure in the foreground often has its back to us. There is no conventional composition, for we seem to look in on a casual scene where a woman may be sweeping the floor or engaged in any mundane task.

FRANS HALS

Frans Hals (1580–1666) specialized in portraits and is known to everyone for his much-reproduced *Laughing Cavalier* in the Wallace Collection, London. Frans Hals was perhaps a facile painter, but he too produced his masterpieces and he had a pleasing fresh approach and the knack of catching not only a likeness but a living one. His paint lives as he uses it to stress the white of a ruff or the curl of a feather; he has a buoyant gaiety which is altogether disarming just at a moment when one is going to accuse him of slickness. What extraordinary individuality he gets into his characters' hands and makes them complement the head!

He certainly captures a moment of dashing cheer as he catches his characters in their Sunday best, but his groups of figures are rather conventionally posed to show off each head to advantage, and the disposition of patches of cold white in cottons and cuffs is apt to be disrupting. Although his extraordinary control over his technique is to be admired, and his direct method of painting was a definite innovation and influenced later painters like Goya and Manet, his portraits are somewhat superficial and are not sympathetic and penetrating character studies such as Rembrandt painted.

REMBRANDT

We have seen Rembrandt's handling of a religious theme, we have seen a drawing, but now let us look at one of his portraits.

An Old Man Seated. *Rembrandt van Rijn* (1606–69). *National Gallery, London* (Plate 83). This reveals the same stillness and quiet that we saw in the *Adoration of the Shepherds*. The old man is deep in thought, completely lost to his surroundings, while a kind of inner radiance emanates from him. Notice the warmth and richness of colour in the robe, the gleam of deep red in the sleeve and the hand silhouetted against the fur collar as it catches the light. Notice too the astonishing modelling of the wrist and the slightly quavering fingers. You feel you know this old man and that you have seen him unobserved. The moment of his being entirely retired within himself is so sensitively conveyed that one scarcely likes to intrude.

Even by simply looking at the three works of Rembrandt we have discussed, we can realize his outstanding genius and his deep sympathy for humanity. He does not paint in the grand manner like Rubens. He does not paint for the Court like Velasquez, he paints for the human race and invests it with immortality. He uses the people around him to illustrate Biblical subjects and he feels the same understanding for the beggar as he does for his son Titus or for The Three Kings.

It has become a cliché, which is not necessarily valid, that great art comes through suffering, but in Rembrandt's case this is true. Admittedly he had a period of prosperity in Amsterdam lasting roughly ten years, in which he was well patronized and revelled in the jewellery and splendid materials of his rich patrons with a Venetian feeling for warmth and glowing colour. He mastered his wonderfully varied technical approach, suiting it to his subject; he developed his free and sure brushwork and his ability to render his theme dramatically without making it theatrical. Rembrandt's real suffering began when his wife Saskia died in 1642. In the same year his famous picture of the *Night Watch* was much criticized because, although a magnificent work of art, it did not give enough importance to each head to satisfy the members of the Guild who commissioned it. This brought about his ruin. His liaison with his housekeeper who looked after him and his son Titus only added to his unpopularity. During the last years of his life his sympathy with his sitters and his insight into their minds and thoughts increased, causing him to produce—in loneliness and obscurity—searching portraits of himself and his family and magnificent renderings of Biblical subjects.

RUBENS IN FLANDERS

Peter Paul Rubens (1577–1640) was almost a contemporary of Rembrandt, but he painted in the grand manner, huge decorations and epic scenes. He paints the human body and delights in great sweeping compositions progressing with the exhuberance manifested in baroque architecture and sculpture (described later). As we saw earlier, in landscape he spreads his vast countryside over countless miles, with a controlled but sweeping rhythm. He entices us progressively to explore, and with amazing skill takes us on his own personally conducted tour of a varied scene, but he does more: he bathes it in a kind of glory.

Rubens was, of course, a splendid portrait painter and he has left us a magnificent self-portrait, at Windsor, of the debonair, brilliant, assured artist that he was, almost a caricature but still a great work of art. His broad black hat is set aslant on his intelligent forehead; his handsome face is glowing with vitality. There is, too, the beautiful, radiant painting of his wife in the *Chapeau de Paille* in the National Gallery, London.

I have stressed Ruben's portraits and his landscapes because his figure compositions constitute for many people a stumbling block to full appreciation of his genius. His characters are sumptuous and his women voluptuous and they often reveal a coarseness which is hard to reconcile with his superb rendering of flesh and powerful building up of architectural unity in a picture. This barrier can often be broken down by first approaching him through his landscapes and portraits; when an appreciation of his brilliant handling of these themes has been acquired, the way is clear to his more difficult epic compositions. These, too, can be approached through his wonderfully confident 'sketches' for compositions, each so complete as to be hardly sketches.

Rubens was a phenomenon in Flemish art; he owes little to his predecessors and much to the Italian masters, particularly to Michelangelo, Titian, and Raphael. He spent eight years in Italy and he managed to combine his admiration for the great Italians with his deep interest in nature and the life around him. Although he emulated the Italians he did not despise a kind of 'noble vulgarity'. His characters sweat and lust and his aristocrats can have the buxomness of peasants. Take a look at his *Judgement of Paris* in the National Gallery, London, and see how superbly he paints the heavily built Flemish bodies so much admired at the time. What a flowing composition this is, exuberant but not restless, perfectly composed within a rich landscape with the sweeping lines of a peacock to link the three goddesses and their judge.

VELASQUEZ IN SPAIN

Velasquez (1599–1660) was born 22 years later than Rubens and so worked entirely in the seventeenth century. His art is timeless, not only for its greatness, but because of its style which might be of almost any country and of any century after the Renaissance. We have already seen the skill with which he handles his paint and the royal flourish of his confident treatment of his patrons' portraits.

There is great satisfaction to be found in his astonishingly brilliant and accomplished technique and no one would be foolish enough to doubt his place in the history of art, but for me he does not rank with painters such as Rembrandt, El Greco, Turner, Cézanne or the great Italians. He does not open up new worlds, or see more deeply or sympathetically into this one. He indulges in no flights of fancy, he glorifies nothing but he records what he sees with an incredible skill which rules out any superficiality.

VERSAILLES

Apart from the art of Claude and Poussin, whose painting was a kind of marriage between French and Italian, since they spent so much time in Italy, seventeenth-century France produced rather pompous portraits and historical pictures for the glorification of Louis XIV. Most of the painters, architects, and decorators were enrolled in the gigantic task of creating the Palace of Versailles in the shortest possible time. The chief honours must go to the architects Le Vau and, later, Jules Mansart (or Mansard) for a stupendous achievement of restrained classical elegance combined with grandeur, and to Le Nôtre, who by his genius for overcoming difficulties and sculpturing the land at his disposal, made landscape gardening into an art. Le Brun, not a very great painter in his own right, was a superb organizer who co-ordinated the whole splendid decoration to give the palace complete unity.

There were no French painters in the seventeenth century to rank with Rubens, Van Dyck, Rembrandt or Velasquez, but there were painters producing works of considerable significance. Though the French did not equal the contribution made by the Dutch in the realm of genre, the three Le Nain brothers were painting domestic scenes which had a kind of nobility, and which lifted this type of picture to great heights.

EIGHTEENTH-CENTURY FRANCE

The French have always been inclined to produce great movements, to have a tremendous influence on art rather than to produce great masters. Even to the layman, several great names come to mind from Italy, Spain, the Netherlands, and England, but when it comes to France, there is a search for the giant, unless it be Watteau; and yet the general public are probably familiar by name with more French painters than those of any other school. Almost anyone, however slightly interested in art, can give the name and identify the pictures of a number of the Impressionists, and also of the much-reproduced and sentimental paintings by Greuze, but neither François Boucher nor Honoré Fragonard were sentimental though some critics consider them superficial.

FRAGONARD

Fragonard (1732–1806) has grace and a kind of perfection. His landscapes are charmingly nostalgic; they are romantic without being over-sweet or prettified. Parklands and ruins overgrown with creepers, elegantly dressed men and women wandering about doing nothing in particular, could be trivial, but they are saved from this by their lovely colour, their unaffected joy in the pleasures of life and the easy grace with which they disport themselves.

The Souvenir. *Fragonard. Wallace Collection, London* (Plate 92). This is one of the most delightfully attractive paintings of this period. Somehow, the graceful, romantic pose of the pretty girl in her delicious pink and white dress, is entirely natural. She is delicately silhouetted against the light sky and her pretty profile is seriously intent on carving the name on the tree while a very French little dog watches earnestly. It is a rococo perfection of flowers, foliage, and silk with creepers entwining themselves around the tree trunk and under the bench. Everything is perfect. There is nothing anyone could wish to alter.

WATTEAU

Antoine Watteau (1684–1721) holds a very special place among the great men not only of the eighteenth century, but of any period, for he manages to produce the sumptuous composition of Rubens, set it in a vast parkland and refine it, then translate it into elegant rococo grace. I say rococo, a term more usually applied to architecture and interior decoration, because rococo was a reaction against pomposity and splendour, against the ponderous and sometimes overstated baroque style. In rococo, a charming dalliance and inconsequence takes charge where roses and shells and garlands almost run riot.

Watteau hints at all the shimmering gleam of silk and satin, but with a light touch, and there is never the robust coarseness of a Rubens nor, it must be admitted, any of the glory.

The Embarkation for Cythera. *Watteau. The Louvre, Paris* (Plate 85). In an age of rather frivolous art of the court which had lost its pomposity and belonged more to the boudoir than to the state apartments and the Church, Watteau accepts the light-hearted scene as though it were on a stage under the glamour of footlights, and he gives it a quality of rapturous beauty as well as a certain magical unreality. This is a world of garlanded statues ghost-like in a park, of huge trees with sweeping branches, of pink cupids and satin bows and misty groves with enchanted islands waiting to be explored; it is no more real than Claude's world, but it is entirely different and has its basis in the world we know. We have all seen places something like these, but Watteau's vision and Claude's vision completely transform them. We can slip easily into the painting, finding more and more to enjoy.

Every figure in the *Embarkation* is just in the act of making a subtle movement forward expressed with an almost dancing rhythm. Each pair or group of figures is rhythmically united, but this rhythm is continued through the rest of the composition to the waiting ship drawn by cupids to the magical islands lost in the mist. The painter conveys a strong sense of excited anticipation among the elegant aristocratic figures moving forward in a kind of slow ballet. This fanciful theme could have been trivial or over-voluptuous by any other hand.

BAROQUE SCULPTURE AND ARCHITECTURE

We tend to think of the baroque style as belonging to the seventeenth century but it did in fact continue well into the eighteenth, covering a period roughly from 1610 to 1715 and merging with eighteenth-century rococo, although rococo was a reaction against it in that the style became much lighter and gayer and was assymetrical. Rococo is a less ponderous and altogether more elegant expression of the baroque style and it owes its name to *Rocaille*, the term for the delicate decoration which uses shell-like forms.

The term 'baroque' is used loosely to denote a new movement in art akin to the Renaissance in its intensity, but revolutionary in that it abandoned the accepted reticences of portrayal, the accepted restraint and influence of classical art. It was at the same time tempestuous and sometimes pompous; it could be heavy-handed, especially in Italy, but it did also have a glorious freedom, a great lifting in exuberant fulsome movement which at times resulted in overstatement. Used monumentally, as in Rome and southern Italy, for great sweeping stairways and splendid fountains such as Bernini's in the Piazza Navona in Rome, the embracing curve of the colonnade to St. Peter's and the cascading fountains at Caserta.

BERNINI IN ITALY

Gian Lorenzo Bernini (1598–1680) was responsible for both the colonnade of St. Peter's, familiar to everyone, and the Four Rivers Fountain in the Piazza Navona in Rome. As with the bronze doors for the Baptistery in Florence, a competition was held for the best designs for this fountain, which had to incorporate an existing Egyptian obelisk. Bernini was not in favour with the new Pope Innocent X, so he was not invited to submit a model; however, he made one and it was placed where the Pope would see it. It immediately aroused great enthusiasm and the commission was given to Bernini. The fountain is an island of rock with figures personifying the rivers Nile, Ganges, Danube, and Plate at each corner surging out of the water. From its peak rises the obelisk. The figures are exuberantly baroque in their dramatic attitudes and their flowing movements and the avalanches of water streaming over the rocks gives an effect of superabundance and splendour.

THE PALACE OF CASERTA

Fountains. *Palace of Caserta, near Naples* (Plate 86). This palace has to perfection the full extravagance of late baroque with its vast rooms and great staircase, but even more fabulous and grandiose is the succession of fountains literally cascading down from a pool on the heights through ornamental groups of figures arranged at different levels.

The normal view is looking up between lawns flanked with trees through fountain rising above fountain to a foaming torrent gushing out of the heights two miles away. At level after level the smooth surface of a pool is broken by great sprays and jets of water, even gushing from the mouths of dolphins. They splash and foam over statues symbolizing the winds and have their greatest effect in the Grand Cascade where the huntress Diana and her nymphs disport themselves, complete with hounds, but there is no architectural background, the statues are set among rocks and natural landscape.

Although the gardens at Versailles are perhaps the most beautifully designed and most deeply satisfying of any in Europe, the master planning of the vista of fountains and pools there seems almost tame compared with this overwhelmingly joyous exuberance at Caserta.

BAROQUE AND ROCOCO IN AUSTRIA, BAVARIA, AND SPAIN

Let us consider some of the manifestations of baroque in Austria.

Melk Abbey. *Jacob Prandtauer* (1660–1726). *Lower Austria* (Plate 87). Even a photograph conveys something of the scenic effect of Melk set on its rock above the Danube and reflected into it. Every line, every mass is organized to add to this tremendous impact. Cream and gold and copper-green, it is perhaps at its most spectacular in autumn when the rolling countryside is bronzed and the russet roofs echo its warmth, but at any time the sight of it is an experience of intense delight and the splendour of the exterior is rivalled by the golden glory of the interior decorations. It is Prandtauer's greatest work and he has exploited the dramatic site; it is a tremendous statement, marvellously complex, yet having absolute unity and a wonderful crescendo that is part of baroque.

This crescendo is even more apparent in the interiors of baroque and rococo abbey churches in Austria and in Bavaria. The church at Wies is a miracle of white and gold and pale colours, stucco and wood and carving all combining to give the richest effect.

At Vorau in the Austrian province of Styria the interior is a fantasy of gold, so exuberant in fact that it is not generally considered to be of the highest order and many critics claim that it is overstated. That it may be, but what an overstatement! Fundamentally baroque, occasional assymetrical details and a certain lightness of touch entitle it to be partially rococo.

An avenue of gold sweeps up from either side, culminating in a fantasy of glittering golden light on the altar, and this is echoed everywhere in controlled exuberance, in the pulpit, in the organ case, and in many of the side chapels. It does not use the Gothic verticals soaring up to the sky, but the masses rise in a kind of adoration and create a paradise of flowers and garlands, saints and angels, rising in a fanfare of trumpets.

Some may consider this to be gold run riot to the point of ostentation, but to others it is the perfect expression of the fullness of life and delight in every aspect of it. The Lady Chapel combines silver and gold; and its Madonna, almost Gothic in her grace, stands beneath a canopy while a small angel holds a crown of stars above her head.

Interior of Our Lady of Four Columns. *Wilten, near Innsbruck* (Plate 89). In contrast to the gorgeousness of Vorau, the church at Wilten is all sober elegance, even to the lovely name of Our Lady of the Four Columns. It is one of the most perfect rococo churches in existence, superbly proportioned, every detail is laid on with the lightest and most sensitive touch: tassels and foliage and flowers, garlands in the most delicate of chains looped to a golden crown. The warm columns are encircled with bracelets of gold and their capitals overflow with gilded flowers as they support an open canopy linked to the crown with garlands of gossamer lightness.

In the Hall of Mirrors in the Amalienburg, in the park of the Nymphenburg Palace near Munich, nymphs swing lightly on the cornices and putti disport themselves, revelling in the flowers which sweep up into the ceiling, letting fall a swag or a garland to the decorative shell-forms below. All this is reflected again and again in the mirrors with their delicate framework. This is no longer baroque, but rococo and eighteenth century.

In many instances the splendid monasteries of Austria and Germany were originally Romanesque or Gothic but were 'baroquified' in the seventeenth century. It is interesting that the earlier styles were considered utterly inferior and it was seldom that efforts were made to preserve any of the former character. Indeed, the main object was to mask it. In comparatively recent years considerable restoration has been carried out to try to preserve the best of both worlds and it is surprising to see how well the styles do marry, especially in the interiors.

The vast and elaborate exterior of the cathedral of Santiago de Compostela in north-west Spain replaced the Romanesque. A riot of extravagant detail makes the relatively sober basic proportions and flat surface of the building disturbingly exciting, but there is none of the serenity of Melk.

MANSART IN FRANCE

Naturally enough such a grand style as baroque influenced the whole of Europe, but in England and France it was tempered by the sobriety of the classical style. Even the extravagance of Versailles was restrained in its classical lines. You have to look at the satisfying lines of the Church of the Invalides in Paris by Jules Mansart to see how classical its lines are: the verticals and horizontals are basically classical and relieved by a controlled ornamentation and gilding and by a grandeur of conception which is baroque. It, too, is superbly sited in an open space at the end of a vista from over the river.

WREN IN ENGLAND

In spite of similarities, St. Paul's Cathedral in London by Sir Christopher Wren (1632–1723) has not the same marriage of baroque and classical features, for the baroque is more or less confined to the west towers and not so much integrated with the classical features. Nevertheless it has all the imposing grandeur of baroque and was indeed well sited when it was originally built.

More splendidly sited than St. Paul's is Wren's Greenwich Hospital, standing majestically on a river bank and, like Melk, reflected in the river. If St. Paul's is a masterpiece of church architecture, then surely Greenwich is one of the finest achievements of a secular building in Europe.

EIGHTEENTH-CENTURY ENGLAND

This has landed us well into the eighteenth century, when Wilson was producing his superb landscapes and a host of other English artists were painting innumerable portraits: usually flattering after the manner of Van Dyck, occasionally more blunt as with Hogarth. Portraits were very much sought after as a status symbol by the new aristocracy, and when carried out by painters such as Gainsborough, Hogarth, and Reynolds, they were indeed usually great works of art.

PORTRAITS

Apart from a few native miniaturists of great ability, England relied on foreign artists for portraits until the eighteenth century. The German, Hans Holbein the Younger, was working in England in the sixteenth century, and in 1632 Charles I made the Flemish-born Anthony Van Dyck his Court Painter on the recommendation of Rubens who had already carried out the superb ceiling decorations in the Banqueting Hall at Whitehall.

VAN DYCK

The influence of a foreign artist of the prestige of Van Dyck, who had been both a pupil and assistant to Rubens, was tremendous and, during the nine years he worked at the Court until his death at the age of 42, he produced an incredible amount of work. He brought the vitalizing force of a great tradition of painting to England where painting had suffered an eclipse in favour of great literature, and he himself absorbed an English gentleness and delicacy far removed from the robustness of Flemish art. His portraits have not the power of Rubens but he certainly has aristocratic elegance. It was he who romanticized portrait-painting in England and imbued his characters with a glamour which is never overdone. He flattered his clients and often set them against a lovely park landscape with the cool, cloud-laden English sky and softly painted trees. The famous *Charles I on Horseback* in the National Gallery is a regally calm figure seated on a stately horse, against a background of noble trees and luminous sky which shows Van Dyck to be a remarkable landscape painter.

Since the Puritans frowned on the visual arts, except for conventional portraits, there was no great incentive for native painters to emerge; with the restoration of the monarchy foreigners were called in and worked for the Court well into the eighteenth century.

HOGARTH

It was not until the time of William Hogarth (1697–1764) that the flourishing school of English painting was established. Unlike Van Dyck, Hogarth would not stoop to flattery. His portraits, brilliant as they are, are not romanticized but very much down to earth, yet he has an unsurpassed freshness of vision and a reasonableness which befitted the 'Age of Reason'. His conversation pieces, which were a kind of parallel to the Dutch genre, were very popular with the English and they were available to a large number of people since he reproduced them by line-engravings. Almost everyone is familiar with his *Marriage à la Mode*, *Rake's Progress*, and *Harlot's Progress*.

REYNOLDS

Sir Joshua Reynolds (1723–92) is more impressive than attractive as a portrait painter, and although he was much influenced by the Italians he shows no great insight into the character of his sitters. He is important in both the history of English painting and in its appreciation not only because he was the first President of the Royal Academy, but also because of his *Discourses* which laid down principles of painting favouring the grand manner rather than Hogarth's direct approach.

GAINSBOROUGH

Thomas Gainsborough (1727–88) appeals to everyone with his light, glowing, sensitive touch, his delicate colour and his rendering of the charm of his sitters. He was forced to paint portraits in order to earn a living, but he preferred landscape-painting and his love of it can be seen in the sensitive handling of his portrait backgrounds.

WILLIAM BLAKE

William Blake (1757–1827) does not really fit into any group or period in English painting, but he was working during the eighteenth century. He rebelled against the 'Age of Reason' with his fanatical hatreds and his fantastic flights of imagination. Basically an engraver and draughtsman, he evolved an intensely personal way of handling paint, a kind of marriage of the definite line of engraving and the texture of oil paint. He was a mystic and a poet—a strange man who had visions and, with a vivid imagination, produced most original and dramatic renderings of his subjects, mainly from the Bible, from Dante and from his own poems.

The Wise and Foolish Virgins. *William Blake. Tate Gallery, London* (Plate 95*a*). Note the fluid rhythm of this interpretation. The five wise virgins seem to flow into the atmosphere and into each other as they sway and their loose robes swing from their limbs; the foolish virgins lament and wail, very much attached to the ground, but even so, their wild movements are dramatic. The landscape undulates behind them; the sky and the angel, in his amazing horizontal flight, emphasize these lines like a flowing river. In everything he depicted, Blake showed a fluid rhythmic line, a definite outline which was essential to the design and colour. Usually rather strange colours were sometimes added arbitrarily. He had a message to give in each of these illustrations, but it was direct and robust, not cloying or sentimental.

THE COUNTRY SCENE

Parallel with the demand for portraiture was a growing demand for landscapes and some of the painters who satisfied this demand carry us on into the nineteenth century, but nevertheless keep an eighteenth-century character. The landowner commissioned a painting of himself, then of his wife and family, his country house, his park. Then he wanted more-or-less topographical records of the surrounding countryside, perhaps with himself out riding, shooting or hunting. He often wanted a portrait of his horse, which George Stubbs (1724–1806) or Benjamin Marshall (1768–1835) could produce to his satisfaction and even create significant works of art in the process.

George Stubbs is certainly one of the greatest sporting painters and had an international reputation for his writings on the anatomy of the horse. So many painters of human animal 'portraits' are content to catch a likeness, to 'copy' nature, which is merely a record and has no value as a work of art. Stubbs was always concerned with making a picture, and his horses are not only anatomically observed but they are painted with sensitivity and conceived monumentally. He was not just a great English sporting painter, he was a genius.

It was in the eighteenth century also that wealthy people took artists with them on their travels to record the countries visited, and alongside all this professional activity they developed tremendous enthusiasm for amateur sketches and water-colour paintings which were, again, largely topographical.

George Morland (1763–1804) supplied an escape from the growing industrialization of the towns and the horrible conditions of the poor with his idealized farm and country-cottage scenes, with sentimental-looking pigs and ponies. Since there is considerable pleasure to be got from these rather cosy thatch and log-fire evocations, we may just as well get what we can from them and, in doing so, admire Morland's skill in composition, in the disposition of light and even in the laying on of paint. Admittedly this is not enough for any lasting satisfaction. Some astringency is needed; some inspiration and a new vision of the countryside would have more impact than this version of some comfortable world which never really existed.

POSSIBLE ESSAYS, DISCUSSION AND RESEARCH

1 Do you think that Watteau compares with the giants of other schools?

2 What are the values and defects of rococo?

3 What do you consider the essential of good portrait painting?

4 Explain the popularity of Frith's *Derby Day* and *The Railway Station.*

5 Compare Dutch and French landscape painting of the seventeenth century.

6 Does Richard Wilson rank above Claude and Brueghel as a landscape painter?

Suggested Further Reading

Bazin, Germain: *Baroque and Rococo.* Thames & Hudson: London, 1964.

Brookner, A.: *Watteau.* Paul Hamlyn: London, 1966.

Cammaerts, Emile: *Rubens, Painter and Diplomat.* Faber & Faber: London, 1932.

Gaunt, Williams: *British Painting.* Avalon: London, 1945.

Gaunt, William: *A Concise History of English Painting.* Thames & Hudson: London, 1964.

Grimschitz, Feuchtmuller, Mrazek: *Barok in Österreich.* Forum Vorlag, 1962.

Hegemann, Hans Werner: *Deutsches Rokoko.* Die Blauen Bucher: Stuttgart, 1956.

Higher, G.: *The Classical Tradition.* Oxford University Press, 1949.

Kitson, Michael: *The Age of Baroque.* Paul Hamlyn: London, 1966.

Lafuente-Ferrari, E.: *Velasquez.* Phaidon: London, 1943.

Lee-Milne, James: *Baroque in Italy.* Batsford: London, 1959.

Masson, Georgina: *Italian Villas and Palaces.* Thames & Hudson: London, 1966.

Rosenberg, J.: *Rembrandt.* Phaidon: London, 1964.

Summerson, J.: *Architecture in Britain,* 1530–1830. Penguin: London, 1963.

Chapter Thirteen

A PERIOD OF TRANSITION

In the main this chapter is devoted to the transition from Classicism to Romanticism and the dawn of Impressionism, but before I discuss these movements I should like to discuss two painters, both strong individualists, and both with some claim to be the first of the moderns.

EL GRECO

El Greco (1541–1614), like Blake in eighteenth-century England, stands apart in the history of art for, although he is classified as being of sixteenth-century Spain, naturally enough, since he was a foreigner, a Greek from Crete, which explains his name (real name Domenikos Theotocopoulos) he was not characteristically Spanish. His work has a Byzantine flavour, as well it might since he spent his early years painting ikons. Yet, in common with a number of others, he could be called 'the first modern painter' because of his daring distortion of the human figure, his direct use of colour-drawing (with full strokes of the brush rather than filling in an outline with colour) to express form, and his brilliant use of artificial light and moonlight.

An imaginative mystical painter, he does not seem to fit into any period, but rather to point the way to modern styles—especially to the art of Cézanne. We have seen his *Agony in the Garden* with all its exaltation of soaring lines and its tragedy stressed by sinister colour. What is astonishing is that in the sixteenth and early seventeenth centuries in Spain this very different approach was accepted and admired though, it must be admitted, with some reservations at times.

El Greco experimented with the juxtaposition of unusual acid-drop colours of green, pink, and yellow, and a new use of an infinite variety of greys, and he had a genius for conveying an unearthly radiance amidst the blackest depth of shadows.

GOYA

Just over 200 years ofter El Greco, the Spanish painter Francisco de Goya (1746–1828) was born. Like El Greco, Goya has been called 'the first of the moderns', but he has also been labelled 'the last of the Old Masters'. This may be because he himself said that he had modelled his work on Velasquez, Rembrandt, and Nature, the third of these being stressed by the fact that he influenced Manet and the

Impressionists. We may justifiably add Tiepolo to Goya's list of masters. Tiepolo, the last of the Venetian decorators, was working on the frescoes in the Royal Palace in Madrid during the 1760's and it was from him that Goya must have acquired his marvellous sense of design, his fresh, spontaneous approach and his genius for apparently mixing his colour with light.

Outside Spain, Goya is best known for his frank, character-searching portraits of famous personalities and for his two paintings of the *Maja Nude* and the *Maja Clothed*, which inspired Manet to paint his *Olympia*.

In Madrid you can see his lovely decorative 'cartoons' for tapestries for the Spanish royal families; these designs are, in fact, oil paintings on canvas.

The Wine Harvest. *Francisco de Goya. Prado, Madrid.* (Plate 93). I find this painting of the harvest the most delightful of the series entitled *The Four Seasons*. The four figures are knit together with the compactness and economy of space of Michelangelo, and yet they are rococo in their graceful, airy gestures, in the range of luminous yellows, pinks and greens and in the 'ballet dancer' impression they give. Note the setting of autumn sky, palely golden, to silhouette the woman's head with the basket of grapes. Her face is illuminated from below and this emphasizes the presence of light reflected from the saffron silk of the man's suit. Note, too, how the two peasants in the vineyard link these main figures with the landscape: one by turning away and drawing them into it, the other by turning towards them and bringing the landscape to meet them. There are miraculous passages of luminous paint in the pearly ground bestrewn with vine leaves, in the transparent purple and white grapes against the sky, in the child's pink sash and white ruff.

FROM CLASSICISM TO ROMANTICISM

Classicism, the adherence to established academic tradition and to rules which were supposed to ensure excellence of execution, was pre-eminent in early nineteenth-century France. This was the natural reaction of revolutionary France against the 'frivolity' of painters like Fragonard. Running parallel to it, and equally to be expected, was Romanticism with its passionate colourful approach.

DAVID AND DELACROIX

Jacques David (1748–1825) was a keen advocate of the new classicism (referred to as neo-classicism) and, later, so was Ingres (1780–1867). The outstanding romantics were Géricault (1791–1824), with his rearing horses and his dramatic *Raft of the Medusa*, and Eugène Delacroix (1798–1863). Delacroix painted in strong, bright colours and rejected the sober understated colours of neo-classicism and the controlled, rather pompous rendering of epic scenes. His was the enthusiastic, dashing approach which reinfused French painting with life.

It was in the Paris *Salon* of 1824 that Constable's *Hay Wain* was exhibited along with the works of other English landscape painters. On seeing this picture, Delacroix repainted his rendering of *The Massacre of Scio* since he was filled with admiration for Constable's fresh colour and his genius for complementing one colour with another to bring out its full value.

From this time onward, French art proceeded from 'movement' to 'movement' and from 'ism' to 'ism'.

In the mid-nineteenth century the landscape painters who congregated near Barbizon in the Forest of Fontainebleu benefited from romanticism to the extent of a greater freedom of handling and a fuller use of colour. The Barbizon school also developed the practice of working in the open air and its members concentrated on an unromanticized and realistic approach to their interpretation of everyday life. In fact they had, in theory, the same artistic equipment and potentialities as the Dutch, but they did not produce the same serene light-flooded statements. Neither Millet, of *Angelus* fame, nor Théodore Rousseau who painted 'portraits' of trees, nor Diaz in his forest glades, attained the Dutch feeling for space and warmth and colour.

COROT

Corot (1796–1875) too, settled in Barbizon in his later years. He is out of favour today for his rather hazy, poetic style, but his genius for laying-on pearly-grey and golden paint is evident even in those paintings which do not represent his best work. His early paintings of the South of France and of the countryside around Rome are luminous and full of atmosphere, although they are decisively stated; they certainly give him a place among the great landscape painters.

THE GREAT AGE OF ENGLISH LANDSCAPE

John Constable (1776–1837) who, as we have seen, influenced French art in the early nineteenth century, and William Turner (1775–1851) were the giants of English landscape painting.

TURNER AND CONSTABLE

Each was entirely different in his approach, though they both produced something which was 'modern' in the sense that it broke right away from the Italian tradition and sought to give an open-air atmosphere, if not actually to paint finished works from nature.

Turner was a city man, brought up in London, adventurous, poetic, and full of imagination. He translated the countryside into a radiant epic scene. He studied light and expressed it more impressively than ever the Impressionists did. He may have painted the

English countryside, but, once on his canvas it was something very much more. His search for the best way to portray light evolved into a genius for creating it in great chasms and storms: light in unbelievable splendour and storms in chaotic frenzy. He could do this even in the gentle medium of water-colour. The Impressionists are midgets beside him, just as the genre and portrait painters of the Dutch school are midgets beside Rembrandt.

You may be overwhelmed by the size and number of the Turners on display in London; you may feel dismayed by the enormous output of his water-colours and sketches, but he is a painter whose work you can go on exploring for the rest of your life and in which you will find something new. Oddly enough, to begin with he was an apparently pedestrian painter of topographical views, and his contemporary Thomas Girtin (1775–1802) often painted a water-colour which was more accomplished; but Girtin died at the age of 27 and critics never stop saying that he might have outstripped Turner had he lived. No one can tell, but I do not believe that Girtin's work had such great potentialities in its limited scale of conception and colour. Admittedly Turner could produce some rather garish paintings, but nature itself can be garish, and with his tremendous output this was inevitable. Who else has ever produced such paintings of light veiling invisible but solid structure beneath it? These are not facile abstracts, neither are his earlier landscapes such as *Crossing the Brook* just repetitions of the work of classical painters like Claude.

Crossing the Brook. *J. M. W. Turner. Tate Gallery, London* (Plate 96). There is nothing revolutionary about this painting, carried out at the height of Turner's career. He is still working in a traditional manner and in a style acclaimed by the Academicians. What first strikes us about this landscape is its perfect composition, its calm, classical atmosphere, almost as though Claude had painted a real stretch of the Italian countryside instead of a fairyland world of his own. Then, almost immediately, we can feel the powerful structure of the painting, the architectural building up of shapes and the decisive, beautifully stated outline of the two trees against the sky. At a guess, this might be northern Italy. It is, in fact, Devonshire, but no landscape has looked less like England. Turner has seen this part of Devonshire as a romantic stretch of light-drenched countryside, a poetic land of infinite possibilities. It has Claude's light coming towards us from the horizon and picking out a curve of river, the top of a bridge and a white dress, but it has none of Claude's dreaminess and no vague statements or diffusion of interest. This is landscape translated into a great work of art. This capacity for revealing the basic structure of nature is evident even in Turner's later works, when light was the 'principal person'.

Snowstorm: Steamboat off Harbour's Mouth. *J. M. W. Turner.*

Tate Gallery, London (Plate 97). This study of the effect of the violent changes in a storm holds more immediate excitement than *Crossing the Brook* and it is more in line with modern taste, but no Impressionist ever charged a painting with such dramatic force; no Impressionist arranged wild swirls of light and cloud in this satisfying ordered way. Note the astonishing rhythm of the troughs and crests of the waves and how they are 'all of a piece' with the clouds, so that the dark ship is suspended in the elements. See the brilliant brushwork which tosses up the peak of water in the right-hand corner and the miracle of light swept around the ship and caught and held by the wind, the rain, and the spray. But look at the *bones* underneath it all and you will understand why Turner had to paint in the manner of *Crossing the Brook* before he could do this.

You have only to glance at a painting by Constable to realize that he was an entirely different character. Constable has more appeal than Turner for a great many people because his direct love of the English countryside even included all its vagaries of weather. It inspired Turner to great heights of poetic feeling and he idealized and re-created it in different terms. Constable could not imagine anything beyond the miracle of the English countryside as he saw it in all its reality: cloud, trees heavy with rain, even in moments of sunshine, and of course all the radiance of hot summer days. More particularly he revelled in the amber light of East Anglia. I do not mean that his interpretation is commonplace, far from it. To me, some of his paintings have all, and more, of the evocative delight of the Impressionists; in particular I admire his superb small sketches in which he shows his genius for catching effects of light and atmosphere and the constantly changing weather.

I could take Constable's painting of *The Valley Farm*, in the Tate Gallery, and compare it with Turner's *Crossing the Brook* as it is roughly the same composition in reverse and deals with the same subject—a stretch of English river scenery. But I am not discussing it here because in doing so I could destroy what is a lovely landscape yet, being so utterly different in conception and result, it does not stand up to comparison with the much greater work. It would be like comparing a good novel with a Shakespeare play. Constable does not attempt here to attain the spaciousness, the selection, the nobility of Turner, and the comparison would make *The Valley Farm* seem a little closed-in, a little over-burdened with foliage and clouds.

Instead, let us consider one of Constable's interpretations of atmospheric conditions over a sweep of open countryside.

Hampstead Heath, Branch Hill Pond. *John Constable, Victoria and Albert Museum, London* (Plate 98). What a wonderful, spontaneous rendering of English countryside! It is so natural and so much as we think we see open heathland, that at first sight it might seem deceptively uncreative, were it not for the impact of the atmosphere. The camera cannot record this. We can *feel* its presence when we are on the spot, but we cannot necessarily *see* it, let alone recreate it. This *is* Hampstead Heath, but it is also a personification in paint of the whole of English weather, with all its vagaries and its subtle enchantment, its pale radiance spread over damp earth. Note, too, the *apparent* lack of composition: the artist seems to be depicting the scene just as he found it; then see how deceptive this is. See the perfect placing of the two poplars on the left and the importance given them by the dark cloud above; this is balanced by the skilfully handled hillock with the interest of the white horse against a dark, the light catching the cart and, above all, the small touches of red in the harness, repeated in a small figure across the pond and, muted in the cattle by the poplar. Without these touches of red, the intensity and variety would go out of the harmony of greens and blues and warm ochres.

What genius to place the tiny snatches of light in the middle distance which carry the eye easily to the horizon! Who else but Constable has ever seen Hampstead Heath quite like this?

Contemporary with these great masters of English landscape painting were the artists who, as already mentioned, made topographical records of English towns and villages, of English parks and the English countryside, in oil and water-colour. Their work has a poetic beauty, a wonderful freshness and spontaneity. Some of these artists developed the technique of water-colour, which the English handled so poetically and so expertly. Obviously water-colour had enormous advantages over oils when painters accompanied the wealthy on their travels, or when they were asked to make paintings of a town or a district on the spot. The very portability of water-colours and the relative speed of handling made this possible. Also, the climate in England is reasonably good for carrying out water-colours in the open air, for, in normal summer weather, they neither dry too quickly nor too slowly, whereas in the Mediterranean heat they dry so quickly that it is very difficult to avoid hard edges or to get the delicate transparent effect so vital to true water-colours. Even so, the water-colour painter who has gained his experience in England often has such a command over his medium that he can overcome these difficulties. Many painters take the easy way out by using gouache: an opaque version of water-colours, which, since white is added, allows of some overpainting or alteration. True water-colour necessitates clear vision, a sure touch and complete confidence if it is to be successful.

THE NORWICH SCHOOL

John Crome (1768–1821), though mainly an oil painter, was the founder of the flourishing school of Norwich, many of whose members painted principally in water-colour. Some of the foremost landscape painters were born in Norwich or worked there. A particularly comprehensive collection of their paintings is on show at the Norwich Castle Museum, and innumerable examples can be seen in public galleries all over the United Kingdom.

Yarmouth Jetty. *John Crome. Norwich Castle Museum* (Plate 99). John Crome, sometimes called 'Old Crome', was the founder of the Norwich Society of Artists in 1803 and exhibited there. He was very much influenced by Dutch painting, but he also had something of Wilson's sense of composition. He combines certain characteristics of these styles with a native or even an East-Anglian freshness. *Yarmouth Jetty* 'smells' of salt and the fresh winds and great broad skies of Yarmouth; this is especially true of the wonderful sky where the clouds seem to be moving and regrouping in the sea air. The figures are a little lacking in structure, but in some inexplicable way, the sea and the sky and the sails have this force.

John Sell Cotman (1782–1842) has a very marked style which does not really fit in with the members of the Norwich school. Although he was born in Norwich, he worked largely in London and his paintings have a most decorative, almost oriental simplicity, with clearly defined flat washes of colour. He was obviously much influenced by Japanese prints.

Durham Castle. *John Sell Cotman. Norwich Castle Museum* (Plate 100). This completely satisfying, almost noble, water-colour has the clarity and grasp of basic patterns of a Japanese print, although it relies for sculpturesque aspect on the stressing of the third dimension. Even so, the planes in shadow constitute other patterns of flat washes of colour. Turn and twist this painting in any direction and it is always satisfactory as a design. Cotman's genius for selection and his grasp of fundamental structure and elimination of all but the essentials raise his water-colours from lyrics to epics. Anyone who has seen Durham Cathedral in its setting can feel its splendour dramatically enhanced by this powerful interpretation of it, accentuated by the miraculous play of light on the water. Could any painter have produced it at that time unless he had seen and been impressed by a Japanese print?

Since we are dealing with nineteenth-century painters in England it seems apposite to mention some artists who favoured the country scene but used it to illustrate a definite theme. Here we should look at one painting of this period which must be dubbed 'academic' in the extreme for its slick technique and acceptance of conventional standards.

Derby Day. *William Powell Frith* (1819–1909). *National Gallery, London* (Plate 90). Anecdotal this painting may be and depicting minor incidents in the lives of a whole cavalcade of people, but the overall conception is grand; there is unity in the general design and interest flows evenly over the composition. There is a Dutch brilliance in the colour and a great deal of skill in rendering the drama of everyday incidents, and it does give a homogeneous picture of a nineteenth-century race crowd. At worst it is an interesting record, at best a lively, well-knit scene with some sensitively painted passages and many that are dexterously handled.

THE PRE-RAPHAELITES

It was in the middle of the nineteenth century that the pre-Raphaelite Brotherhood was founded, but we have already looked at some of the paintings produced by members of this group. They did at least express some ideas and they did take a stand against what they considered to be slavish dependence on the ideals of the great painters of the Renaissance. Instead, they drew inspiration from the ideals of the Middle Ages, but they were too much involved with minute detail and too little in simplifying a theme. They were too much interested in the 'simple life'. A kind of autumnal melancholy pervades their landscapes and a nauseating innocence emanates from most of the women. Nevertheless, some of these paintings do give considerable pleasure, mainly because of the appeal of Victoriana, not because they are great works of art in themselves. Millais, Holman Hunt, and Rossetti were the founders of the Brotherhood. Later Millais became President of the Royal Academy and was knighted, whereas Rossetti worked with Morris and Burne-Jones, and Holman Hunt concentrated on religious paintings.

TREATMENT OF LANDSCAPE AT DIFFERENT TIMES COMPARED

Now that we have considered a number of paintings of the countryside, I am choosing some from different periods and giving my opinion of them.

Let us look back, first of all, to the fifth-century mosaic of *The Good Shepherd* (Plate 28). Here the landscape background serves as something for the sheep to stand on and against, and the rocks make a throne for Christ and terraces so that the whole of each sheep can be seen. The flowers and plants and the shrubs are treated decoratively but there is a slight feeling of recession.

We have seen how Gentile da Fabriano used a flower-bespangled background in his *Adoration of the Magi*, decorating the skyline with castles and painting the animals with exquisite care (Plate 46), but let us now see how Benozzo Gozzoli (1420–98) deals with the same subject nearly forty years later in Florence.

The Journey of the Magi (detail). *Benozzo Gozzoli. Medici Chapel, Riccardi Palace, Florence* (Plate 101). Gozzoli has used members of the Medici family as the Kings and painted them round the walls in a splendid procession; the horses' trappings, the pages' clothes and the Kings' magnificent apparel give us a detailed record of a procession in fifteenth-century Florence. The painting is fascinating rather than a great work of art, although some of the details are a delight. The landscape background is overcrowded like a botanical garden and the rocks are carved out in an irritating series of holes like a Gruyère cheese. The whole painting, winding steeply up the rocks, is so complicated with animals and trees and plants as to have no rhythm, no satisfying progression, no real coherence. The young Lorenzo on his horse is a charming portrait, but the other figures are commonplace. However much we may criticize this as a work of art, there are very few people who do not feel compelled to seek out some of the individual details or to be intrigued by the amazing amount of information that is given.

Look again at Brueghel's *Fall of Icarus* (Plate 78) which, were it not for the minute figure, would be a country scene rather than a landscape background, and see how much more there is here to enjoy and experience; how much more real observation and atmosphere and what a far more satisfying interpretation of nature it is.

In seventeenth-century France, Claude still clings to a story with rather ridiculous figures.

Italian Landscape. *Claude Gellée. Birmingham Art Gallery* (Plate 102). The figures here are rather unfortunate and do nothing to help the composition, indeed they are distracting. So too, are the cattle which look like blown-up hides. Above this weak foreground is a wonderful middle and far distance: an idyllic luminous world of complete tranquillity, where two trees are so perfectly placed that it is impossible to imagine them a fraction of an inch removed.

We have seen how in seventeenth-century Holland painters were no longer shy of making landscape the whole theme.

An Extensive Landscape. *Philipe Koninck* (1609–56). *Southampton Art Gallery* (Plate 103). Koninck shows us a countryside of wide cloud-swept sky, its billowing masses contrasting with the firm horizontals of the vast flat land which stretches for miles, caught by gleams of sunshine, then darkened by deep shadow. The whole panoramic view is carefully constructed so that the eye sweeps gently forward from the foreground to the horizon.

Now that many of Koninck's pictures have been cleaned, we can see that they are harmonies of green and blue and gold. Those which still retain their old varnish are glowing with amber light contrasted with deep browns and reds: not by any means unpleasing, but hardly what the painter intended.

Landscape. *Chang Jo-ch'êng. Ch'ien-lung period* (1736–95) *of Ching Dynasty, China. Gulbenkian Collection, Durham* (Plate 104). This painting in colours on a silk hanging scroll is a kind of composite landscape incorporating essential and permanent features of nature. It is not a particular place at a definite date. Clouds, trees,

118. The Windmill.
Vincent Van Gogh.
Glasgow Art Gallery and Museum.

119. The Customs House.
Henri Rousseau.
Courtauld Institute Galleries, London.

120. *Top*. **Ferme ton Armoire. Jean Lurçat.**
Southampton Art Gallery. Rights Reserved A.D.A.G.P., Paris.

122. *Left*. **The Inattentive Reader. Henri Matisse.**
The Tate Gallery, London. © by S.P.A.D.E.M., Paris.

121. Church at Longpont. Maurice Utrillo. Southampton Art Gallery.
Southampton Art Gallery. © by S.P.A.D.E.M., Paris.

127. *Top.* **Le Pont Neuf, La Nuit. Albert Marquet. Musée de L'Art Moderne, Paris.**
Archives Photographiques—Paris.

128. *Left.* **They're Biting. Paul Klee.**
The Tate Gallery, London.
© by S.P.A.D.E.M., Paris.

130. Two Forms. Ben Nicholson.
Southampton Art Gallery.

125. *Top*. **Painting 1952.**
Jackson Pollock.
The Tate Gallery, London.

126. Still Life with Fish.
Georges Braque.
The Tate Gallery, London.
Rights Reserved A.D.A.G.P., Paris.

123. The Apprentice. Georges Rouault. Musée National de l'Art Moderne, Paris.
Archives Photographiques—Paris.

124. Self Portrait with Seven Fingers. Marc Chagall.
Stedelijk Museum, Amsterdam. Rights Reserved A.D.A.G.P., Paris

131. Whaam!
Roy Lichtenstein.
The Tate Gallery, London.

129. An Island. L. S. Lowry.
Manchester City Art Galleries.

124a. Battle.
Wassily Kandinsky.
The Tate Gallery, London.
Rights Reserved A.D.A.G.P., Paris.

132. Supernovae. V. Vasarely.
The Tate Gallery, London.

B. (*Top*). **Stained glass at Viktring, Austria.**
Landesfremdenverkehrsamt Klagenfurt.

F. Tympanum at Moissac.
Photo Boudot-Lamotte. French National Tourist Office.

C. (*Left*). **Van der Weyden.**
Triptych, Beaune.
St. Michael
French National Tourist Office.

D. (*Top*). **Georges Seurat.**
Ville d'Avray.
Maisons Blanches,
Walker Art Gallery, Liverpool.

E.(*Right*). **Tiger. Mu Ch'i.**
Reproduced by courtesy of the Trustees of the British Museum.

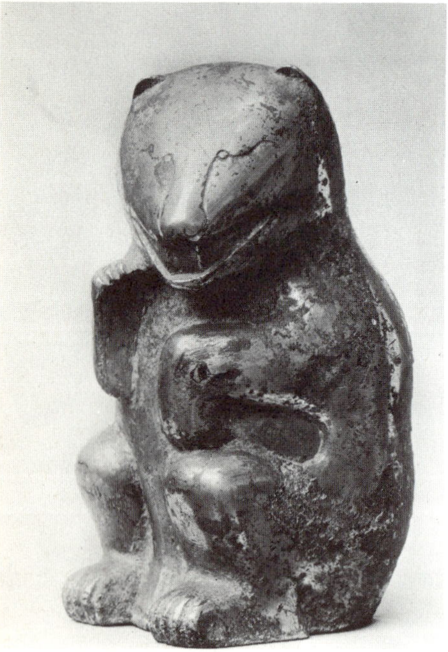

G. *Left*. **Chinese Han dynasty. Gilt Bronze Bear.**
Reproduced by courtesy of the Trustees of the British Museum.

I. *Right*. **Young Man (Greek). Statue of a**
Reproduced by courtesy of the Trustees of the British Museum.

J. (*Top*). **William Blake. Nebuchadnezzar.**
The Tate Gallery, London.

V. Henry Moore
Seated Woman.
By courtesy of the Laing Art Gallery, Newcastle upon Tyne.

H. Two Cheetahs (Lombard).
Reproduced by courtesy of the Trustees of the British Museum.

Hell. Hieronymos Bosch. N
Museo del Prado, Madrid.

Madonna of the Rose Garden. Stefano da Zevio. Verona. (*Top right*) M.
Mansell Collection.

The Three Dancers. Picasso. Q.
The Tate Gallery, London.

Work. Ford Madox Brown.
Manchester City Art Galleries.

Harvesters. Keith Vaughan.
Reproduced by permission of the Birmingham Museum and Art Gallery.

I. Hitchens. R
Forest Edge No. 2.
The Tate Gallery, London.

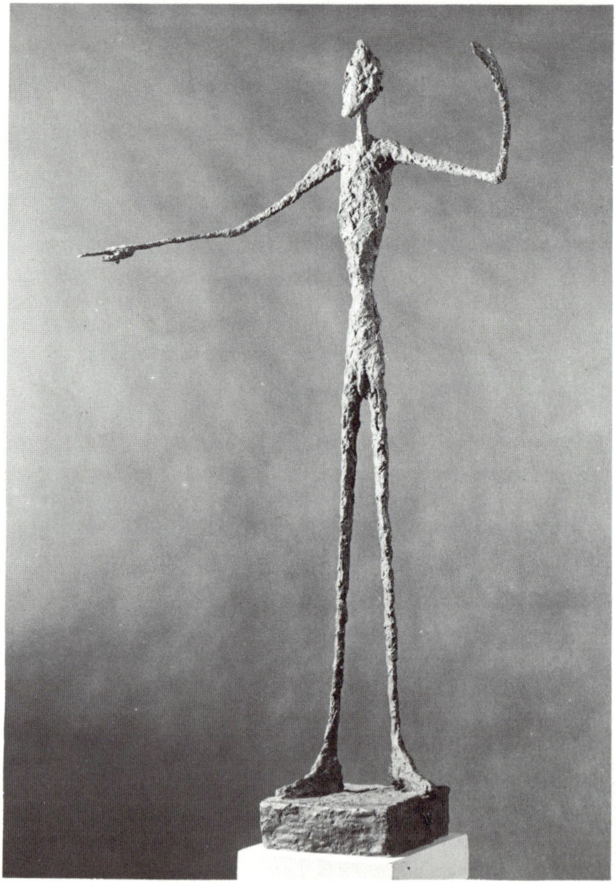

A. Giacometti. T.
Man Pointing.
The Tate Gallery, London.

Battle. Albrecht Altdorfer. O
Pinakothek, Munich.

The Washerwoman.
Daumier. The Louvre. P
Archives Photographiques—Paris.

Jade Bodhisattva, Ming. U
The property of the Gulbenkian Museum of Oriental Art, University of Durham, Great Britain.

La Ville Pétrifiée.
Max Ernst. S
Manchester City Art Galleries.
© by S.P.A.D.E.M., Paris.

torrents, rivers, and flowers are decoratively arranged in a long strip which can be looked at progressively. There is no architecturally conceived composition within a framework intended to make a dramatic impact immediately. Instead there is a completely satisfying rhythmic pattern and every part of the picture is complete in itself, the space being as important as the details.

In Chinese painting much is left to the imagination of the beholder. There is no foreground as such, there is no middle distance and no horizon; instead there is infinity. The land, the sky, the clouds, the water, and the mountains are one. They are not seen in perspective by the human being standing at the foreground. The universe is spread out for you to savour in all its infinite variety, and man—in this case two minute creatures in a junk—is an infinitesimal part of it and at the mercy of the elements.

Norfolk Wherries. *Peter de Wint* (1784–1849). *Southampton Art Gallery* (Plate 105). In this water-colour, painted about half a century later, Peter de Wint, a contemporary of Turner, also spreads the countryside before us and conveys spaciousness, but not infinity. This is a Norfolk waterway at one particular spot at a definite time of day and season of the year. Nevertheless it has been influenced by the art of the Orient, more particularly by Japanese woodcuts, just as Cotman's water-colours were. There is a breadth of vision, a simplification of mass and a handling of the difficult medium of water-colour as skilful and sure as the Chinese handling of ink. This painting of Norfolk makes its own timeless appeal and, like the Chinese landscape, it suggests that the broad sky and flat expanse continue beyond the painting. Where it is immediately recognizable as a Western work of art is in its topographical nature and its stressing of the third dimension.

English Autumn Afternoon. *Ford Madox Brown* (1821–93). *Birmingham Art Gallery* (Plate 106). Although Ford Madox Brown was never a member of the pre-Raphaelite Brotherhood, their profound influence on him is obvious from this picture. There is a certain appeal in this painter's choice of a natural, simple subject, with no drama, no focal point of epic interest. Instead he stressed rather obviously the gentle cooing doves mating on the dovecote, and the conventional Victorian lovers with a sentimental-looking woolly dog on guard. His real interest seems to have been in rendering in detail every known European tree and shrub, overcharged with autumn foliage. There are some patches of beauty in this picture: the grouped trees, left centre, are monumentally stated and, to the left again, the single poplar, wispy at the top, is gently stirring.

This is a panoramic view and our reason tells us that the horizon is far away since it is painted according to the rules of linear and aerial perspective, but we do not *feel* the distance. We are stifled and crowded in with trees, condensed into an airless region, and there is none of the unifying grandeur which the gold and red and brown of autumn imparts to any sketch of the country. You may well say that Altdorfer's *St. George* (Plate 75) crowds us into a wood, that is what the artist meant us to feel. His *is* a painting of a dense forest and he achieves his object. Ford Madox Brown gives us only the superficials, apart from his successful rendering of the mellow glow of autumn in the colour.

TREATMENT OF ANIMALS COMPARED

We have found that landscape has an important part to play in a large proportion of paintings of all kinds and at the same time we have seen that animals and birds have also been rendered with sympathy and a keen sense of observation. If we confine our period to historic times this is evident in all the donkeys in the various interpretations of the *Flight into Egypt* that we have described, and in the horses and the ox and the ass in the Magi scenes. We have also found that, in the eighteenth century, animals, and more particularly horses, could constitute the subject of a picture. They form an important part of the composition in Daumier's *Don Quixote*.

Don Quixote and Sancho Panza. *Honoré Daumier* (1808–79). *Courtauld Institute, London* (Plate 107). There has been no space to discuss Daumier's contribution to nineteenth-century French painting, but he has such a great appeal to me that I cannot leave him out. He has the power to express in paint, *continuous* movement more convincingly than anyone before Matisse, who with his rhythmic outline explored possibilities for the moderns. Daumier was obliged at that time to use familiar forms and so had less scope for experiment. Don Quixote *is* arrogantly tensing his muscles, his horse *is* cocking an ear forward; it *is* proceeding with an awkward gait. Sancho Panza *is* urging his plodding beast. All four are in *continuous* action. This you will find in every painting or drawing by Daumier. In sculpture, Donatello's figures have this quality: his *David is* relaxing a leg and taking the weight; he is *moving*, not caught in a completed movement. Of necessity many free-standing sculptured figures are in repose, but that does not mean that they are devoid of life.

EQUESTRIAN STATUES

Let us look at some equestrian sculpture from different periods.

Mounted Warrior. *Greek. About* 550 B.C. *British Museum, London* (Plate 108). This bronze statue is only about a foot high, but what astonishing vigour is conveyed with strict economy of detail. How proudly the horse steps forward and how firmly the rider is seated! The movement of the legs is not correct, but the sense of action is.

Note with what genius the sculptor has conventionalized the mane and forelock to add to the horse's proud bearing and how the merest incision conveys the jawbone and a single line slims the head.

We have already considered the Roman equestrian statue of *Marcus Aurelius*, so now let us see what the Chinese could do with a horse and rider in the golden years of the T'ang Dynasty.

Polo Player. *Earthenware. T'ang Dynasty* (618–906). *Gulbenkian Collection, Durham* (Plate 109). There is such perfection in this interpretation of the combined action of horse and rider that any attempt at description is pretentious. Suffice it to say that more than 1,000 years ago a Chinese sculptor could model a horse in clay in all its nobility and all its power, and could convey controlled, determined actions. This is not just a model of a polo player on a horse: the figure is part of the horse in the marvellously co-ordinated movement. It is a 'horse-and-rider'. For me, there is all the wisdom and all the culture of a great civilization in this small earthenware figurine.

Compared with Chinese genius a very charming and skilful German carving may seem an anticlimax.

Christ riding upon an Ass. *South German, late fifteenth century. Victoria and Albert Museum, London* (Plate 110). This composition in painted limewood was made for use in Palm Sunday processions and has great charm by virtue of its simple statement. There is some incongruity in the rather naïve, nervous donkey with the huge ears and the figure of Christ where the carver has become absorbed in his skill in handling wood. I find the modelling of the knee through the drapery an overstatement, and the anatomical rendering of the feet is too harsh. On the other hand there is a majesty in the simple treatment of Christ's body and head. Forget all that I have said and look again. This time the impact could be of a stupid but, lovable, toy-like donkey, overawed by the majesty of its rider.

Now look at Verrochio's sophisticated, completely confident handling of the statue of Colleone, the proud, successful general on a splendid horse (Plate 54). See how admirably this conveys all that that the sculptor was commissioned to do, and then reflect how the German carving also achieves what the artist set out to do.

POSSIBLE ESSAYS, DISCUSSION AND RESEARCH

1 How far was Goya an innovator?

2 Do you think that water-colour give a better 'fleeting' impression of the countryside than oils?

3 Compare one of Cotman's water-colours with a Japanese print.

4 Compare Constable and Turner.

5 Find three other equestrian statues and assess their value.

Suggested Further Reading

Binyon, Laurence: *English Water Colour Painters*. A & C. Black: London, 1962.

Boase, T. S. R.: *The Oxford History of English Art. Vol. X*, *English Art*, 1800–70. Clarendon Press: Oxford, 1959.

Brion, Marcel: *The Art of the Romantic Era*. Thames & Hudson: London, 1966.

de Montmorency, Miles F.: *A Short History of Painting in England*. Dent: London, 1933.

Finberg, A. J.: *The Life of J. M. W. Turner*. Clarendon Press: Oxford, 1961.

Gaunt, William: *The Pre-Raphaelite Tragedy*. Cape: London, 1946.

Leslie, C. R.: *Memoirs of the Life of John Constable*. Phaidon: London, 1969.

Ruskin, John: *Modern Painters*. (Various editions.)

Wilenski, R. H.: *English Painting*. Faber & Faber: London, 1933.

Chapter Fourteen

IMPRESSIONISM

Despite the furore when Impressionist painting first appeared in the second half of the nineteenth century, there were a few sympathetic critics and, gradually, patrons materialized. The men and women painters belonging to this group are now accepted as the 'Old Masters of Modern Art', and this century has been completely conquered by them, not only for their intrinsic appeal, but for their ever-increasing commercial value.

MANET AND THE SALON

Edouard Manet (1832–83), who was not an Impressionist, usually figures in books about Impressionism because he was an innovator. He abandoned the traditional slow, meticulous building-up of a picture from monochrome to full colour with carefully graduated tones. He set brilliant light against deep shadows, making his use of black of great importance. He reduced half-tones to the minimum and painted his own direct vision of a subject, making each stroke of the brush put on the exact colour or tone he wanted, without feeling his way through the building-up of layers. His palette and his way of painting were very much influenced by the Spanish, particularly Velasquez and Goya, and he also admired the direct painting of Frans Hals.

Manet was certainly associated with the Impressionists, and for a while he painted in their lighter style, abandoning the use of black for lighter, clearer colour, but he did not exhibit with the group.

Musique aux Tuileries. *Manet. National Gallery, London* (Plate 111). This picture, though it shows touches of Manet's genius in the quality of painting, is more an interesting record of the time than an inspired production. It recalls the years of the Second Empire when society flocked to listen to music among the trees in the palace gardens. It shows us also portraits of the immaculate Théophile Gautier and of Baudelaire as well as of Manet himself. As a painting it is crowded and airless, and the bare trunk of the tree in the centre divides the composition in two, even though this is modified by the charming touch of the two children playing at its base. It does, however, give us the atmosphere of fashionable Parisiens gathered together in the gardens which, even in our own time, are a reflection of contemporary life. Here is the elegant Paris with its well-dressed, gracious people in a setting of shaded walks and flowers: the Paris that was shocked by the extraordinary ideas of a handful of young men at the beginning of their careers.

Edouard Manet belonged to this Paris in so far as his social life and his family were concerned, but, as we have already seen, he was not in sympathy with its narrow conception of art; he wanted to invest painting with a new vitality, awakening it from the lethargy into which it had fallen during the first half of the century.

Until 1863, when Manet's painting *Le Déjeuner sur l'Herbe* caused so much comment, those of his paintings which had been shown to the public had not excited any great hostility. When this picture, refused by the official Salon, was shown in the *Salon des Réfusés* the critics were filled with indignation and the public was unable to accept it as a serious work of art.

In the light of our more catholic twentieth-century taste, it is difficult to understand quite why this painting met with such violent criticism.

Déjeuner sur l'Herbe (sketch for painting in Louvre). *Courtauld Institute*, *London* (Plate 111*a*). To our eyes, used to all kinds of exaggerated experiments in the art, even the sketch is simply a picture composed on traditional lines, with figures obviously painted from life in the studio, and placed in a landscape setting. These people are unaffected by the foliage above them, which would surely be casting flickering shadows over their bodies, and the nude girl is in full light although the ground on which she is seated is in deep shadow. The little figure in the middle distance is a delightful study of a woman bathing, but is so high in tone as to seem the same distance from us as the three main characters. It may well be that Manet wished to emphasize the figures as a group and to focus our attention on the people rather than on the landscape, a device used by him in several compositions.

Nevertheless the painting is lacking on architectural unity and is, in fact, a series of separate studies which make up a work of no very great appeal. There are lovely passages such as the glimpses of brilliant blue sky through the leaves, the light on the curved shoulders of the bather, the harmony of the greens of the water and the vivid still life of fruit and drapery in the foreground. Over the entire canvas the laying on of the paint is fresh and brilliant and each figure is fully alive and 'contemporary'. This was the real cause of the trouble. To choose an idyllic theme of bathing and feasting in a wood was a splendid idea, provided that it was suitably idealized, but to people it with ordinary men and women and to add a nude model was almost obscene. They were, in fact, hardly ordinary people, as one was Manet's brother, the other his future brother-in-law, and the nude was the enchanting Victorine Meurand, the painter's favourite model.

Manet, who was not endowed with a lively imagination, had taken a traditional theme, based his composition on a design used many times by the old masters (notably Giorgione and Raphael) and brought its whole interpretation up to date. The astonishing result is that the impact upon us of a rather 'old-fashioned' picture—a picture somewhat outdated. No painting of a very high order has this effect. *Le Déjeuner sur l'Herbe*, then, is not a great masterpiece, but it is of paramount importance in the history of art and to students of technique. To the general public of today, it must seem quite an ordinary painting, unlikely to cause violent criticism or great applause.

ASPECTS OF IMPRESSIONISM

Impressionism has come to mean rather sketchy 'unfinished' painting of landscape, still life, portrait and genre, carried out by artists working in the last quarter of the nineteenth century in a style which revolted against the conventional manner of building up in the studio and finishing according to academic traditions. The true Impressionists attempted to portray the play of light on objects and even made light the 'principal person in the picture'. They intensified colour by using pure pigments in juxtaposition so that the eye of the beholder merged them and created new ones, rather than mixing colours on the palette and thus losing some of their brilliance. They even saw colour in the shadows. Clear outlines or even contours were lost in an effect of trembling light, and one group, known as neo-Impressionists, developed the use of primary colours to the extreme limits of using spots or points of colour (for instance, their tiny dots of red and blue, seen at a distance, give the effect of violet). This group is also referred to as the Pointillists.

SEURAT AND POINTILLISM

Georges Seurat (1859–91) was the leader of neo-Impressionism; his early work consisted principally of drawing, working out on rough-grained paper the masses of shadow and the light planes. He used no outline, but composed entirely in mass, perfectly assessing the value of contrasts. The result was completely satisfying, with no hint of the blur which might so easily have weakened his drawing. His forms pulse with life, and glowing shapes emerge from a strangely impressive world of shadows. His experience and skill as a draughtsman gave added power to his paintings.

The Bathers. *Seurat. National Gallery, London* (Plate 112). This picture of the banks of the Seine at Asnières was painted in 1883–4, and was the result of much intensive study. It is not a stiff or formalized picture, and although mounted gives the impression of being something conceived almost spontaneously. The painting as a whole has complete architectural unity even though Seurat has not used a uniform technique throughout. Where he found it appropriate to use large sweeping brush strokes he has done so, and where a more meticulous treatment would give the desired effect, he has employed it. The painter has achieved an astonishing feeling of a hot day: the heat haze rising over the river, the figures all rendered more or less inert in the sun; they all gaze ahead in a kind of trance, save the one little figure standing in the water with his back to us. This small boy holds our attention well within the framework of the composition, and if he were not there the balance would be upset.

These statuesque bathers emanate light. They are not only bathed in it, they radiate it from their bodies. The sailing boat with its decisive white triangle cut clean against the dark trees arrests our attention before it wanders off out of the picture. Even the little dog in the foreground turns his head to stare into the distance—towards the country. Seurat found his new theories about painting entirely absorbing, and he worked all day and often right through the night to perfect some detail of composition. Like Van Gogh, he worked with great intensity.

Monet, Renoir, Sisley, and Pissarro were all members of the group though they were also involved in its various ramifications and even experimented with the later movements of neo-Impressionism. Degas exhibited with them, but he loathed painting in the open air and was not interested in landscape as such. Degas and, later, Toulouse-Lautrec were intensely interested in drawing, and were superb draughtsmen seeking out every type of person from the circus, the theatre, the brothels, the cafés, and the street. They were absorbed in catching the passing moment, never composing their subjects into a 'picturesque' group but capturing them in the act of stepping into or out of a bath, practising for the ballet, sodden with absinthe in a café, asleep in bed.

MONET

Road under Snow at Honfleur. *Claude Monet* (1840–1926). *Louvre, Paris* (Plate 113). This is a painting of the road to the Saint Siméon farm where Monet and his friends used to take their meals when they were little more than students. Along the snow-covered road a horse and cart are moving into the distance where dark trees, their branches heavily laden, are patterned against the sky—a grey-green sky warmed by the faintest orange glow which relieves the icy grip of the wintry scene.

It was at Honfleur, too, that Monet caught the brilliantly sunny effect of snow in *The Magpie*. This is a painting of a bird sitting on a rickety gate in a hedge, which throws decorative shadows over the snowy field. Trees, with their dark branches silhouetted against the sky, are heavy with snow, and half veil the farmhouse and distant fields. In this second painting, perhaps more than in any other, Monet conveys his delight in the snow, in the contrast of the biting frost and the flooding sunlight which turns the fields into a carpet of glistening ice.

DEGAS

La La at the Cirque Fernando. *Edgar Degas* (1834–1917), *National Gallery, London* (Plate 114). Degas' genius for suspended movement is apparent in this painting. He has solved a very difficult problem of composition, for he gives the effect of the set as it would appear to an audience looking up to the point from which the acrobat hangs by her teeth from a cord. He manages to do this without giving us a crick in the neck or lessening our suspense and our admiration of her perfect balance. The lovely subdued pale gold, dusky red and brown, with its cooling touches of grey, are a perfect foil for the theatrical, shining silk of her pale-violet costume. All this adds to the dramatic effect of the curious little figure suspended above our heads. Degas somehow manages to convey the feeling that she is perfectly in control of the moment, with a tenseness shown principally by the crossing of the ankles which keeps up our excitement in this critical moment of her act.

With Degas we see 'snapshot' composition for the first time in art. He dispenses with the conventional arrangement of figures and objects to form a complete scene, and instead often gives us fragments of figures chopped off by the edge of the canvas. We can now have actual happening recorded as in *Absinthe* in the Louvre, where the woman 'happens' to be centrally placed, but her companion's toe, his elbow, and part of his pipe are out of the picture; in the foreground we have the sharp corner of a table. Similarly *La La at the Cirque Fernando* is not conventionally 'composed'.

In the right hands this style of composition has architectural unity and is, of course, carefully planned with exactly the right amount of stressing to make a dramatic impact.

RENOIR

Auguste Renoir (1841–1919) painted pretty girls, pretty gardens, and pretty flowers. Sometimes his voluptuous, rather gross, pink bodies can be cloying, but his paintings of delightful young women—and men—enjoying themselves at a dance or on the river are such infectious delights and the paint is laid on with such loving care and richness, as though he himself were endowing his characters with all their youth and charm and excitement, that they do not become sentimental or 'chocolate box'.

In 1879, when he was working at Bougival, Renoir met his future wife, Alice Charigot. She was his favourite model, and her portrait occurs again and again in his pictures. She looks particularly delightful in the *Luncheon of the Boating Party*, where she sits fondling the little dog. Enchantingly feminine in her dark silk dress and straw hat trimmed with a profusion of ribbons and flowers, her charm is accentuated in contrast to the muscular rower behind her. Her beautifully shaped hands look transparently delicate against the rough coat of the dog. Opposite her, astride the chair, is Caillobotte, the collector and amateur painter. This whole picture glows with the brilliance of a colourful event. The painter has endowed his friends with the splendour of eighteenth-century France or Venice, and though they are dressed for a day on the river, the scene has the aspect of a gala occasion.

TOULOUSE-LAUTREC

The Bed. *Henri de Toulouse-Lautrec* (1864–1901). *Louvre, Paris* (Plate 115). In this wonderful painting Toulouse-Lautrec gives us sleep and rest in a curious intense way. These two people have not just ceased to be awake but are actively sleeping. Every line of the bed clothes and the crumpled pillow accentuates this feeling and yet never in any way detracts from the heads, which are the focal point of the painting.

In his *Clownesse*, also in the Louvre, the figure is vitally alive and awake. The composition is bold and arresting; the crescent of yellow frilling, broken only by the white wig, is continued in the swinging bow. The powerful drawing of the arm in action and the extraordinary subtle twist at the elbow show great strength, and we have the feeling of a remarkable individual of extraordinary vitality. The colour is brilliant, with much more body colour than this artist usually employed.

SISLEY AND PISSARRO

Alfred Sisley (1840–99) who was English by birth, was no great innovator, but he was consistently an Impressionist all his life, and although his technique intensified, it did not change. His painting has great appeal and he is one of the most popular of the group. He interpreted the delightful countryside near Paris in terms of lovely effects of sunshine in summer and winter, and his paintings have an especially nostalgic charm now that this enchanting scenery is rapidly being obliterated by encroaching suburbs. Sisley was certainly not a facile follower of the Impressionists, but he himself did not make any great discoveries in the technique of painting, though he always preserved his own personality.

Nothing at all dramatic is ever expressed by Sisley. He has a calm acceptance of nature as he sees it, and always seems to find it in a charming, smiling mood. He did not confine his themes to the countryside, but obviously enjoyed painting towns and villages and was particularly interested in snow effects. His pictures hardly seem startling to us now, but they aroused bitter criticism when they were painted. Curiously enough, his colour scheme, which seems so natural, was considered to be completely untrue. Obviously his critics were comparing it with the heavy tones of the early nineteenth-century landscape painters.

Snow at Louveciennes. *Alfred Sisley. Courtauld Institute, London* (Plate 116). Snow, with its quality of reflecting and holding light, was a favourite theme of the Impressionists and Sisley interpreted it in the most natural, attractive way. This painting has caught one moment in time during a period of snow, a moment all of us have witnessed but with Sisley's all-embracing eye.

Camille Pissarro (1831–1903) was the 'grand old man' of Impressionism. The oldest of them all, he was loved and respected by everyone, and some critics were most enthusiastic about his painting. You can judge the truth of this by looking again at *The Edge of the Village*, the landscape we have already discussed (Plate 82). Octave Mirbeau, in his series of articles, *Des Artistes*, wrote:

> 'Landscape . . . as rendered by Camille Pissarro, that is to say, the enveloping of form by light . . . is then a modern invention. Guessed at by Delacroix, more strongly felt by Corot, attempted by Turner in impressions of splendid, barbaric beauty, it only has its place in art, in a completely realized form, with Camille Pissarro and Claude Monet.'

Nevertheless Pissarro lived in abject poverty for most of his life and he was beset by disaster: first by the German invasion of 1870 when his store of paintings was destroyed, and then by eye trouble which finally caused blindness.

Cézanne, Van Gogh, and Gauguin are often referred to loosely as Impressionists, but Cézanne rebelled against the tenuous painting of Monet and was a post-Impressionist. He put bones and structure back into landscape; he painted form and he expressed form with colour. Van Gogh used a robust outline for all his characters, his light is strong and often harsh; his trees, his flowers, even a field of grasses and weeds, all have individual character. His forms are not lost in light like Monet's. Gauguin, too, exploited a definite outline to stress the pattern of his painting and he used brilliant flat colour. Not even the least knowledgeable could confuse the painting of Cézanne, Van Gogh or Gauguin.

CÉZANNE

Cézanne felt drawn to the Impressionists because of their independent outlook; but he himself had very different aims, chief among them being to express volume and the basic solidity of the things around him. With this aim, he struggled to combine brilliant, clear colour.

Throughout the history of art there has always been a compromise with colour and form. It is obvious that a painter who wishes to stress colour will have to sacrifice some of the shadow areas in order to do so. If, for instance, a painter wishes to stress a large area of red, say in a child's dress, the greatest area of clear red will be obtained by leaving out all shadows. This is the practice of oriental painters who do not, as a rule, concern themselves with the third dimension and therefore do not bother to elaborate the folds of drapery by shadows. Alternatively, if the painter is preoccupied with form, he will want to show the roundness of the body under the dress and the shape of the folds by shadows; thus, unless he is one of those artists who can suggest form by the subtlety of his outline, he will quite obviously reduce the area of clear red.

Most painters have come to a compromise with this problem, but as a generality they all show a bias towards stressing either form or colour. For instance, the Florentines, who were natural sculptors, were preoccupied with form and stressed this rather than brilliant colour. The Venetians were surrounded by the exotic glowing colours of the East and by glittering mosaics; naturally they were painters rather than sculptors, and they stressed colour rather than draughtsmanship.

The Impressionists, and more particularly Claude Monet, were concentrating on colour and light to such an extent that some of their paintings were almost formless and shimmering misty 'impressions', with no attempt to define the objects painted. Cézanne felt that this technique had reached its logical limits, that it could not be developed any further without becoming entirely nebulous. As he was naturally classical in his outlook and deeply impressed by the fundamental and permanent qualities of everthing he saw, he wanted to restore this basic structural quality to painting. His whole artistic life was given up to resolving the problem of combining brilliant, clear colour with solid form.

Grande Arbres au Jas de Bouffon. *Paul Cézanne* (1839–1906). *Courtauld Institute, London* (Plate 117). Cézanne is another example of a painter whose genius cannot be questioned. We have only to compare the trees in this landscape with those in Pissarro's for it to be immediately to the latter's detriment. Pissarro's is a charming, slightly vague 'impression'. Cézanne's is a powerful statement. His trees have a basic structure and form; they are monumental and, even though simplified, we can feel the 'woodiness' of the trunks and the softness of the foliage. With remarkable economy he conveys the third dimension dramatically. How definitely flat the ground is and how convincingly he stresses the vertical plane of the trees. This is perhaps the best example that we have seen of a monumental approach to painting and also of complete architectural unity in the composition.

VAN GOGH AND GAUGUIN

The familiar golden landscape of Van Gogh, when he has taken a few fields, a strip of fencing, a haystack and a blue cart, give us a miracle of brilliant sunshine. He takes us across burning fields to the comparative coolness of the distant blue-green hills which roll away to the horizon. Ochre, apricot, orange, gold, primrose-yellow, vermilion, and saffron follow each other in a pattern across the canvas, a pattern relieved by deep-green foliage, the vertical lines of a sun-drenched white house, the blue of a painted cart. He achieves the flat pattern and clear colours of the Japanese print; but unlike the eastern artist, he plants our feet firmly on the ground and leads us into a landscape on a particular day, at a particular time, and pours the hot sunshine over us.

Who else but Van Gogh has ever felt so intensely the force and life in a group of thistles, or a jug of sunflowers? Who else could take a rush chair and invest it with such personal appeal? It is a special chair, a chair the artist used and left his pipe on; it has a special texture and is worn; it is solid and simple and useful, and part of the equipment that Van Gogh needed in his life as a painter.

The Windmill. *Vincent Van Gogh. Glasgow Art Gallery* (Plate 118). Here is a forceful, dramatic rendering of a simple theme depicted with all the intensity of Van Gogh's vision, attacked vigorously and set down on canvas spontaneously but imbued with great power.

Paul Gauguin (1848–1930) felt no such inspiration in his immediate surroundings in the gentle landscape of the Île de France, nor did the average model to be found in Paris appeal to him. Brittany was the obvious choice for him, for he always longed to work somewhere primitive and simple without the sophistication of town or the suavity of well-trodden country. The bare splendour of Brittany and the Breton peasants with their uncomplicated lives were the stimulus he needed, so he spent the summer at Pont-Aven. Living was cheap there and innkeepers were used to supply the needs of hard-up painters. Gauguin himself said: 'When my clogs strike this granite ground, I hear the low, dull powerful sound that I seek in painting.'

The artists who gathered at the famous Gloanec Inn where Gauguin took lodgings immediately recognized him as a leader. It was here, in Pont-Aven in 1888, that Gauguin painted his lovely picture entitled *The Swineherd*, now in a private collection in New York. Although this does not seem to represent any particular spot, it does give, in what is perhaps a composite picture, the atmosphere of the district and is much gentler than some ofhis later paintings. The paint is glowing but soft, and has only a hint of the exotic colours he was to employ later. Against a luminous blue sky strewn with pink clouds, hills that are a patchwork of red earth and rough green grass, sweep down to the valley. Pink, golden, and green trees are grouped round a little white church tower, and dark poplars form a background to the simple white houses with their dark roofs. In the foreground the swineherd in his blue smock and brown trousers stands on the rough, grassy field with yellow pigs snuffling at his feet. The whole painting has a delightfully rustic feel and gives the atmosphere of simple, unspoilt, countryside.

On the repeated invitation of Van Gogh, Gauguin went to Arles in the South of France and the two friends worked together for some weeks. Van Gogh had a project for establishing a school of painting where artists would work together, pooling their ideas, and he was anxious that Gauguin should be its director. During this period there is no doubt that Gauguin influenced Van Gogh's work to some extent, encouraging him to give an added grandeur with simplified areas of flat colour. It must be remembered though that Van Gogh was at that time feeling the impact of Japanese painting, and this would also have inclined him to concentrate on simplification, flat colour, and rhythmic design. Van Gogh, we know, aroused Gauguin's interest in the art of Japan which had a strong appeal for a man with such an instinctive feeling for decoration and love of clear colour with the minimum of shadows.

These two painters undoubtedly had a deep affection for each other, but Gauguin was overbearing and very difficult to get on with, while Van Gogh, as we know, was subject to long periods of deep despair and violent brain storms. After a few weeks the two men quarrelled.

Gauguin's *The Yellow Christ* painted in Brittany in 1889 is a deeply moving picture of a Calvary set in a flaming countryside of gold and yellow, cooled by the black and blue and white dress of the simple peasants kneeling beneath it. This was the first of his symbolic pictures in the new manner which he was later to develop during his stay in Tahiti.

Gauguin went to Tahiti because he felt that he had exhausted Brittany and hankered for something more primitive, more colourful and more exotic; all this he found in the South Sea islands where he spent the last years of his life.

The public was horrified by the 'crude' colours of Gauguin's Pacific paintings, but was becoming a little reconciled to his earlier work. His paintings of Brittany glowed, but not with the astonishing areas of flat colour unrelieved by shadow, which gave his Tahitian canvases such an overwhelming brilliance. Gauguin found the landscape and the people just what he needed as subjects, and he was able to develop his wonderful sense of decoration and intensify his colour. The clearly defined shapes of exotic plants were a delight to him and the simple, but graceful, native girls in their patterned cotton sarongs furnished him with all the models he needed.

Everyone is familiar with Gauguin's South-Sea paintings and it is difficult to form any opinion without colour, but since there are numerous books about him with excellent coloured reproductions, it is best to study one of these.

ROUSSEAU

Henri Rousseau (1844–1910), referred to as 'Le Douanier' since he was a customs official, painted in his spare time and on retirement. He was almost exactly contemporary with Cézanne, but although he was associated with the Impressionists, he was no great revolutionary. He was entirely self-taught and painted the only way he could, in a completely unselfconscious, naïve style. He was so obviously fascinated by everything he saw, that he represents nature as though he were looking at it for the first time. He really did have the eyes of an exceptional child.

Rousseau's fresh vision did not prevent him from composing his pictures with the utmost care, and although his early attempts are amateurish in the sense that he had only the vaguest knowledge of perspective, proportion, and construction, his later works are a marvel of intricate design. While he was a customs officer he was already painting portraits and landscapes, and after he had left the service his memory of it provided him with subject-matter, for he painted pictures of the Customs House and of the country round about.

The Customs House. *Henri Rousseau. Courtauld Institute, London* (Plate 119). This painting was carried out some years after he had retired, and although it has the atmosphere of the suburbs of Paris, it is largely imaginary for there was no such undulating country in the district where he worked. Somehow Rousseau invests this rather dull suburb of Paris with a mysterious quality, almost as though he were trying to enliven a dreary quarter by telling a fairy tale about it for children. For some unknown reason the painter stands one of the officials on the roof of the Customs House, as if he were looking into the distance to warn of the impending arrival of some supernatural procession. The plain iron gate remains expectantly open and the whole painting foreshadows the Surrealist movement which was to chose its subjects from the dream and thought world.

Rousseau was an ardent pacifist, although he did not concern himself in any way with politics, and in the early 1890s he painted his great picture of *War*, now in the Louvre. This is probably the only picture he painted of violent action, apart from the rather static animal fights in the forests and his curious, ballet-like rhythmic footballers. In this strangely moving composition a vast black horse, with mane and tail flying, ruthlessly carries a white-robed figure bearing a sword and a torch over tortured figures of the dead and dying, already being preyed upon by huge black carrion birds. The horse is silhouetted against a clear blue sky, broken by fiery red clouds and slashed across by the stark branches of blasted trees. Despite the horror and destruction he portrays, in some curious way there is a strong feeling of triumph in the symbol of war rushing across the world.

Although 'le Douanier's' work was admired by the advanced painters of the period, it was regarded by conventional artists and the general public as a joke. Today we look upon this kind of art as a serious contribution to painting. It is 'primitive' in so far as it sees the world untrammelled by the technical achievements of the Renaissance; it is 'folk art' in so far as its subjects are in most cases simple ones dealing with peasants' pastimes, children, animals and village life, and it employs bright colours and a generally unsophisticated style. However, 'naïve' seems the best title for these painters who emerge from time to time with little relation to contemporary movements. Its exponents see everything as if for the first time, and they are not bothered with such things as perspective or the relative size of people and objects. Like all serious painters, they paint as they see or feel—the only way they can paint.

If this is a valid way of painting, why should not children's art be termed great? A child's painting can and often does include some of the qualities that contribute to the making of a great work of art, such as disposition of colour, dramatic effect, and the freshness of vision of the naïve painter; but a child does not co-ordinate these qualities into architectural unity. He records, and in doing so, he adds a child's imagination. He sees freshly because he has not seen very much or very often; so does the folk artist. Rousseau and a few others like him acquired complete control of their medium, observed nature meticulously for years, contributed their own remarkable imagination and yet still kept the ability to look at everything with a new vision.

ACHIEVEMENTS OF THE IMPRESSIONISTS

But what did all these nineteenth-century painters have in common? They all had different personal approaches to painting, but they did share broad aims and they all belonged to what amounted to the first modern movement in art (a movement which is still going on). They developed a style of painting which is followed by a large number of artists today who continue to paint the more-or-less familiar scene.

All of them had been directly or indirectly influenced by the newly-awakened interest in oriental art, especially in coloured Japanese woodcuts. They had seen that a cat watching a peony could be a fitting subject for a picture; even a single spray of blossom or a delicately brushed-in bamboo shoot could be as acceptable as an elaborately arranged bowl of flowers or still life. European artists had hitherto considered these things too trivial to constitute subjects for painting and only worthy of inclusion in the background.

Until the middle of the nineteenth century, members of the general public had little chance of seeing any pictures: the Salon was not open to them, so their opinion was never asked or given. When, eventually, outsiders were admitted, they were faced with this revolutionary painting which even most critics disliked. Naturally enough, they were bewildered and the outcry was much greater than it is today when new ideas are expressed. More and more members of the public are now taking an interest in pictures and have considerable discernment, even if they are neither collectors nor critics. People who visit galleries are used to shocks and, it must be admitted, many of them are afraid to say what they dislike for fear of being considered unsophisticated.

The Impressionists had a new public to contend with, and it is largely due to the battle they won against its opposition that today's public is willing to look at and even try to understand the strangest forms of expression. Obviously the evolution of painting would have continued by some means, as nothing but great calamity can prevent this, but someone had to bring about a change.

There is no painter today who does not owe a tremendous debt of gratitude to the Impressionists. Today's artists are able to put before the public the most revolutionary theories because the Impressionists liberated them from the shackles of the past. But there is a risk of overestimating the quality of a painting just because it is by an Impressionist. Some of the lesser members of the movement produced only mediocre pictures, and even the great names painted some failures. The only defence is to use the greatest of the Old Masters as a yardstick to keep a sense of proportion with these most immediately appealing pictures.

We like to look at the world of the last century as a live world, a world we could live in with enjoyment, and it is the capacity of the Impressionists to show us this world, in living terms, that makes their work of such appeal to us. Those nineteenth-century painters who turned away from the original aims of Impressionism, or never embraced them, take us into equally exciting worlds and reveal the fundamental structure of nature and its basic, glowing colours.

As we have seen in Holland in the seventeenth century, the genre painters presented the beauty of the everyday scene, a house or courtyard, as an escape from the confined existence of winter in the sombre Dutch homes, when the weather and the state of the roads made contact with the outside world difficult. These painters spread a soft golden light over the tiles and furniture, over silks and velvets and feathers; they brought out the glowing reds and warm browns, the gilded threads in brocade and the contrasts of white linen. In common with the Impressionists, they loved light and sought inspiration from near-by scenes, but they were not experimenting like the French of two centuries later. The lesser among them were rather smug: happy in the restricted field of competent achievement. Except for the few, they did not seek to discover new worlds, nor were they enthusiastically trying out new methods of technique, new forms of expression.

Superficially, perhaps, these Dutchmen have points in common with the nineteenth-century French, but in actual fact the excitemen of the opening-up of new worlds by the Impressionists was rivalled only by the excitement of the Florentine artists of the Renaissance. These Florentines were inspired by the enthusiasm of discovery, by the excitement of increasing knowledge of technique, by the wonder of the world around them in which they were so intensely interested, and by the vaster scope of the new themes used for a painting, provided by the gradual acceptance that pagan subjects were worth illustrating as well as Bible stories.

With just such enthusiasm and growing excitement, the progressive spirits of the latter half of the nineteenth century attacked the problem of representing on canvas the fleeting moment, the change effected by differences of light and shade, by the varying atmosphere of every hour of the day. There has been so much written about these men, so many novels and articles romanticizing them, that they would be almost hackneyed were it not for the excellent biographies and letters which have restored the balance. In many instances the painters led uneventful lives and they were so preoccupied with their work that their existence was often a narrow one. Their struggle to perfect their art and gain recognition was in itself colourful. Extreme poverty is not romantic; neither is failure, unless it is accompanied by splendid courage.

POSSIBLE ESSAYS, DISCUSSION AND RESEARCH

1 Do you find Manet's work revolutionary?

2 Does the technique of Pointillism gain more than it loses?

3 Choose any Impressionist painting to hang in your home, and give reasons for your choice.

4 Do you prefer Renoir's interpretation of the French scene or Toulouse-Lautrec's?

5 In what way is Le Douanier Rousseau's work more stimulating than a child's painting?

6 Which Impressionist is to your mind the greatest painter?

7 Do you think that the Impressionists stand up to comparison with the Old Masters?

Suggested Further Reading

Bazin, Germain: *The Impressionist Painting of the Louvre* (translated from the French). Thames & Hudson: London, 1958.

Lake, Carlton, and Maillard, Robert: *A Dictionary of Modern Painters* (translated from the French). Methuen: London, 1956.

Lynton, Norbert: *The Modern World.* Paul Hamlyn: London, 1965.

Rewald, John: *Histoire de l'Impressionisme.* Albin Michel: Paris, 1955.

Vollard, Ambroise: *Souvenirs d'un Marchand de Tableaux.* Albin Michel: Paris, 1948.

Wilenski, R. H.: *Modern French Painters.* Faber & Faber: London, 1944.

(There are innumerable lives of the individual Impressionists in most Public Libraries.)

Chapter Fifteen

A BRIEF SURVEY OF ARCHITECTURAL TRENDS FROM THE EIGHTEENTH CENTURY TO THE PRESENT DAY

EIGHTEENTH-CENTURY ARCHITECTURE IN BRITAIN

While eighteenth-century baroque architecture merged into rococo in all the countries of western Europe (especially France, Austria, Germany, Italy, and Spain), Great Britain, as usual, continued her own evolution. (The Dutch, nevertheless, contributed materially to the creation of the Georgian style of architecture.) In the mid-eighteenth century, the Adam brothers visited Italy and the ruins of Diocletian's Palace at Split in what is now Yugoslavia, and so they created their own style of architecture and decoration inspired largely by what they had seen in the course of their travels.

THE ADAM BROTHERS

Robert Adam (1728–92), helped by his brother, James, transformed the face of residential London and indeed of England, lavishing meticulous care on exterior and interior so that every detail, including the furniture, was beautifully designed and finished.

JOHN NASH

He was followed by John Nash (1752–1835), a very different type of architect, who was more interested in the general effect and broad planning than in detail. Best known for his wonderful conception of Regent Street and Regent's Park with its villas and terraces picturesquely sited, he also designed cottages and large and small houses in every conceivable style.

REVIVALS: CLASSICAL AND GOTHIC

In the early years of the nineteenth century, the Classical revival was manifested in architecture as well as in painting and sculpture in the countries of western Europe. Public buildings were erected in the form of Greek or Roman temples with colonnades and pediments and friezes, though the decoration in France in particular was supposedly copied from Ancient Egypt.

The Gothic revival which followed was a natural reaction against the austerity of the Classical revival. Architects and painters drew their inspiration from the Middle Ages. Pseudo-Gothic churches were built all over England, France, and Germany. The House of Commons was a neo-Gothic palace which was soon to be rivalled by St. Pancras Station with its amazing skyline; criticized and despised in the first half of the twentieth century, these buildings have come into fashion again largely owing to the writing of Sir John Betjeman.

The great defect of the Gothic revival was that the craftsmen of the Middle Ages had disappeared and the decoration was repetitive.

During the nineteenth century there was a great wave of restoration of Gothic buildings which had fallen into decay or were in danger of doing so. In France, Viollet-le-Duc (1814–79) restored a large number of buildings but few of them are really successful and most of them give the impression of Gothic revival rather than true restoration. He believed in architecture being functional, but he also believed that Gothic architecture was the most truly functional of all styles, and the eventual reaction was to cultivate simplicity, sometimes an arid simplicity. He was responsible for the restoration of both Notre Dame and the Sante Chapelle in Paris, and also of the great fortress city of Carcassone.

ART NOUVEAU

Before the period which favoured simplicity there was a short-lived enthusiasm for *Art Nouveau*: a movement against revivals of any kind. This movement influenced America as well as Europe, and was particularly popular in England, Belgium, and parts of Spain. It sought to invent new forms, or rather take inspiration directly from natural forms, and to use these in freedom from traditional rules, to such an extent that right-angles were non-existent. Wavy lines and natural, curved and over-emphasized plant forms were used: tulips and roses and tendrils, which in their turn became conventional and stylized. The Metro stations in Paris were built at this period and the wavy lines can be seen in the not-unattractive arched entrances, particularly around Montmartre.

In Spain, Antonio Gaudi (1852–1926) designed the exaggerated shapes of the church of the Sagrada Familia in Barcelona. It is an extraordinary florescence of general Gothic lines but obeying none of the rules of Gothic proportions. There is so much confusion, so much contradiction and such a wealth of wavy, over-life-size decoration that, to me, it is overwhelmingly horrific. To many it is a real achievement in liberated technique and freedom of expression. Its style is certainly not arid.

THE ADVENT OF STEEL

It was considerably before this time—at the end of the eighteenth century—that the new building material, steel, was being employed for industrial buildings and for engineering projects. John Nash used steel with brick for the exotic Brighton Pavilion, and indeed this immensely strong material opened up all kinds of possibilities for experiment.

THE CRYSTAL PALACE

The new partly steel architecture had a link with Gothic cathedral architecture since steel girders served the same purpose as stone ribs in vaulting; and the walls, relieved of their load-bearing functions, could now be of glass. The Crystal Palace, built in Hyde Park in 1851 and later moved to South London (where it was destroyed by fire in 1936), was a huge glass building supported by a framework of steel. This vast transparent building was functional; it was erected as an exhibition hall and served its purpose admirably, but it was not without beauty: beauty of proportion and the dazzling beauty of glittering glass held in control by the satisfying horizontals, verticals and curves of the steel. It also had the added advantage of reflecting the brilliance of firework displays and appearing excitingly palatial when glowing with artificial light.

We have seen the superb tower built in a lacework of steel by Eiffel in Paris. Claude Monet was inspired to paint an impression of the steel framework interior of the Gare St. Lazare, and suspension bridges show how graceful as well as practical this material can be in use.

REINFORCED CONCRETE

By the middle of the nineteenth century the use of reinforced concrete (steel girders cased in concrete) led to further developments in the building since now the steel was protected from oxidization. It is surprising that buildings did not immediately aspire to new shapes with the possibilities of the new material, but much architecture (particularly domestic architecture) clung to the old rules of proportions and did not indulge in any great flights of fancy.

WILLIAM MORRIS

Horrified at the increase in industrial buildings, at the general industrialization of England, and dissatisfied with the standard of architectural design, William Morris (1834–96) had a very simple red-brick house built for himself. He found difficulty in furnishing it in the taste he required, so he created a firm to produce well-designed furniture, textiles, wallpapers, stained glass, and carpets, all of which were to be hand-made. He closed his eyes to the possibilities of machine-made goods and wanted to recapture the skill of the medieval craftsman. He also had the impossible ideal of making this available to everyone. It was of course far too expensive for the average man, let alone the working man who was only too glad to get cheap, machine-made goods, even if they were badly designed.

Morris certainly had a beneficial influence on the design of textiles and wallpaper, simplifying it to being two-dimensional, and generally uncluttering the elaborate, fussy ugly lines of everyday objects. He failed, for me, not only because he was looking back to past achievements, but because he had no vision and he was out of touch with his own period. He had the boring quality of 'good taste' which rules out flights of imagination or exciting new discoveries. Like Robert Adam a century earlier, he wanted everything in keeping, but on an almost rustic scale, certainly not on an elegant one.

However the influence of Morris's simplicity spread over Europe and resulted in conscious planning of domestic architecture, of planning areas surrounded by countryside, of pleasant suburbs with gardens built away from factory smoke.

I have already mentioned the fact that alongside the new buildings of steel, necessarily different because they fulfilled entirely new needs (factories, railway stations, etc.), the diehards still insisted on following tradition in brick and stone decorated with outworn designs.

In spite of the widespread influence of William Morris, there was still no solution to the problem of artists and architects co-operating with the industrial age and no directive as to the use of the new materials. William Morris offered an escape, or at best a halt in the increasing influence of the machine.

GROPIUS AND THE BAUHAUS

It was Walter Gropius in Germany who developed his ideas for well-designed everyday products and put forward propositions for the mass-production of housing. He built a factory which incorporated the basic principles of twentieth-century architecture. This style, known as International Modern, departed from the classical tradition of proportion, adopted assymetrical design and the use of the cube as a basic shape, usually unrelieved by decoration, with enormous windows running horizontally along the walls which were rendered in blinding white. Everyone is familiar with this type of building which has been produced all over the world during this century.

Gropius was also influenced by the American architect Frank Lloyd Wright (1869–1959), although the latter's approach was intensely individual within the general new principles and he favoured the use of decoration. It was Wright who developed the 'prairie' house with the delightful low, spreading buildings to be seen in the United States.

Daring innovations in factory and office design gained Gropius the post of head of the School of Arts and Crafts at Weimar, which he soon converted into the Bauhaus ('the house of building'). Gropius brought to the Bauhaus the most progressive painters, sculptors, architects, and designers of the day to make a concerted effort to produce building for working in with the same enthusiasm and unity of purpose that created the medieval cathedrals. Even he was still clinging to medieval principles, but he gradually changed from his enthusiasm for the ancient crafts to preoccupation with industrial design. When the Nazis assumed power, the Bauhaus was discredited and Gropius left Germany, but he continued to design contemporary buildings of great distinction all over the world and is still an important influence in the teaching of the principles of great architecture.

Students of the Bauhaus were versed in all the crafts and studied the nature of the material at their disposal. From this has grown the contemporary artist's insistence on texture in all the arts.

LE CORBUSIER

The best-known mass-producer of housing in Europe is Le Corbusier (real name: C. E. Jeanneret), who is also the most inventive, if not the greatest of modern architects. His style continually changes and it is impossible even to dwell on his achievements here. As a generalization he is an 'irrational' architect producing entirely new skylines, with windows, doors, and towers placed apparently at random. His 'mushroom' roof is the most obvious of his individual features. He is also responsible for the idea of setting a series of skyscrapers in parkland.

RESTORATION AND REBUILDING AFTER THE SECOND WORLD WAR

The contemporary insistence on texture is particularly apparent in the large number of buildings restored or rebuilt all over Europe after the ravages of the Second World War. I can only mention one or two instances here, but one of the most moving is the new basilica erected in Cagliari, Sardinia, to replace the prized ancient church of Cosma and Damiano, on which Pisan, Aragonese, and Renaissance styles had left their mark. The new church is ultra-modern in style, and glass, metal, and concrete contrast with the elegance of marble and limestone. The architect has miraculously married the Gothic pattern with something of the splendour of the Byzantine. Internally the basilica has vastness and simplicity. Its proportions suggest the nobility and permanence of a Greek temple but the architectural form is completely modern. Since this is by a Florentine architect, the texture of the stone is stressed with true Tuscan feeling.

Churches, town halls, and schools have been erected or restored in the modern idiom in Germany and Austria. In Austria, in particular, the importance of the craftsman has been fully maintained in splendid stained glass and carved wood, and a unity has been maintained by well-designed furniture and textiles.

In a new village in southern Italy, built to replace one washed away by floods, the very modern, very simple, colourful church is accepted and admired by the Calabrian villagers who have probably never seen any architectural style but the over-elaborate, fussy, interior of their former church, cluttered with finery and images. The new one is flooded with light and glows with brilliant ceramics and glass contrasted with stone and wood. Here is an example of something eminently suited for its purpose being immediately acceptable.

We are tired of the cliché that a modern house is a 'machine for living in', that a factory or office is a machine for working in and a church is a machine for worshipping and getting together in; but there is much truth in it. The weakness here is, I believe, in overstressing the machine aspect, and insisting on everything being suitable—in fact in 'good taste'. Most people welcome a little fun, a little exuberance, and there is even a place for 'prettiness'. One daringly crude touch of colour, such as a grotesquely ornate piece of Victoriana, can enhance the effect of lovely antiques, and painters have discovered how a brilliant touch of red, placed with genius, can bring out the subtle colours of a picture and increase its 'life'.

We admire the lovely proportions, the perfect siting and the simplicity of Greek temples and theatres; but the ancient Greeks, if they could see them in their present state, would presumably find them rather boring. Otherwise they would not have cluttered the Sacred Way with crowds of statues; they would not have 'embellished' the Temple of Zeus at Olympia with gilt and colour and statues; they might not even have produced the superb carvings to decorate the Parthenon.

EMPLOYMENT OF PROGRESSIVE ARTISTS

To begin with, as in all revolutionary movements, modern architecture was oversimplified and inclined to be stark. Now, however, the aims of the Bauhaus seem to have materialized to the extent that when there is a great architectural project like Coventry Cathedral, progressive artists are commissioned to work on it together. Moreover, a new impetus has been given to crafts such as stained glass and tapestry which were in decay at the beginning of the century; and artists of the status of Marc Chagall (in Jerusalem) and Georges Braque (in Normandy) are commissioned to design windows.

RENAISSANCE OF STAINED GLASS AND TAPESTRY

With the new materials made possible by technical research, the stained-glass worker has an infinite variety of colours at his disposal. He is no longer confined to binding fragments together with lead, for glass can be cast within concrete blocks; it can also be used in several layers to intensify colour with the employment of transparent adhesive, and fibre-glass is available in every colour and tone. In the hands of inspired artists these materials open up endless possibilities.

There has also been a renaissance in the weaving of tapestry, inspired by Jean Lurçat in France (Plate 120). He has returned to the simple basic colours and hand dyeing used in the Middle Ages and he designs in the modern idiom, paying great respect to the limitations and possibilities of his medium.

Now that toughened glass can be used far more extensively, huge office blocks and flats can now appear to be almost entirely of glass, reflecting light and glittering in the sunlight; blocks lit by thousands of electric bulbs at night turn built-up areas into cities of enchantment.

In the huge new exhibition building at La Défense, in Paris, glass is the most obvious element; but at the Unesco buildings, also in Paris, it is the mosaic decorations by Joan Mirò which give them such distinction.

For me the best feature of modern architecture is that it is functional but not starkly so, and it makes use of the wealth of new materials to create new textures, new shapes, and heights unattainable before. New materials have made skyscrapers a possibility almost anywhere; new materials have made huge sweeping roofs a possibility too, and coloured plastics have made attractive decoration comparatively cheap.

JOHN RUSKIN

Lack of space makes it impossible to enumerate the large number of architects of genius of this century. Although I have been forced to confine myself to a general survey, I have not mentioned the great influence of John Ruskin (1819–1900) mainly because, though strong, it was backward-looking. In essence it was an assertion that the final word in architecture had been said, and only needed repeating with modifications and the maintaining of standards of craftsmanship.

CONTRIBUTION BY ENGINEERS AND DESIGNERS

I have not thought it apposite to dwell on the amount of very dull building in the way of dwelling-houses, apartment blocks, and suburbans churches in some regions, and I have not even listed the many great traditional architects of our time. I must, however, mention the tremendous contribution made by engineers in their own field and in co-operation with architects, and the exhilaratingly lovely roads and bridges and pylons which enhance the countryside instead of spoiling it.

Many designers too, have risen magnificently to the needs of the time with beautiful shapes for cars, ships, and aeroplanes, and they will doubtless keep up this standard in designing for the space age.

POSSIBLE ESSAYS, DISCUSSION AND RESEARCH

Describe how you would plan:

1 A garden city.

2 A festival exhibition.

3 An imaginary riverbank in a town.

4 An airport.

5 A council estate in a small town of historic interest, mainly half-timber mixed with a little Georgian.

Suggested Further Reading

Flemming, J.: *Robert Adam and his Circle*. John Murray: London, 1962.

Naylor, Gillian: *The Bauhaus*. Studio Vista, Dutton: London, 1968.

Pevsner, Nikolaus: *Pioneers of Modern Movement (from William Morris to Walter Gropius)*. Faber & Faber: Londin, 1936.

Richards, J. M.: *An Introduction to Modern Architecture*. Penguin: London, 1940.

Summerson, John: *Georgian London*. Penguin: London, 1962.

Summerson, John: *John Nash*. George Allen & Unwin: London, 1950.

Chapter Sixteen

MODERN ART

Until recently, the vast majority of people have been convinced that the painter's job was to represent familiar forms. Even when photography deprived the artist of the need to record the world around him in paint or stone, they continued to hold fast to this idea, conceding that it could be the artist's very personal view if he did not take too many liberties.

After all, it may still be argued that however perfectly a colour photograph can truthfully reproduce a particular object or a particular place, it cannot comment more than to the extent to which the operator of the camera chosses his viewpoint, his moment. The artist, good or bad, cannot help commenting, even if inadequately. He has to put down, with the first line or brush stroke on a given surface, what he thinks about the subject. Though he may be limited in his capacity to do this, each painter will do it differently. Thus it is obvious that there is still a place for the artist to record and comment on the things around him; but recording and commenting is not enough, unless he infuses something new into it. We have seen how the minor Dutch painters were mainly concerned with recording, making an inventory, and how tiresome the lesser works of the pre-Raphaelites became with their prosaic rendering of details.

THE EXPANSION OF PATRONAGE

The familiar world has already been painted superbly, and for hundreds of years subject-matter has been more or less dictated by the different types of patron at different periods. Prehistoric art, we can guess, was in the service of magic and the supernatural; cave painting, whether symbolic or realistic, was to placate unspecified gods and demons, to work a spell to increase the animal kingdom for the hunter and to promote fertility. In ancient Greece, art was in the service of the gods, in the idealizing of perfection in human and animal form, and the State was the patron. In the Byzantine world, the Emperor and the Church were the patrons, and religious themes were demanded by the Christian religion. In medieval times, the Church was still the patron of art dedicated to the glory of God, but this art had also to be of moral value to the congregation and its message understood. As far as the main theme was concerned the artist was not free to paint the things he wished to paint. This was also true with art for the Court, which ran parallel to and sometimes merged with art for the Church. The Renaissance and the widening of interest in art outside religion increased competition for the artist's services, with the result that he began to have more say as to how he should paint.

By the sixteenth century, a large number of churches and cathedrals had already been built and fully decorated, so inevitably the demand for purely religious art slackened, and the State and the Court were the chief patrons who needed artists to erect and decorate civic buildings and palaces. In seventeenth-century Holland, as we have seen, the wealthy merchants took over as patrons and there was virtually no demand from the Church. In eighteenth-century England, it was the Court and the aristocracy; but by the nineteenth century, patrons with power to dictate terms dwindled and the humbler patron took over: an individual collector from any walk of life, who might commission a portrait or a landscape, but was more likely to buy from the artist's accumulated works. In England, at any rate, the individual patron gained ground, and in recent years the number of small private collectors has grown enormously.

GREAT CHANGES IN THE APPROACH TO ART

However many painters may be dubbed the 'First of the Moderns', the real break (as distinct from recurrent reactions against academic art) came with Cézanne, for it was he who led the way for the twentieth-century revolution in art. He marks the end of six centuries of painting during which artists strove to represent nature as seen by the normal human eye, to interpret it by means of forms familiar to everyone, albeit more keenly observed by the artist.

CÉZANNE, THE FIRST MODERN

Cézanne made very definite statements about the things he saw, and the third dimension was an essential ingredient of his painting. In order to render form convincingly, he simplified it to the cube, the sphere, the cone, and the cylinder; so to that extent he was a Cubist, though the Cubist movement, as such, did not materialize until after his death. He fully realized that he was opening up new worlds which would almost certainly be more deeply explored by his successors, as indeed they were, more particularly by Picasso and Braque.

It is at this point that art, instead of following a direct course within certain accepted limitations, becomes diffused. Far more experience and perception are needed to differentiate between what is good and what is bad; what we like and what we hate, and why. Painters and sculptors no longer feel that the representation of familiar forms in one way or another is the only truth. They no longer feel obliged to render, say, a tree or a head as most people see it.

L'ÉCOLE DE PARIS

The change came about conveniently with the beginning of the twentieth century, at a time when Paris was becoming the centre of the art world to which artists from every country flocked. *L'École de Paris* describes the 'school' of painting made up of the work of these artists of different nationalities, many of whom began movements of importance but who had in common a modern approach to art and stressed its decorative rather than figurative aspect. In its narrower original form, *L'École de Paris* was composed of a group of refugees, mainly Jewish, whose circumstances and sympathies brought them together, but it is now loosely used to cover the work of painters nurtured in the stimulating atmosphere of twentieth-century Paris.

UTRILLO

Maurice Utrillo (1883–1955) may be mentioned here since he was painting in the present century, but he does not stylistically fit in with any group. His mother, the artist Susan Valadon, persuaded him to paint as occupational therapy, an occupation which soon became a necessity to him, and his paintings of suburban streets are now familiar to everyone.

Church at Longpont. *Maurice Utrillo. Southampton Art Gallery* (Plate 121). Utrillo has chosen to paint a church, not a particularly beautiful one, and he paints it as though it were a portrait, investing it with real character. More than that, he imparts definite texture to the wall surface and in some curious way the sketchy dark patches of window and doors draw one inside the building and make it more three-dimensional. Utrillo used plaster as paint when he wanted to give a matt brilliance of snow or plaster walls and he scraped and scratched it to get the best effect. Even though he does not often paint figures, when he does employ them, as here, they play an important role, however incidental they may seem. Remove them and the whole painting loses vital balance and the nervously moving bare branches of the trees lose a vital contrast.

From this period onwards, the number of movements gains impetus and there are so many that I can only enumerate a few.

THE FAUVES

Fauvism was the first real movement of the twentieth century. Its members explored the great possibilities of flat patterns and pure, violent colour; they also deliberately distorted shapes. It began when a number of painters with similar aims exhibited together at the *Salon* of 1905. Their works were considered so garish and distorted that they were hung together in one room and were dubbed *les fauves* (the wild beasts). These men were joined by others and included Matisse, Braque, Marquet, Derain, Vlaminck, and Rouault, all painters who have made their individual contribution to modern art. Matisse certainly ranks among the foremost painters of the century, if he is not indeed *the* foremost.

MATISSE

Henri Matisse (1869–1954) began his painting life conventionally, studying and copying paintings in the Louvre, but he also made studies from nature and came under the influence of Impressionism. He was soon to change his style and to be more influenced by Cézanne and Seurat, both of whom experimented in their different ways beyond Impressionism. When he was criticized as the leader of the Fauves, he was employing brilliant colour in simplified flat shapes; he had reduced his painting to pure-colour harmonies and rhythmic, expressive lines.

Matisse contrives to give an amazing sense of space by relating areas of pure colour in such a way they seem almost to hang in the atmosphere; he does not make use of perspective, but preserves the plane of the flat surface on which he is working. He is able to suggest great space and a range of lyrical colour by the juxtaposition of pure colours and the simplification of shapes, rejecting everything which is not essential to his purpose. With a few thick flowing black lines, as in the Matisse Chapel at Vence, he can express all that is necessary, and even leave the faces blank. There is the most astonishing unity in his compositions and the most utterly satisfying cadences of colour which owe much to oriental art and also, paradoxically enough, to the tradition of the Old Masters. Like the Old Masters, he prepared his subject with numbers of sketches and studies; he thought out his composition so thoroughly that it was at his finger tips and he could transfer it in absolute freshness to his chosen surface.

When finally unable to paint through infirmity, he produced lyrical colour harmonies with cut-out shapes arranged as areas of pure colour. He can convey, in paint, the velvet density of a night sky through an open window with what appears to be a patch of black, but varied so subtly as to be hardly noticeable. He can also convey a trembling light with an area of pure colour, and he makes such an area intensely exciting in its own right.

The Inattentive Reader. *Henri Matisse* (1869–1954). *Tate Gallery, London* (Plate 122). There is a comforting feeling of complete oneness in this lyrical painting. The patterning of the floor, the line of the mirror, the flowers, the panels of the door, the curves of the drapery, and the armchair all flow together, and the dark eyes and far-away expression conveyed with such miraculous economy are as convincing as the *Portrait of an Old Man* by Rembrandt (Plate 83). There is the same utter quietness, though Matisse effects it by entirely different means.

VLAMINCK

Maurice Vlaminck (1876–1958) gives excitement but of a different kind: his landscapes are charged with electricity and are wildly dramatic as if on the verge of an electric storm. A few trees, an ordinary stretch of road become a setting for some possibly epic event and the picture is full of a kind of expectancy.

ROUAULT

Georges Rouault was dramatic too, but in a tragic, rather heavy way, despite the brilliant jewel colours he used: jewel colours outlined in thick black reminiscent of stained glass. He was indeed first apprenticed to a stained-glass worker and he himself, towards the end of his life, designed windows. He expresses deep feeling and distorts and exaggerates to intensify this. He was a natural expressionist, though Expressionism as a movement is more generally associated with German painters and especially with the Norwegian, Edvard Munch, who worked in Berlin and produced frenzied pictures of intense emotion.

The Apprentice. *Georges Rouault* (1871–1958). *Musée National de l'Art Moderne, Paris* (Plate 123). A broad black outline, simple dark shadows and brilliant areas of light make this a very powerful head, but there is also subtlety in the marvellously handled paint. The actual laying on of the paint in layers of rich impasto gives a glowing effect. There is something of Rembrandt's genius for making light emanate from the face, though Rouault approaches his subject in a simpler, broader way and lacks Rembrant's delicacy and subtlety of colour. This is a haunting and rather tragic study of a serious, youthful workman.

CUBISM: PICASSO AND BRAQUE

It was Picasso and later Braque who created Cubism and took the revolutionary step against representation of the visual appearance of nature as distinct from distorting it. The whole structure of objects was analysed, giving several fragmentary views at once, and arranged to keep the two-dimensional unity of the painting surface. The Cubists no longer wanted to take you into a picture in the three-dimensional sense of a landscape by Hobbema; neither did the mainly decorative and colourful style of the Fauves satisfy them. This 'analytical' Cubism was followed by a second phase, 'synthetic' Cubism, in which painters arranged coloured forms in juxtaposition and superimposed them on each other, giving the effect of space and also often suggesting easily recognized objects such as jugs, bottles, fruit, and violins associated with the painting of still life.

Still Life with Fish. *Georges Braque* (1882–1963). *Tate Gallery London* (Plate 126). There is very little colour in this Cubist painting. The bottle and the fish are familiar forms, as they must be if they are to have any impact as such in the complexity of the style where shapes are overlapping to give the effect of recession in space. There is no conventional perspective since the objects are seen from several points and organized in space to give a complete representation. Keep looking at this picture and you will find it *is* organized in space—vast space.

We have discussed Picasso's painting of the *Goat's Skull, Bottle and Candle* in Chapter Two, but it is impossible to form any opinion of this astonishing artist's work by looking at one painting, for throughout his long life his style has undergone many changes. He came to Paris at the beginning of the century when the painters of *L'École de Paris* were experimenting with new ideas, and he himself portrayed the shabbier, more poverty-stricken aspect of the Paris street-scene in sensitive line and sad, cool, colour—this was his 'blue period'. He painted a happier side of Paris—street musicians and harlequins—in warmer pinks and yellows, his 'pink period' but he was still a more-or-less representational painter. Then he began to formulate ideas outside the scope of the decorative, colourful contribution made by the Fauves and he found Cubism, inspired by Cézanne. Picasso's Cubist paintings were followed by a series of monumental pictures of nudes depicted as though they were carved out of stone and very three-dimensional. In the 1930s he was distorting the human figure and dislocating it to show the violence, the senselessness and cruelty of war; he produced the famous *Guernica* to reveal to the world his horror at the Spanish Civil War and his own devotion to the cause of peace.

Picasso's intense interest in ceramics has brought about a renaissance in the production of pottery in the South of France where so much of his work can be seen in this form, in delicate drawings, in sculpture and in vast wall decorations.

Growing interest among progressive painters and sculptors in the bold, simplified art of the African Negro gave the right atmosphere for the development of Cubist ideas which opens the way to modern art movements all over the world.

It is quite impossible to enumerate all the other 'isms' of the first half of the twentieth century, or for that matter, all the subsequent movements in art. It has become a habit to pin a label on everything, but artists are individuals and though they may, at times, belong to a 'movement' they will almost certainly either react against it or modify it to their own needs and begin another movement. I can therefore only mention a few of the more important trends in art.

EXPRESSIONISM

In contrast to the coolly calculated character of Cubism, Expressionism is emotional, even hysterical. Expressionism in its widest sense applies to the art of any individual at any period who distorts forms and intensifies colour to appeal to the emotions. This is notably exemplified by Van Gogh, but the Expressionist movement of the twentieth century was more consciously and obsessionally concerned with the emotional and often tragic aspect of life, and is especially associated with artists working in central Europe.

So far I have not discussed abstract art because, although it plays such an important part in the twentieth century, used broadly the term can be applied to a wide diversity of painting and sculpture and can cover all non-representational works. A dozen modern movements can come under its broad heading.

Constructivism, which concerned sculpture and developed from *collage* (the practice of attaching various materials to a surface, used by Cubists and others), was mainly a Russian movement of assembling a variety of materials such as glass, wire, metal, in relief or hanging in spatial relationship. This died out in Russia in the political upheavals of 1921 but had considerable influence on architecture especially in the use of materials such as perspex.

In the early years of this century there began a definite trend towards abstract art, in which a large number of painters took part. It is almost impossible to define the difference between good and bad abstract art. How does one evaluate a painting which, although it may arise from some natural form, does not evoke it for the spectator? How much more difficult it becomes when this develops into non-representational art—that is, colours and shapes with no reference to known objects. The difficulty here is that painters with abstract convictions can be involved in both abstract and representational art; at the same period there were, and even today there are, many painters who produce representational or impressionistic pictures as well as abstract.

Painters from any of these concurrent styles or movements can be great artists. After all Matisse, now recognized as a great master of contemporary art, painted abstracts at the end of his life.

'Abstraction' is the great stumbling-block for evaluating modern works of art, for there are no longer any boundaries, there are no longer the fixed rules which for hundreds of years had been accepted by all painters. Even symbols had the significance of a decipherable language. Painters and sculptors had to curb their way of expressing themselves and were restricted to a familiar world because their art was representational and even a symbol represented something.

RESPECT FOR MEDIUM

There are at the same time limitations imposed by medium upon an artist. For instance, water-colours cannot produce the richness of oil paint; nor for that matter, can fresco. Jade has to be ground into shape because it is so hard: some stones are softer than others and therefore more easily shaped, though the very softness may be an obstacle. All great artists have respected their medium and have let it influence their execution, and this has been a kind of compromise. For centuries there was a tug-of-war between colour and form, then Cézanne attempted to express form with colour and the Impressionists sacrificed form to trembling light. Anyone who has looked at the countryside in the bright sunlight of noon knows how it drains colour away.

Modern movements are biased in favour of allowing the medium to take over. In carving wood, the grain takes charge and dictates the shape, even to the extent of deciding the proportion, but the carver may, instead of compromising in carving some familiar form, create something entirely new, non-representational and abstract, but nevertheless with a life of its own. The Old Masters were concerned with representing natural forms, each in his own individual way, stressing as he thought fit this or that aspect, but always concerned with 'putting over' something readily intelligible and always concerned with his patron's wishes. They were not generally preoccupied with themselves as artists or with consciously expressing themselves. They were artists and had as much artistic temperament as our contemporaries, but they were mainly concerned with doing a professional job of work and in overcoming the difficulties of their media. The modern painter is usually seeking a style in which he can best express himself, and only in the broadest sense does this style come from the circumstances of his birth and century.

ABSTRACT ART: KANDINSKY

Abstract art stresses the actual quality of paint, colour, and pattern, and perhaps the freest and most poetic of these painters is Wassily Kandinsky who has a kind of dream quality: meteoric, disturbing, and imaginative. Since Kandinsky's work appeals to the emotions, it is termed 'Abstract Expressionism', a term which is also applied to Action painting.

Battle. *Kandinsky* (1866–1944). *Tate Gallery, London* (Plate 124*a*). This is probably the first abstract work to be painted (1910); a kind of calligraphy, a kind of doodling, but not a thoughtless one and certainly a form of 'expression'. Kandinsky is consciously expressing his thoughts and making a short cut through familiar shapes to their basic curves and lines in such a way as to make an emotional effect. Here we have the basic lines of cavalry, a castle, spears, and birds arranged to create a satisfying but emotionally disturbing composition, further stressed by haunting colour. But both Cubism and Expressionism can be disturbing, though Cubism is just as likely to be calmly satisfying

Perhaps 'disturbing' is the keynote of much significant contemporary art. For if art in no way disturbs the senses nor intensifies their reaction, it can hardly be of significance. In many ways, contemporary or abstract art is a kind of essence of all that has gone before. The Old Masters, because of the times he lived in, needed a female body if he wanted to express a sensuous curve; the two things were essential and indivisible, but the contemporary artist can dispense with the body and produce either in sculpture or in painting, a sensuous curve. The painter of an eighteenth-century topographical picture had the buildings where domes supplied rounded lines, the façade produced vertical lines, pediments gave angles, and these were almost unconsciously interrelated by the artist to make a satisfactory picture of architecture. The modern artist can suggest architectural unity with these basic lines and without the building. Whether what he does is worth while, whether it has real significance in the history of art, or whether it is merely experimental and therefore a contributary influence, cannot be decided from as near by as we stand today.

Once again, if you are lost, may I suggest that you use the old yardstick, a rather less rigid one now since there is no longer any doubt that artists like Matisse, Picasso, Braque, Henry Moore, Barbara Hepworth, Piet Mondrian, Joan Miró, Kandinsky, Brancusi, Marini, Ben Nicholson, Sidney Nolan—to mention only a very small number, and none of them young—are undoubtedly masters of modern art. Most of these artists were involved in many revolutionary movements and all of them have evolved from one means of expression to another during their artistic career. Although not every one of their works is necessarily of the first order, they have all produced masterpieces; but so, too, have less sensational artists such as Ivon Hitchens, Paul Nash, Augustus John, Epstein, Manzu, Giacometti, and Lowry.

SURREALISM: CHAGALL

Surrealism, which is not abstract since it represents recognizable forms, has been used by many artists of the past: that is to say they have taken subjects from the world of dreams and fantasy, the world of the unconscious where anything may happen.

The modern movement was an outcome of the short-lived anihilistic *Dada* movement of nonsensical, hysterical, 'shocking' art which crystalized into the expression of the subconscious irrational world. Surrealists are taken up with presenting this world often so precisely that their painting becomes academic and is representational. When Magritte paints one of his odd creatures, the component parts, however fantastic in relation to each other, are realistically painted. Salvador Dali works with slick academic smugness, although he is really an exhibitionist like the protagonists of the *Dada* movement.

Chagall's dream world cannot fail to delight in its evocative nostalgia. This is a dream world we are all partly familiar with. Who has not experienced this strange sensation of vertical floating at some time, and the merging of time and events? This is a delightful, innocent fantastic art, but I doubt if it enlarges many people's experience, except possibly in its harmony of colour.

Self Portrait with Seven Fingers. *Marc Chagall* (*b.* 1887). *Stedelijk Museum, Amsterdam* (Plate 124). Everything is in this picture: Chagall's dream, memories of his childhood, folk-lore and the influence of Cubism apparent in the disrupting of shapes to emphasize pattern and fantasy, also stressed by unusual colours and a 'phantom' treatment of figures. There is a lilting beauty in the arrangement of the shapes and passages of delight such as the debonair knotting of the tie, the ghostly rose in the buttonhole, his native town Vitebsk in the clouds, and the Eiffel Tower against a velvet night sky.

ACTION PAINTING: JACKSON POLLOCK

The American painter Jackson Pollock is the name mainly associated with Action painting, and there is no doubt that he has produced some exquisitely delicate intricacies of pattern, an interweaving of curves and lines and spirals, firmly, under control and certainly not haphazard. In Action painting, the artist expresses *himself*, not any subject. He can pour the paint on canvas on the floor, he can run a roller over it, direct it this way or that until he arrives at what satisfies him. The result is partly accidental, but can be something quite lovely, something in common with mosaic (although it must be admitted, a rather purposeless mosaic).

Painting 1952. *Jackson Pollock* (1912–56). *Tate Gallery, London* (Plate 125). No one can be in any doubt that this is an Action painting. Pollock is *expressing himself* in paint. He claims to be in control of the paint which is poured on, rubbed on, scratched over and directed by him compulsively. This is a direct approach dispensing with any form of representation, making more or less violent marks on a surface and presenting those impulses to the spectator. In theory anything as direct as this should be immediately understood; but is it? There is certainly a fascination in 'entering into' this painting, for it has remarkable depths through intricate lines of tangled patterns. The definite 'blot' of spilt paint in the middle serves to push back the rest of the painting. Look at this for a long time and if you feel it is accidental and could be done by anyone: try on a small scale and then compare the two. Like it or not, it is significant in that it goes beyond all other forms of abstract art in being a physical expression. The obvious reaction against this loose technique is Hard-edge painting, a movement which originated in America and, as the name implies clearly defines the areas of different colour.

KINETIC ART AND OP ART: VASARELY

Kinetic art is the name given to 'moving' art, to mobiles which make patterns of light and shade as they move. All kinds of effects can be produced with coloured lights on moving assemblages and glass, arranged to give moving reflections; glinting materials hung on invisible nylon threads can give a great variety of changing patterns. It is quite impossible to give any idea of these in a reproduction, but some examples of 'Op' or Optical art do photograph quite well, and depend on optical reactions for their effect. Victor Vasarely is the leader of this group, and even in reproduction his dazzlingly black and white *Supernovae* has a disturbing impact and seems to explode. There is a perpetual interplay of inverse patterns: black on white, white on black, all appearing to move so that the spectator has to keep looking and exploring the surface (Plate 132).

Bridget Riley's painting of *The Fall* produces vertigo at first in its extraordinary piling up of descending water, and then it gradually becomes dramatic.

MINIMAL ART

Minimal art is self-explanatory as it reduces everything, including form and colour, to a minimum. It practically annihilates art. It uses drab, unpleasant colours or white; it breaks down form. It is non-commercial in that it happens only once: a pile of ashes and twisted wire, exhibited and then abandoned.

The exhibition entitled 'The Art of the Real' at the Tate Gallery in June 1969, showed works by American minimal artists, but also works of immense size into which one could literally 'enter' since they surrounded the spectator. Some other exhibits seemed to me to be those things which one can see at any time on a railway station (piled up boxes), in a market (sheep pens) or along any corridor. Perhaps it is necessary for some people to see, in a picture gallery, a long corridor wall with two or three stripes of colour before they can understand what happens to this colour as it gradually disappears from view. Perhaps the interrelation of blocks of white, spiralled up like a staircase, has to be studied closely, but surely most perceptive people have absorbed these things in everyday life.

Behind this art is the idea that paint itself, in all its varied possibilities of colour and texture, can be a work of art and need not depict anything and, above all, need not be confined within a rectangle or a given flat surface. So, instead of entering into a painting mentally and accepting what the artist has to say, the spectator can literally walk round and inside some of these 'paintings' and sense their message. It does not seem to me to be more than a message which is normally absorbed in the daily round.

QUALITY OF COLOUR IN CONTEMPORARY ART

Nevertheless the quality of paint, the actual, almost living, quality of the colour itself is, I am sure, one of the great contributions made by contemporary art. Some painters, notably the

Russian-American Mark Rothko, have a genius for a magical laying-on of paint in 'bleeding' veils of radiant colour. This does not often seem to me to be enough to constitute a work of art; it is only part of the truth. The stained-glass workers might as well have assembled vast sheets of glowing glass instead of using them to create decorations of exquisite beauty. Indeed, some modern glass workers do use glass without depicting anything, but they vary the shapes and make a definite design.

So, it seems to me that part of contemporary art is only part of the answer, just as Cézanne found that the light and pure colour of Impressionism was only part of the answer. Matisse used shapes of singing colour and rearranged them significantly. This tremendous power of the contemporaries of making a seemingly flat area of colour have a definite entity, might be harnessed by someone to produce works of tremendous force. As yet, except in the hands of Rothko, Victor Pasmore, and a few others, I cannot see that an area of colour can be made sufficiently significant to hold its own as a work of art; but neither is it negligible.

Today art tends to be international, and a movement may be followed for a time by painters of different nationalities and decades. Nevertheless there is a national thread discernible in that, for instance, France keeps elegance, however many excesses she indulges in; England keeps poetic delicacy; Germany a violent exaggerated realism; Italy a tradition of great draughtsmen and sculptors.

In the main this book deals with the contribution made to art by the different countries of Europe; moreover, during the nineteenth century both the United States and the countries of the British Commonwealth tended to produce painting and sculpture along traditional European lines. Today, however the English-speaking nations overseas do contribute definite 'movements' of their own to the international achievement.

AUSTRALIAN PAINTING

Being basically of British extraction, the Australians painted in the British tradition during the nineteenth century and well into the twentieth. Being also largely Celtic rather than Anglo-Saxon, the work showed signs of imagination and passion but did not produce anything new or exciting. Now a change has come about. Since just before the Second World War, the Australians have contributed a considerable number of names to the list of significant painters. There has been a flowering of exceptional artists who have not only added to the sum total of artistic achievement of the present century, but who have also revealed Australia to us and made a national contribution to international art. They had a background of splendid prehistoric cave art to draw on, and the primitive 'folk' art of contemporary aborigines has proved a vigorous influence of particular appeal to modern painters; but there is an excitement, a depth of feeling, a fantasy, and a richness of colour peculiar to modern Australians.

Arthur Boyd, Russel Drysdale, Sidney Nolan, and Brett Whiteley are international names. Whiteley's picture, *Untitled Red Painting*, in the Tate Gallery, exemplifies his powerful handling of colour and so loses a great deal in black-and-white reproduction. This is true of many of the best Australian pictures, since the intensity of colour is an essential factor.

POP ART AND ROY LICHTENSTEIN

The most important and widespread influence of the second half of the present century is 'Pop' art, which evolved independently in the United States and in England. Pop art is a kind of shock art combined with a more sophisticated approach to folk-lore. It brings art into the service of expressing the brash world of commercial competition, of advertising and mass media. It blows up posters to a colossal size; it stresses the trivial and banal. It can be stimulating and satirical; it can be simply boring.

Whaam! *Roy Lichtenstein* (*b.* 1923). *Tate Gallery, London* (Plate 131). This example of Pop art overwhelms me with its size and brashness, rather in the same manner as the church of the Sagrada Familia in Barcelona. It does make a statement about the tremendous importance advertising has assumed in a materialistic world and therefore has some significance in portraying and interpreting certain facets of contemporary life. There is certainly a case for art to reflect the times we live in; but the world of synthetic materials, of substitutes, of computers, of the television camera and the cinema, is only a part of our civilization. There are still vast areas of countryside to delight in, unsullied by ice-cream cartons; there are still poets and musicians. There is still a place for the creation of new worlds rather than the reflection of the more material and shallow aspects of life; and the view of the world as a vast brash advertising screen seems to me a limited one. Pop art is, to me, only part of the truth. The Old Masters and the established masters and potential masters of today do more than this: they may disturb as well as stimulate and satisfy; they may extend your experience and influence your life, and above all they do add something to the stature of mankind.

There is still a place, even in a materialistic world, for the expression of human emotion, human aspirations and suffering; there is still a place for expressing the limitless fund of nature and for exploring the new areas of space, and new worlds which are opening up every year. Now that man has reached the moon, future painters may have the universe for their inspiration, and indeed many Abstract and Surrealist painters have already more than hinted at its vast potentialities.

It might seem from these last pages that movements are more important than individuals, but this is not so. It is the contribution of the individual painter which is of the highest value, for that remains when the movement itself has fulfilled its purpose and died, or developed into something new. As we have seen with Picasso, the style of a painter of significance modifies and develops, and far more space than is at my disposal would be needed to discuss even some of the facets of each artist's work. I have therefore, in most instances, only been able to hint at some of their achievements and now, when I describe one work from each of four modern painters of accepted worth, I must make my own choice and leave out a number of equal achievement.

FOUR MODERNS

BEN NICHOLSON

Two Forms. *Ben Nicholson* (*b.* 1894). *Southampton Art Gallery* (Plate 130). Though Ben Nicholson does at times combine abstract and representational painting, in this picture he has relied on abstraction. It is a carefully planned geometric painting dependent upon its perfect proportions and relationship of colour and light and dark areas.

ALBERT MARQUET

Le Pont Neuf, La Nuit. *Albert Marquet* (1875–1947), (Plate 127). Marquet was one of the original Fauves, but he tended more towards Impressionism. In this night scene he gives us a wonderful effect of velvety blackness and scintillating light, light of differing qualities in the lamps, the headlights, the reflections in the river, and the glittering lights across the river. Note the quality of the brushwork on the road over the bridge and the essential light rectangle of the bus to carry you over to the other side.

PAUL KLEE

They're Biting. *Paul Klee* (1879–1940). *Tate Gallery, London* (Plate 128). This is a light-hearted amusing painting carried out with a rhythmic, sensitive line that is almost continuous in its flow. The figures, the fish, the nets, the sea, and the boats are all miraculously combined to give the essence of fishing and also to produce a lovely, satisfying pattern.

L. S. LOWRY

An Island. *L. S. Lowry* (*b.* 1887). *Manchester Art Gallery* (Plate 129). Both Klee and Braque can convey great space without perspective, yet Lowry gives it to us by employing a representational style, by depicting objects in an extraordinary isolation. This painting has no figures, a fact which adds to the frozen desolation, though this painter can include figures and isolate them as well. He uses areas of space as the Chinese do.

EXPERIENCE AND NEW DISCOVERIES

Although in these last pages, I have been able to choose only four paintings, the choice for you is limitless. You can seek out examples for yourself in galleries and museums everywhere; you can look at the exhibitions arranged annually by many art schools and try to discern work of promise; you can use your judgment and develop your own taste. I do not believe that anyone is born with 'taste'; it is something acquired with a great deal of effort, a great deal of experience and a great deal of enjoyment.

Whatever your reactions have been in reading this book, you must have formed some opinions of your own; you must have disagreed with some of mine. I hope that you have been filled with a desire to see more and more, and to find out about the achievements of artists in countries outside the scope of this book. But above all I hope that you are now prepared to enlarge your experience, to accept the strangest modifications and even distortions of the world you know, provided that they really do have significance and really do open up new horizons and are not simply exciting because they are novel.

If your sensibilities are to be gradually sharpened to discern between the worthwhile and the trivial, you will need a new awareness of the possibilities of line and space and colour. When you have this, you will find that you inhabit a new world, a world of infinite possibilities where not only familiar forms are presented in a new light, but where both familiar and unfamiliar forms are related to light and atmosphere and boundless space.

In the latest phases, the best of contemporary art is an appeal not only to the intelligence and to the senses, but to the imagination. So you will find beauty not only in everyday things, as Van Gogh did in his familiar old rush chair and his pipe, but also in the creations of your own imagination. As we are shown visions of entirely new worlds, we come to understand that each of us can create new forms of beauty if only in our minds.

POSSIBLE ESSAYS, DISCUSSION AND RESEARCH

1 Compare Keith Vaughan's *Harvesters* (Plate *V*) with Ford Madox Brown's *Work* (Plate *W*).

2 Compare and assess Giacometti's *Man Pointing* (Plate *T*) and the *Jade figure of a Bodhisattva* (Plate *U*).

3 *The Three Dancers* by Picasso (Plate *Q*) is a great acquisition by the Tate. Do you agree?

4 Give an appreciation of Plate *P*.

5 Give an appreciation of Plate *R*.

6 Give an appreciation of Plate *S*.

7 Can you suggest country of origin and date of Plates *M*, *N*, and *O*?

Suggested Further Reading

Bazin, Germain: *A Concise History of Art*, Vol II. Thames & Hudson: London, 1964.

Lippard, Lucy R.: *Pop Art*. Thames & Hudson: London, 1966.

Lynton, Norbert: *The Modern World*. Paul Hamlyn: London, 1965.

Newton, Eric: *The Arts of Man*. Thames & Hudson: London, 1963.

Penrose, Roland: *Picasso, his Life and Work*. Gollanz: London, 1958.

Pringle, John Douglas: *Australian Painting Today*. Thames & Hudson London, 1965.

Read, Herbert: *A Concise History of Modern Painting*. Thames & Hudson: London, 1959.

There are numerous books on individual modern artists, in particular in the series by Thames & Hudson. The Skira books include monographs and volumes on Impressionism, Fauvism, and Cubism.

Appendix One

ART GALLERIES AND MUSEUMS IN GREAT BRITAIN

Birmingham: *City Museum and Art Gallery*, Congreve Street.
Departments of art, archaeology, and ethnography. (Mon. to Sat. 10–6; Sun. 2–5.30.)

Bristol: *City Art Gallery*, Park Street.
Collection of old and modern paintings and sculpture, and a fine collection of Chinese works of art, English Delftware, silver, and glass. (Weekdays 10–6.)

City Museum, Queen's Road.
Department in classical and British archaeology, enthnography. (Weekdays 10–6.)

Cambridge: *Fitzwilliam Museum*, Trumpington Street.
Old and modern masters. Ceramics, prints, coins. Collections of music and medieval manuscripts and art library. (Weekdays 10–5 [10–4 Sept. to April] Sunday, picture galleries only, 2–5 [2–4 Sept. to April]. Closed first Wed. in each month.)

University Museum of Archaeology and Ethnology, Downing Street.
Archaeological collection illustrating the old Stone Age in Europe, Asia, and Africa. Britain from prehistoric to Roman times. Prehistoric America. Ethnographical material from America, Africa, and Oceania. (Weekdays 2–4. Mornings for students by appt.)

University Museum of Classical Archaeology, Little Street.
Representative collection of casts of Greek and Roman sculpture. (Mon. to Fri. 9–1, 2.15–5.)

Dundee: *City Museum and Art Galleries*, Albert Square.
Flemish, Dutch, French, and British painting. (Weekdays 10–6; Winter 10–5.)

Durham: *Gulbenkian Museum of Oriental Art and Archaeology.*
Chinese pottery and porcelain, fine Chinese and Tibetan paintings, Chinese carved jades and hardstones, Chinese and Japanese sculpture, bronzes, robes, hangings, swords, and screens; sculpture from India and Tibet, and Indian illuminated manuscripts and paintings. (Mon. to Fri. 9.30–1, 2.15–5; Sat. and Sun. 2.15–5.)

Glasgow: *Art Gallery and Museum*, Kelvingrove.

Extensive collection of Old Master paintings, including works by Rembrandt, Giorgione, Rubens, Bellini, Maitre de Moulins, etc. Four galleries of British paintings from the sixteenth century to the present day, and a gallery of nineeenth- and twentieth-century French paintings which contains works by Delacroix, Picasso, and Matisse. Also on view: *Christ of St. John of the Cross* by Salvador Dali. European and Oriental art objects including silver, porcelain, glass, bronzes, and costume. Burbell collection of tapestries, furniture, porcelain, stained glass, silver, etc., contains outstanding treasures of Gothic art. Archaeology: Neolithic, Bronze Age, and Roman material. Ethnography: implements, clothing, weapons, religious and ceremonial objects relating to primitive and civilized societies. (Weekdays 10–5, Sun. 2–5.)

Leeds: *City Art Gallery*.

An extensive collection of water colours; nineteenth- and twentieth-century British and French paintings; modern painting and sculpture. Leeds and Staffordshire pottery. (Weekdays 10.30–6.30.)

Temple Newsam

Tudor-Jacobean house with Georgian decorations containing excellent examples of seventeenth- and eighteenth-century English furniture. Collections include European paintings, Chinese porcelain, and English silver. (Daily: May to Sept. 10.30–6.15 [10.30–8.30 on Wed.]; Oct. to April 11.30–6.15 or dusk.)

Liverpool: *Walker Art Gallery*, William Brown Street.

Notable collection of European paintings, famous for the early Italian and Flemish pictures. The later Italians, Dutch and Germans, and the English school from Holbein onwards are well represented. They include fine examples by Signorelli, Rembrandt, Hogarth, Zoffany, Stubbs, and Wilson; twentieth-century paintings and sculpture. (Weekdays 10–5 [Thur. 10–9 April to Sept.].)

London: *British Museum*, Great Russell Street.

Comprising the National Museum of Archaeology, Art and Ethnography, the collection of prints and drawings and the National Library. The museum departments are: Coins and medals; Egyptian antiquities; Western Asiatic antiquities; Greek and Roman antiquities; British and medieval antiquities (including ceramics); Oriental antiquities (including ceramics); and Ethnography. The Library departments are: printed books; manuscripts; Oriental printed books and manuscripts; prints and drawings. (Weekdays 10–5. Sunday 2.30–6.)

Courtauld Institute Galleries, Woburn Square.
Courtauld collection of Impressionist and Post-Impressionist paintings. (Weekdays 10–5; Sun. 2–5.)

Dulwich College Picture Gallery, College Road.
Excellent examples of Rembrandt, Rubens, Claude, Poussin, Gainsborough, Watteau, Lancret, etc. Collection of Spanish paintings and of small Dutch paintings. (Tues. to Sat. 10–6 [closes earlier in winter]; Sun. 2–5 [Summer only].)

Horniman Museum, London Road, Forest Hill.
Enthnographical exhibits. (Tues. to Sat. and Bank Holidays 10.30–6; Sun. 2–6.)

The Iveagh Bequest, Kenwood.
The paintings include a fine Rembrandt self-portrait, Vermeer's *Lady Playing a Guitar*, and works by Van Dyck, Hals and Cuyp as well as English eighteenth-century paintings by Reynolds, Romney, and Gainsborough. (Weekdays 10–7, Sun. 2–7 [closes earlier in Winter].)

National Gallery, Trafalgar Square.
Representative collection of Italian, Dutch, Flemish, Spanish, German schools; French painting up to 1900; a selection of British painters from Hogarth to Turner. (Weekdays 10–6; Sun. 2–6.)

The Queen's Gallery, Buckingham Palace.
Paintings, furniture, and other works of art from the royal collections. (Tues. to Sat. and Bank Holidays 11–5; Sun. 2–5. Admission 2*s*. 6*d*.)

Tate Gallery, Millbank.
The National Collection of British painting, modern foreign painting, and modern sculpture. Special collections of Turner, Blake, and the pre-Raphaelites. (Weekdays 10–6; Sun. 2–6.)

Victoria and Albert Museum, Cromwell Road.
An outstanding art museum comprising collections of fine and applied arts of all countries, periods, and styles. The European collections are mostly of art from early Christian times to the nineteenth century. Series of special rooms display masterpieces from all periods. (Weekdays 10–6; Sun. 2.30–6.)

Wallace Collection, Manchester Square.
Paintings of the French, Spanish, Italian, Flemish, Dutch, and British schools. Miniatures, sculpture, furniture, armour, goldsmiths' work, ceramics, and other works of art. (Weekdays 10–5; Sun. 2–5.)

Newcastle: *Laing Art Gallery and Museum*, Higham Place.
British oil paintings and water colours from the seventeenth

century onwards. Egyptian and Greek antiquities; pottery and porcelain; glass, silver, ironwork, arms, and armour; costumes; textiles and local historical exhibits. (Weekdays 10–6 [Tues. & Thurs. 10–8]; Sun. 2.30–5.30.)

Nottingham: *City Museum and Art Gallery*, The Castle.
Museum of ceramics. Art gallery with paintings and drawings (mainly English) from seventeenth century to present day. Special collections of works by the Nottingham-born artists Thomas and Paul Sandby and R. P. Bonington. (Weekdays 10–6.45 [closes earlier in Winter and on Fridays]; Sun. 2–4.45.)

Oxford: *Ashmolean Museum of Art and Archaeology*, Beaumont Street.
British, European, Mediterranean, Egyptian, and Near-Eastern, archaeology; Italian, Dutch, Flemish, French, and English oil paintings, Old Master and modern drawings, water-colours and prints; miniatures; European ceramics, sculpture and bronzes; English silver. Chinese and Japanese porcelain, painting and lacquer. Chinese bronzes, Indian sculpture and painting. Tibetan art, Islamic pottery and metalwork. (Weekdays. 10–4; Sun. 2–4.)

Sheffield: *Graves Art Gallery*, Surrey Street.
Presents an introduction to British and some interesting examples of European painting. Gainsborough, Turner, Landseer, Whistler, Sickert, Epstein, Paul and John Nash, Leonardo, Murillo, Morales, Cézanne, Corot. Large collection of English water-colours. (Weekdays 10–8; Sun. 2–5.)

Southampton Art Gallery, Civic Centre.
Specializing in British painting, particularly contemporary; some French nineteenth-century and Continental masters. (Weekdays 10–7; Sun. 2–5.)

Wakefield: *City Art Gallery*, Wentworth Terrace.
Contains paintings, sculpture, drawings and prints; some Old Masters; eighteenth-century English water-colours and drawings. Emphasis on modern school. (Weekdays 11–6; Sun. 2.30–5.30.)

Appendix Two

ART GALLERIES AND MUSEUMS IN AUSTRALIA AND NEW ZEALAND

Sydney:	*National Art Gallery*, The Domain. Mainly Australian art; collections of Japanese prints and Primitive art.
Melbourne:	*National Art Gallery*, Swanston Street. Magnificent permanent collections of European and Oriental art; excellent Impressionists.
Brisbane:	*Queensland Art Gallery*, Gregory Terrace.
Adelaide:	*National Gallery of S. Australia*, North Terrace. Permanent collections of pre-Raphaelites and English water-colours.
Perth:	*West Australian Art Gallery*, Beaufort Street.
Hobart:	*Tasmanian Museum & Art Gallery*, 5 Argyle Street.
Auckland:	*Auckland City Art Gallery*, Wellesley Street.
Christchurch:	*Robert McDougall Art Gallery*, Botanical Gardens, Rolleston Avenue. Permanent collection of Old Masters, modern painting, and sculpture; special exhibitions.
Dunedin:	*Dunedin Public Art Gallery*, Logan Park. Painting and sculpture; Old Masters.
Gisborne:	*Gisborne Art Gallery & Museum*, Stout Street. Small collection, mainly consisting of the work of New Zealand artists.
Hamilton:	*Waikato Art Gallery*, Victoria Street. Permanent collection, mainly consisting of the work of New Zealand artists; temporary exhibitions.
Napier:	*Hawke's Bay Art Gallery & Museum*, Hershell Street.
Timaru:	*Aigantighe Art Gallery*, 49 Wai–iti Road.

Wanganui: *Sargeant Art Gallery*, Queens Park.

Wellington: *National Art Gallery*, Buckle Street.
Permanent collection of Old Masters and modern works; very fine English water-colour section.

ANSWERS

Suggestions as to how to answer some of the questions in Chapters 2–9. By Chapter 10 you will certainly have found your own way of dealing with them.

Chapter 2

1 How far does each sculptor exploit and respect his material? One is in relief; one is in the round. One is built up; one is cut away. They both serve religion.
2 What is the difference between a masterpiece of painting or sculpture and a good copy? What are your reactions to 'dead' and 'flowing' lines in any work of art? Can you find any copy that stimulates you?
3 Does knowledge of a picture add to its stimulus or merely to its interest?
4 Take various examples and see if the distinction is always clear cut.
5 When it is machine-made? When it is repetitive? When it is mass-produced? Or does it overlap?
6 What is the most a camera can do? What is the most a human mind and hand can do?
7 Size. Purpose. Quality of life. Flow of movement.
8 Should a tapestry be 'flat'? Does perspective play any part in a tapestry design? Can subtle changes of tone and colour be given? Can you imagine a naturalistic sky or feathery trees in a tapestry?
9 What are, for you, the essentials of a stimulating painting? How far do these paintings possess them?

Chapter 3

1 Intensity of colour. Ease of handling. Permanence. Portability. Setting.
2. Plants? Very small subjects? Architectural subjects? Dürer. Rembrandt. Michelangelo. Leonardo.
3 Personal choice.
4 Consider their conditions of life.
5 Spontaneous. Basic essentials only. Done by hand of master—not assistant.
7 What is each sculptor trying to express? How far does he succeed? One is in round, one is in relief.

Chapter 4

1 Find a book with good reproductions and see how far very early patterns have meaning.

3 Are they a monument *to* someone or something, or are they for the *use of* someone or something? Would you perhaps call them 'monumental architecture', or can you think of some other term?
5 Variety of shape. Size. Intention of builders. Setting.
6 Naturalistic? Formal? Different treatment in different media. Both convincing? Both creative?
7 Consider the entirely different approach of each. Depth. Atmosphere. Design. Architectural unity. Imagination. Are they both true to nature? If so, do they express different truths?

Chapter 5
1 Setting. Limitations of wall paintings. Purpose. Quality of life. Flow of design. Colour.
4 Consider first impact, growing interest, satisfaction, continuing and increasing enjoyment or waning interest.
5 Are the possibilities of the materials fully exploited? How far is the effect the same in a church? Which is more dramatic, more truly decorative, serves the purpose of telling a story best, or are they both as effective in their own way?
6 Consider the 'job' each has to do. Should they be complementary? Should they both have grown with the centuries or be in one style for the best effect?
7 As in Question 4; also consider size and viewpoint of each.

Chapter 6
1 Limitations and possibilities of each medium. Are they all basically making patterns? Can they all serve the same purpose?
2 How is the human figure approached? Are both imaginative? Grotesque? Ideal? Freely treated?
3 Consider the basic principle of the styles. Do they all strive towards the same ends?
4 Dramatic force. Grace. Sensibility. Treatment of drapery. Proportion. Distortion.
5 Consider setting and materials available as well as architectural quality.
6 Make sketches or diagrams.
7 Find examples with and without landscape. See if some (*Book of Kells*) are more powerful without landscape; or if others (*Books of Hours*) are more interesting, more appealing and more decorative with landscape. Do both have an equal impact?

Chapter 7
1 Compare with a detailed manuscript and find out where it differs. Impact? Dramatic force? Architectural unity? General conception? Study of character? Treatment of detail? Rendering of texture?
2 Take examples from different countries.
3 Show change of approach to nature and to subject. Compare with Byzantine, early Christian, Carolingian.

6 A: *Seated Woman*. Henry Moore. Newcastle.
B: *Stained Glass*. Viktring, Austria.
C: *St. Michael Triptych*. Rogier Van der Weyden. Beaune, France.
D: *Maisons Blanches, Ville d'Avray*. Seurat. Walker Art Gallery, Liverpool.
E: *Tiger*. Mu Ch'i (thirteenth century). British Museum, London.
F: *Tympanum of St. Pierre*. Moissac, France.
G: *Gilt Bronze Bear*. Chinese (Han Dynasty). British Museum, London.
H: *Two Cheetahs*, Lombard (*c*. 1400). British Museum, London.
I: *Statue of a Young Man*, Greek (490 B.C.). British Museum, London.
J: *Nebuchadnezzar*. William Blake, Tate Gallery.

Chapter 8

2 Does it 'get in the way'? Does it seem forced? Does it help the design? Increase the impact? Is it essential to this particular painting? Or is it sufficient that it has come off magnificently?
4 International Gothic? Naturalistic? Realistic? Dramatic?
5 Consider the *function* of tapestry.
6 Look for qualities of design, of decorative detail, of colour, of story-telling, even of recording. Look for charm and imagination, freshness of outlook. Be constructive rather than destructive.

Chapter 9

1 Historical background. Different approach. Colour. Form.
2 Composition. Dramatic force. Sensibility.
6 Treatment of form? Realism? Idealism? Naturalism? Power? Sensitivity?
7 Consider basic principles of all three, and how far they achieve these. Is it more elegant? More impressive? More intellectual? Has it more unity? Is the decoration more satisfying? Less interesting? Less moving?

Chapter 16

4 Plate *P*: *The Washerwoman*. Daumier. Louvre, Paris.
5 Plate *R*: *Forest Edge No. 2*. Ivon Hitchens. Tate Gallery, London.
6 Plate *S*: *La Ville Petrifiée*. Max Ernst. Manchester.
7 Plate *M*: *Madonna of the Rose Garden*. Stefano da Zevio (fifteenth century). Scaliger Castle, Verona. Plate *N*: *Hell*. Hieronymus Bosch (*c*. 1450–1516). Flemish. Plate *O*: *The Battle of Alexander*. Albrecht Altdorfer (1480–1538). German.

Index

Aachen, 60
Abstract art; Abstract Impressionism, 180, 181, 186
Academic art, 144
Action painting, 181, 183
Adam, James, 166
Adam, Robert, 166, 169
Aerial perspective, 109
African art, 8, 179
Agrigento, 48
Ajanta caves, 40
Alexandrovac, Lady of, 34
Altamira caves, 30
Altarpieces, 64
Altdorfer, Albrecht, 114
  St. George, 114, 148
Amelienburg, Hall of Mirrors, 132
Amiens Cathedral, 89
Ancient Middle East, the, 36
Animal painting, 135, 148
Assyrian art, 37
Australian painting, 186

Barfreston, Kent, 62, 65
Baroque, 97, 112, 129, 130, 131, 132, 166
Basilica, 52, 53
Bauhaus, 169, 171
Bayeux tapestry, 21, 22
Bellini, Gentile, 105, 108, 109
Bellini, Giovanni, 105, 108, 109
Bellini, Jacopo, 104
Benin bronzes, 8
Bernini, Gian Lorenzo, 130
  Piazza Navona, 130
  St. Peter's, Rome, 130
Betjeman, Sir John, 166
Blake, William, 131, 135, 138
  Wise and Foolish Virgins, 135
Book of Hours, *see* Manuscripts
Botticelli, Sandro, 96, 97, 112
  Birth of Venus, 97
  Nativity, the, 97
  Primavera, 96
Boucher, François, 128
Brancusi, Constantin, 182
Braque, Georges, 171, 175, 176, 178, 182, 187
  Still Life with Fish, 178
Brighton Pavilion, 167
Bronze casting, 22
Brueghel, Pieter, 115
  Fall of Icarus, 116
  Hunters in the Snow, 116
  Return of the Herd, 116
Boyd, Arthur, 186
Brunelleschi, Filippo, 79, 80, 93
  Pazzi Chapel, 93
  Sacrifice of Isaac, 80, 93
  San Lorenzo, 93
  Santa Maria del Fiore, 93
  Santo Spirito, 93
Burne-Jones, Sir Edward, 145
Byzantine art, Byzantium, 54, 106, 138

Cagliari, Sardinia, 170
  Church of Cosmo and Damiano, 170
Camera obscura, 120
Canaletto, 112, 120
  Grand Canal, 120
Canterbury Cathedral, 9, 10, 11, 12, 62
Capitals, *see* Romanesque, Gothic, etc.
Carcassone, 167
Carolingian art, 60
  Christ in Majesty, 60
Carpaccio, Vittore, 107, 108
Cartoons, 100, 102, 152
Carving, 19
  Ivory, 19
  Wood, 22, 181
Caserta, Fountains of, 130, 131
Castelfranco, 10
Casting, 22
Catacombs, 52
Cavallini, Pietro, 74, 77
Cave paintings, 31, 32, 33, 185
Cefalù Cathedral, 25
  Christ Pantocrator, 25
Ceramics, 13, 22, 23, 179
Cézanne, 4, 127, 138, 157, 158, 175, 177, 179, 181, 185
  Jas de Bouffan, 158
Chagall, Marc, 171, 182, 183
  Self portrait with Seven Fingers, 183
Chalices, 57
  Early Christian, 57
  Tassilo Chalice, 57
Charlemagne, 60
Charlemagne's crown, 58
Chartres Cathedral, 67
Chiaroscuro, 100
Chinese art, 40, 188
  Ch'ing, 43, 146
  Sung, 42
  T'ang, 13, 23, 42, 149
Cimabue, 74
Classical revival, 166
Classical style, 132, 133
Classicism, 166
Claude, *see* Lorraine
Collage, 180
Composite order, 48

Composition, 100, 102, 105, 110, 112, 115, 135, 141, 143, 144, 147, 154, 155, 158, 161
Commercial art, 6
Concorde, the, 22
Concrete, reinforced, 168
Constable, John, 140, 142
Valley Farm, 142
Hampstead Heath, 142
Constantinople, *see* Byzantium
Constructivism, 180
Conversation pieces, 134
Corinthian order, 47
Capitals, 93
Corot, Jean Baptiste, 140, 157
Cosimo, Piero di, 95
Death of Procris, 95
Court art, 86, 104
Coventry Cathedral, 171
Crafts, 6
Crivelli, Carlo, 106, 107, 108
Beato Serretti, 107
Crosses, 64
Cross vaulting, 64
Crucifixes, 63, 64
Crystal Palace, 167, 168
Cubist, Cubism, 175, 178, 179, 180, 181, 183

Dadaism, 182
Dali, Salvador, 182
Danube, School of, 114
Daumier, Honoré, 148
Don Quixote and Sancho Panza, 148
David, Jacques, 139
Degas, Edgar, 154, 155
Lala at the Cirque Fernando, 155
Delacroix, Eugène, 139
Delphi, 48
Derain, André, 176
Designers, 172
Donatello, 93, 94, 148
David, 94, 148
Gattamelata, 94
St. George, 94
Doric Order, 47
Drawings, 20, 115
Drysdale, Russell, 186
Duccio, 75
Maestà, 75
Dürer, Albrecht, 114, 115
Four Horseman of the Apocalypse, 26
Mountain Landscape, 115
Durham Cathedral, 62
Dutch painting, 27, 118, 146, 163, 174

Early Christian art, 51, 52, 53, 54
École de Paris, l', 175, 176, 179
Egypt, 37
Pyramids of Giza, 37
Queen Nefertiti, 38
Seated Scribe, 37, 38
Two Daughters of Akhenaton, 39
Eiffel Tower, 10, 168
El Greco, 106, 112, 124, 127, 138
Agony in the Garden, 106, 138
Engineers, 172
Engravings, 21
Epstein, Jacob, 182
Etruscan art, 8, 9, 49, 50
Tomb of Trinclinion Musicians, 50
Winged Horses, 8, 9

Fabriano, Gentile da, 81, 104, 105, 108
Adoration of the Magi, 81, 104, 105
Fauves, Fauvism, 176, 178, 179, 187
Fine Arts, 6
Fra Angelico, 94
Flight into Egypt, 94
Fragonard, Honoré, 128, 129
Souvenir, the, 128
Francesca, Piero della, 95, 109
Nativity, 95, 97
Resurrection of Christ, 96
Frescoes, 17, 18, 26, 83, 102
Frith, William Powell, 144
Derby Day, 144
Frontality, 95, 110

Gainsborough, Thomas, 133, 134
Galla Placidia, Mausoleum of, 55
Gaudi, Antonio, 167
Sagrada Familia, 167
Gauguin, Paul, 158, 159, 160
Swineherd, 159
Yellow Christ, 160
Georgian architecture, 166
Genre, 124, 134, 163
Géricault, Théodore, 139
Raft of Medusa, 139
Ghiberti, Lorenzo, 79, 80
Gates of Paradise, 79
Queen of Sheba, 80
Sacrifice of Isaac, 80
Giacometti, Alberto, 182
Giorgione, 10, 108, 109
Madonna Enthroned, 10
Tempest, the, 109
Giotto, 74, 77, 78, 83, 111
Flight into Egypt, 78, 94
Giotto's Tower, 79
Girtin, Thomas, 141
Gonçalves, Nuno, 73
Altarpiece of St. Vincent, 73
Gothic architecture, 64, 65, 66, 92
Gothic painting, 81, *see also* International Gothic
Gouache, 11
Goya, Francesco, 125, 138, 139
Maja Clothed, 139
Maja Nude, 139
Wine Harvest, 139
Gozzoli, Benozzo, 145
Journey of the Magi, 145
Greek art, 49
Apollo, 49
Birth of Aphrodite, 13
Parthenon, 24, 47

Greek orders of architecture, 47
Greenwich Hospital, 133
Greuze, Jean Baptiste, 128
Gropius, Walter, 169
Guardi, Francesco, 112, 120, 121,
Sta Maria della Salute, 121

Hals, Frans, 125
Laughing Cavalier, the, 125
Hard-edge, 183
Hepworth, Barbara, 182
Hitchens, Ivon, 182
Hobbema, Meindert, 119, 178
Avenue, the, 119
Hogarth, William, 133, 134
Harlot's Progress, 134
Marriage à la Mode, 134
Rakes Progress, 134
Holbein, Hans the Younger, 133
Hooch, Pieter de, 124, 125
Hunt, William Holman, 7
Hunter, art of the, 31, 32, 33

Iffley church, 62
Ikons, 15
Illuminated Manuscripts, *see* Manuscripts
Impressionism, Impressionists, 4, 121, 128, 138, 140, 142, 153, 180, 181, 185
Indian art, 40, 41
Ajanta caves, 40
Radha and Krishna, 41
International Gothic, 77, 86, 104, 111
International modern architecture, 169
Invalides, church of, Paris, 132
Ionic order, 47
Italian painting, Schools of, 74

Japanese prints, woodcuts, etc., 40, 43, 144, 147, 158, 160, 162
John, Augustus, 182

Kandinsky, Wassily, 181, 182
Battle, 181
Kastoria, Greece, 54
Kells, Book of, 25
Kinetic art, 183
Klee, Paul, 187
They're Biting, 187
Klosterneuberg, Monastery of, 64
Konnick, Philipe, 146
Kremsmunster, Monastery of, 64

La Défense, Paris, 172
Landscape, 114–124
as a background, 73, 116
in Flemish painting, 74, 116
in Italian painting, 74, 116
Le Brun, 128
Le Corbusier, 170
Le Nôtre, 128
Leonardo da Vinci, 98, 99, 109
Cartoon for Virgin and Child with St. Anne and St. John the Baptist, 99
Mona Lisa, 101

Le Vau, 128
Lindisfarne Gospel, 57
Lithography, 21
Lloyd-Wright, Frank, 169
Lorraine, Claude, 116, 117, 119, 122, 127, 129, 141, 146
Italian Landscape, 117
Lowry, L. S., 182, 187
Island, an, 187
Lurçat, Jean, 171

Madox-Brown, Ford, 147, 148
Magritte, René, 182
Major arts, 22
Manet, Edouard, 125, 138, 151, 152, 153
Le Déjeuner sur l'Herbe, 152
Olympia, 138
Mansart, Jules, 128, 132
Mantegna, Andrea, 105
Agony in the Garden, 105
Manueline architecture, 68, 69
Manuscripts and Books of Hours, 56, 70, 81
Anglo-Saxon Psalter, 57
Book of Kells, 25, 57, 58
Book of Yarrow, 57
Lindisfarne Gospel, 57
Rossano, Codex, 56
Sforza Book of Hours, 70
Très Riches Heures du Duc de Berry, 70
Vienna Genesis, 56
Winchester Bible, 57
Manzù, Giacoma, 182
Marini, Marino, 182
Marquet, Albert, 176, 187
Le Pont la Nuit, 187
Marshall, Benjamin, 135
Masaccio, 83
Expulsion from Garden of Eden, 83
Materials, 6
Matisse, Henri, 148, 176, 177, 182, 185
Inattentive Reader, the, 177
Matisse Chapel at Vence, the, 177
Medici Chapel, Florence, 145
Medici Lorenzo, 92, 145, 146
Medieval Glass, 9, 10, *see also* Stained Glass
Megalithic monuments, 34
Melk Abbey, Austria, 131, 132, 133
Messina, Antonella da, 108
Metro stations, Paris, 167
Michelangelo Buonarroti, 98, 99, 100, 139
Madonna and Child, St. John and Angels, 101
Pietà, 101
St. Peter's, Rome, 130
Milan Cathedral, 92, 93
Millais, Sir John, 87, 107
Ophelia, 87, 107
Minimal art, 184
Minoan art, 20
Minor arts, 6, 22

Mirò, Joan, 172
Modern Media, 20
Mondrian, Piet, 182
Monet, Claude, 154, 157, 158, 168
Road under Snow at Honfleur, 154
Magpie, 154
Moore, Henry, 28
Reclining Figure, 28
Morland, George, 135
Morris, William, 145, 168, 169
Mosaic, 18, 19, 25, 26, 54, 55, 56, 74, 104, 145
Museums,
Amsterdam, Stedelijk Museum, 183
Athens, National Museum, 49
Birmingham Art Gallery, 121, 146, 147
Cagliari, Sardinia, Museum of Cagliari, 35
Cambridge, Fitzwilliam Museum, 60
Dublin, Trinity College Library, 25
Durham, Gulbenkian Collection, 146
Florence, National Museum, 79
Bargello National Museum, 79, 94
Ufizzi, 81, 96, 102
Glasgow, Glasgow Art Gallery, 159
Graz, Austria, Joanneum, 8, 89
Leeds, City Art Gallery, 28
Lisbon, Lisbon Museum, 73
Liverpool, Walker Art Gallery, 14, 122
London, British Museum, 8, 13, 24, 27, 37, 70, 104, 148
Courtauld Institute, 90, 148, 152, 156, 158, 161
National Gallery, 14, 71, 84, 85, 95, 97, 99, 101, 102, 105, 106, 107, 109, 110, 111, 114, 117, 119, 120, 125, 126, 127, 133, 144, 151, 153, 155
Tate Gallery, 14, 87, 135, 141, 177, 178, 181, 183, 184, 186, 187
Victoria and Albert, 41, 142, 149
Madrid, Prado, 27, 114, 138
Manchester, Manchester Art Gallery, 187
Munich, Alte Pinakothek, 102, 114
Norwich, Norwich Castle Museum, 144
Oxford, Ashmolean, 39
Padua, Scrovegni Chapel, 78
Paris, Cluny Museum, 88
Louvre, 27, 37, 102, 104, 115, 119, 129, 154, 161, 177
Musée des Monuments, 64
Musée National d'Art Moderne, 178
Rome, Museo delle Terme, 13
Siena, Cathedral Museum, 75
Palazzo Publico, 76
Southampton Art Gallery, 146, 176, 187
Tarquinia Museum, 8, 9
Vienna, Kunsthistorisches Museum, 116
Venice, Accademia, 108, 109

Naïve painting, 160, 161
Nash, John, 166, 167
Nash, Paul, 182
Neo-Impressionists, *see* Pointillists
Nicholson, Ben, 182, 187
Two Forms, 187
Nolan, Sydney, 182, 186
Norman architecture, 61
Norwich School, 122, 143
Norwich Society of Artists, 144
Nuraghe, 35, 36
Nymphenburg Palace, 132

Oil painting, 17, 108
Olympia, Temple of Zeus, 171
Op art, Optical art, 184
Orders of architecture, 47
Oriental art, 39, 40, 41
Orvieto Cathedral, 171

Paestum, 48
Partheon, 24, 48
Pasmore, Victor, 185
Patenir, Joachim, 114
Charon Crossing Stix, 114
Patrons of the arts, 92, 117, 118, 174, 175, 181
Persian art, 40
Picasso, Pablo, 14, 175, 178, 179, 182, 187
Goat's Skull, Bottle and Candle, 14, 179, 187
Guernica, 179
Pisa, 78
Pisanello, Antonio, 85, 104
Vision of St. Eustace, 85, 104
Pisano, Andrea, 79
Baptistery doors, 79
Pisano, Giovanni, 78
Pisano, Nicola, 78
Crucifixion, 78
Pisano, Nino, 79
Pissarro, Camille, 119, 154, 157, 158
Edge of the Village, the, 119
Pointillists, Pointillism, 27, 153, 154
Pollock, Jackson, 183
Painting 1952, 183
Pop art, 186
Post-Impressionism, 4, 157
Poussin, Nicolas, 117, 122, 127
Prandtauer, Jacob, 131
Monastery of Melk, 131
Pre-Columbian art, 23
Prehistoric art, 8, 17, 23, 24, 30, 31, 32
Altamira, 30
Bronze Cult Chariot, 8
First Farmers, 33
Hunter, 31, 32, 33
Lascaux, 23
Nuraghe, 35, 36
Pyrenees, 31

Prehistoric art—*cont.*
Stonehenge, 34, 35
Vitkovo, 34
Primitive art, 30

Raphael, 98, 99, 101, 102, 127, 153
Knight's Dream, 102
La Belle Jardinière, 102
Madonna of Bullfinch, 102
Madonna of the Meadow, 102
Ravenna, 54, 55, 56, 60
Real, Art of the, 184
Reinforced concrete, 168
Rembrandt, van Ryn, 27, 97, 112, 118, 124, 125, 126, 127, 128, 138, 141, 178
Adoration of the Shepherds, 97
Girl Sleeping, 27, 112
Night Watch, 126
Old Man Seated, 125, 177
Renoir, Auguste, 154, 155
Luncheon of the Boating Party, 155
Representational art, 4, 5, 180
Reynolds, Sir Joshua, 133, 134
Riley, Bridget, 184
Fall, the, 184
Rococo, 112, 130, 132, 166
Roman art, 50, 51
Marcus Aurelius, 51
Romanesque capitals, 11, 12, 65
Romanticism, 138, 139
Rossano Codex, 57
Rossetti, Dante Gabriel, 145
Rothko, Mark, 185
Rouault, Georges, 176, 178
Apprentice, the, 178
Rousseau, le Douanier, 160, 161, 162
Customs House, 161
War, 161
Royal Academy, 4, 134, 145
Rubens, Sir Peter Paul, 112, 119, 124, 126, 127, 128, 133
Chapeau de Paille, 126
Chateau de Steen, 14, 109
Judgement of Paris, 127
Ruskin, John, 172

St. Bartholomew's, London, 132, 133
Sainte Chapelle, Paris, 68, 167
St. John's Chapel, Tower of London, 62
St. Paul's, London, 132, 133
St. Peter's, Rome, 101, 130
St. Trophime, Arles, 65
St. Vincent Altarpiece, 73
Salon des Refusés, 152
Salon, the, 4, 162, 176
Salonica, *see* Thessalonika
Salvator Rosa, 117
San Marco, Venice, 104
Santiago da Compostella, 132
Savonarola, 96
Saxon architecture, 61
Sechau, 63
Seurat, Georges, 27, 28, 153, 154
Bathers, the, 153
Circus, the, 27, 28, 153, 154
Sforza Book of Hours, 70
Simone, Martini, 14, 15, 75, 76
Finding of Christ in the Temple, the, 14, 15
Guidoriccio da Fogliano, 76
Sinopie, 18, 26
Sisley, Alfred, 154, 156
Snow at Louveciennes, 156
Sistine Chapel, Rome, 101
Sphinx, 37
Sporting pictures, *see* Animal painting
Stained glass, 9, 19, 66, 67, 171, 178, 185
Steel, 10, 167
Stonehenge, 34
Stubbs, George, 135
Sumeria, 36, 37
Imugud from Ubaid, 37
Surrealism, Surrealist, 161, 182, 186

Tapestry, 12, 13, 21, 22, 69, 88, 89, 171
Tarquinia, 8, 50
Tassilo Chalice, 57
Taste, 5, 7, 188
Tempera, 17
Thessalonika, 54
Tiepolo, Giovanni Battista, 112, 120, 139
Tintoretto, 110
St. George and the Dragon, 110
Titian, 108, 109, 110, 127
Bacchus and Ariadne, 109
Topographical paintings, 135, 143
Toulouse-Lautrec, 154, 156
Bed, the, 156
Clownesse, 156

Uccello, 84, 85, 86
Rout of San Romano, the, 84
Unesco building, Paris, 172
Utrillo, Maurice, 176
Church at Longpont, 176

Van Dyck, Sir Anthony, 124, 128, 133, 134
Charles I on Horseback, 133, 134
Van Eyck, Hubert, 87
Adoration of the Lamb, 87
Van Eyck, Jan, 71, 73, 86, 87, 108
Marriage of Giovanni Arnolfini and Giovanna Cenani, 71
Van Gogh, Vincent, 154, 157, 158,159, 160, 179, 188
Windmill, the, 159
Vanvitelli, Luigi, 131
Vasarely, Victor, 183
Supernovae, 183
Vasari, Giorgio, 98, 99
Vatican, the, 102
Victoriana, 171
Viollet-le-Duc, 167

Vlaminck, Maurice, 176, 177
Vorau, Abbey of, 131, 132

Water colours, 20, 135, 141, 143, 147
Watteau, Antoine, 112, 128, 129
Embarkation for Cythera, 129
Whitely, Brett, 186
Untitled Red Painting, 186
Wies, 131
Wilson, Richard, 121, 122, 133, 144
Snowdon from Llyn Nantlle, 122
Wilten, Our Lady of Four Columns, 132
Winchester Bible, 57
Wint, Peter, de, 147
Norfolk Wherries, 147
Wren, Sir Christopher, 132, 133
Greenwich Hospital, 133
St. Paul's Cathedral, 133

Yarrow, Book of, 57
Yugoslavia, 33, 34

Zuccarelli, 117